Mutual Benefit Evaluation of Faculty and Administrators in Higher Education

Mutual Benefit Evaluation of Faculty and Administrators in Higher Education

William J. Genova
Marjorie K. Madoff
Robert Chin
George B. Thomas

TDR Associates, Inc.
Newton, Massachusetts

Ballinger Publishing Company ● Cambridge, Mass.
A Subsidiary of J.B. Lippincott Company

This book is printed on recycled paper.

International Standard Book Number: 0-88410-165-7

Library of Congress Catalog Card Number: 76-6875

Printed in the United States of America

Library of Congress Cataloging in Publication Data
Main entry under title:

Mutual benefit evaluation of faculty and administrators in higher education.

  Bibliography: p.
  Includes index.
  1. College teachers, Rating of. 2. College administrators, Rating of. I. Genova,
William J.
LB2333.M87   378.1'22   76-6875
ISBN 0-88410-165-7

Contents

Preface

This book is a practical guide for developing programs of faculty and administrator evaluation in colleges and universities. It describes operating principles, summarizes research, and displays exemplary practices. The prototype of this book was developed by Training, Development, and Research (TDR) Associates, Inc., a consulting group located in Newton, Massachusetts, under contract with the Massachusetts Advisory Council on Education (MACE: see Appendix D). Copies of this prototype were distributed to all degree-granting institutions in Massachusetts in September 1975. Because it has been so well received in Massachusetts, and because of the interest expressed in it by many people in other states, we decided to make it available in this hardcover edition.

The book contains many rating scales that are available for use *only* if ordered from their sources. These sources are identified in the resource sections of chapters 2 and 3.

We wish to express our thanks to the many students, faculty, administrators, and others within and outside Massachusetts who contributed to this book, some of whom served on a Project Advisory Committee (see Appendix C). Our special thanks go to Ronald J. Fitzgerald, Director of Research, MACE, for his thoughtful guidance (see Appendix B); Mark T. Munger, Senior Associate of McBer and Company, Boston, Massachusetts, who developed Chapter 4 under subcontract to TDR Associates, Inc.; Dean K. Whitla, Director, Office of Instructional Research and Evaluation, Harvard University, for his assistance in instrumentation; and Robert C. Hayden of the Educational Development Center, Newton, Massachusetts, for assisting with our field visits.

William J. Genova, President
TDR Associates, Inc.
Newton, Massachusetts

Introduction

Our conviction that faculty and administrators can be evaluated in ways that will benefit all the constituencies of a college or university community—students, faculty, administrators, and members of the governing body—is reflected in this book. This theme is highlighted in the title and has guided our selection of the research and practice summarized within. And, to the degree that each constituency becomes a real and convinced beneficiary, faculty or administrator evaluation becomes a way of translating the rhetoric of renewal into concrete procedures for the improvement and support of instruction.

Mutual benefit is not, however, an automatic outcome of faculty or administrator evaluation, but rather the result of careful and guided planning by all of the constituencies involved. When any constituency has not been involved in such planning, its later participation has typically been one of uneasy ritual, conditioned by the absence of perceived self-benefit.

We describe in some detail the purposes, principles, and procedures of mutual benefit evaluation. We give examples of alternative approaches, from which a specific evaluation program can be constructed to fit the needs and climate of a particular institution. For those who are interested in applying these guidelines to the establishment of mutual benefit evaluation programs on their campuses, we suggest seven stages of action.

1. The Initiative
If you see the potential value of mutual benefit evaluation on your campus, you can initiate an attempt to enhance an existing program, or develop a new program. Whatever your role—student, faculty member, administrator, or governing board member—your interest can spark members of each constituency into a mutual exploration of the topic. For maximum effectiveness, your advocacy should be channeled through the existing representative groups: the student and faculty associations, the administration, and the governing body.

Their mutual sanction and full support of a formal exploration of the topic is essential to the eventual establishment of evaluation programs that will result in benefits to all.

2. A Representative Study Group

Once such an exploration is initiated and sanctioned, we suggest the formation of a study group of from eight to twelve members, composed of representatives of each of the four constituencies. The study group members can be appointed, elected, or volunteer, and each constituent group need not be equally represented. Its work should be supported by the provision of some released time and recognition (e.g., study credits for students, service experience in the dossiers of staff), and its efforts should be visible to all members of the campus community. Each member of the study group should be provided with a copy of this book and the group should have a budget of several hundred dollars for the purchase of sample materials, postage, telephone, reports, and other expenses. In addition, the study group should have access to previous evaluations on its campus for its assessment of the strengths and weaknesses of the existing faculty or administrator evaluation program.

3. Consideration of Mutual Benefit Evaluation

Each member of the study group should read Chapter 1 and the chapter that applies to the group's immediate concern; e.g., faculty evaluation in conventional education programs (Chapter 2), administrator evaluation (Chapter 3), or faculty evaluation in competency-based educational programs (Chapter 4). The purposes, principles, and procedures of mutual benefit evaluation presented in the book should then be discussed by the study group members. The study group should subsequently examine the existing evaluation program against the principles described in those chapters, looking for areas where improvement is both feasible and important. The Faculty Evaluation Program Inventory in Appendix A may assist in this process.

4. Recommendations

Based on its examination of any existing faculty or administrator evaluation program, and on its review of mutual benefit evaluation, the study group should make specific recommendations for improvement. Alternatively, it may decide to recommend no changes, but rather to endorse the continuation of the existing program. Whatever the recommendations, they should be written up and distributed to all members of the campus community. For this purpose a summary can be distributed to all members, with several copies of a detailed report made accessible for their review.

5. Campus Discussions

If the study group recommends improvements in existing faculty or administrator evaluation programs, it should hold hearings soon after its recommendations have been distributed. These hearings should provide a forum for resistance and self-interest—as well as advocacy—to emerge. The genuinely open airing of problems and real concerns at this stage will allow for participatory decisions and eventual acceptance. Study group members should expect to give time and effort to share their resources and understandings, as well as listen carefully to others' concerns. The study group members must be patient and responsive to questions and suggested modifications, and may find the prevailing climate such that acceptance of a small pilot effort for the subsequent academic year may be a realistic accomplishment.

6. Decision

Before the recommendations of the study group are put into practice, either in their original or modified form, we strongly recommend that they be formally endorsed by the representative student and faculty associations, the administration, and the governing body. This empowerment by the campus constituencies is not the end, but the beginning, of what should be a stimulating and mutually beneficial venture for all.

7. Program Renewal

Anything new will eventually go stale, and must therefore be continually and critically reviewed, and revitalized from time to time. In the case of mutual benefit evaluation, the most crucial sign of natural erosion will appear when one constituent group comes to view another group as the sole beneficiary of the process. This may happen naturally as a result of changes in group membership, where new members will have to experience the benefits before they will develop a stake in the process, and experienced members will aspire toward new and more meaningful benefits. Procedures for the continual renewal of evaluation programs are described in this book and they should be incorporated into the recommendations made by the study group.

Chapter One

Assumptions and Operating Principles

A campus committee is typically formed to plan the details of a new or revised faculty or administrator evaluation program. The committee members first familiarize themselves with the literature in this area, and send to other campuses for rating scales and sample procedures. This is a time-consuming process that is often rushed by the pressure for action, and may not be guided by tested principles of operation. For such committees, this book accomplishes the first task, and lays out a general framework and operating principles for comprehensive evaluation programs.

The book was developed between September 1974 and August 1975, in several stages. First, a literature search identified previous work on a national scale—books, articles, people, and programs related to faculty and administrator evaluation in higher education. Second, telephone interviews probed (with people and places identified in the literature search) for current research and practice. Third, materials (such as program descriptions and rating scales) were collected from colleges, universities, business organizations, government agencies, and educational institutes and centers involved in the general area of personnel evaluation. Fourth, certain research findings and personnel evaluation practices were selected as "exemplary" (e.g., consistent with the theme of mutual benefit evaluation) by the TDR Associates staff, in consultation with prominent experts in the field. Fifth, field visits to over thirty colleges and universities in Massachusetts identified current practices and concerns. Sixth, the selected research and practice was written up, and the draft chapters were pilot tested with students, faculty, and administrators from public and private colleges and universities in Massachusetts, and were subsequently revised on the basis of their critique and suggestions.[a]

[a] A one-day conference was held in western Massachusetts in February 1975, in which teams of one student, one faculty member, and one administrator from each of twelve colleges and universities reviewed the faculty evaluation chapter (Chapter 2). In April 1975, the administrator evaluation chapter (Chapter 3) was reviewed by twenty-five administrators

Because of the variety of institutions of higher education for which this book was prepared, no single evaluation program will be uniformly suitable. The approach is therefore general and eclectic. Within a general framework of operating principles and procedures, and issues—such as affirmative action and confidentiality—that must be discussed and resolved by those planning evaluation programs, examples of specific research and practices are used as illustrations. Particular institutions can develop their own unique evaluation program by combining selected elements of established programs. Making a "local translation"—selecting rating scales, developing specific procedures, adopting or adapting practices from other places—will produce a program consistent with local institutional needs and conditions.

Evaluating people is a serious business. At stake for the persons evaluated are self-esteem, job security, assignments and promotion, and future careers. For students, the quality and usefulness of their education depends in large part on the institution's capacity to identify and maintain staff excellence. For the institution itself, its very survival will more and more depend on its purposefulness and quality of instruction. In our view the choice in evaluating people is not whether to be "hard" or "soft," but how to be fair to both individual and collective concerns. So the task is not to fit individuals into some abstract notion of an organization, but to build the organization around its human resources.

In more expansionist times, openness and collaboration for collective aims among students, faculty, administrators, and others associated with institutions of higher education were more possible than today. Higher education is no longer a growth industry in this country. And, partly because of retrenchment and other national trends, openness is giving way to guardedness; collaboration is giving way to competition.

We believe, however, that there is sufficient mutual benefit from faculty and administrator evaluation for students, faculty, administrators, and others to make openness and collaboration among these constituencies not only possible, but necessary for survival in an increasingly competitive environment. We urge that colleges and universities form study groups of students, faculty, and administrators for the purpose of planning new or improved evaluation programs. And we suggest the deliberations of these groups, and the programs they recommend, be made visible to their constituencies and ratified by them before being implemented. Without such a ratification process a program's benefits may remain obscure.

On many campuses evaluation is viewed quite differently by each of the three major constituencies—students, faculty and administrators. Each currently sees the *others* as the principal beneficiaries of the process.

---

and faculty members from eastern Massachusetts. These chapters, and the chapter on faculty evaluation in competency-based educational programs (Chapter 4), were also reviewed by the Project Advisory Committee, which met three times during the project.

During our visits to colleges and universities in Massachusetts, we asked the three groups whom they found to be the principal beneficiaries of present faculty evaluation programs. The typical responses were:

Students:	Faculty benefit most.
Faculty:	Administrators benefit most.
Administrators:	Faculty benefit most.

We do not know how universal these opinions are, because our sample of less than 100 persons was small and selected, and our intention was to explore rather than to undertake systematic survey research. But the responses are surprisingly consistent: none of the major constituencies names itself as benefiting as much as the others, and none sees the students as principal beneficiaries. When we probed beyond the initial responses, some of the reasons became clear.

Faculty View. Until quite recently, many faculty were willing to look on faculty evaluation as a useful tool for self-development and the improvement of instruction. But the expansionist times that fed that point of view are over. Now faculty tend to see evaluation as a weapon—real or potential—used by administrators to make critical personnel decisions. It is difficult to talk about development and improvement when so many jobs are on the line. Faculty members are apprehensive that diagnostic information, originally solicited for self-improvement, will now become part of a personnel file for the purpose of administrative decisions only.

Administrator View. Administrators are directly responsible for critical personnel decisions. As they see it, most faculty evaluation programs, as they presently exist, are not very helpful because faculty tend to protect each other. Until evaluation programs become more rigorous, and discriminate better among those who are being evaluated, administrators will continue to be forced to make impressionistic judgments based on very incomplete data. In addition, administrators frequently bemoan the present lack of student interest in faculty evaluation. In general they feel that their personnel decision-making responsibilities are growing in importance, while the information on which they must base their decisions is becoming less useful to those decisions.

Student View. The late-sixties enthusiasm on the part of students in the evaluation of faculty performance is disappearing. Despite the availability of carefully developed evaluation instruments, and the presence of procedures to facilitate course evaluation, students on most campuses are willing to invest very little energy in faculty evaluation. Students we interviewed said that they want to support good teaching, and to help faculty improve instruction. Students are resentful about being a continual *source* of information because they are skeptical that anyone—administrator or faculty—is *listening*. They see little evidence of the impact of their participation.

As evidenced in this book, the technical elements of mutual benefit evaluation programs are readily available. It contains student evaluation instruments, peer observation forms, and other well-tried information-collecting instruments and procedures from all over the country.

But collecting the information is only a very small part of a faculty or administrator evaluation program. The information must be used within a context that produces benefits for all the principal constituencies on a campus. Without such benefits, which give each group a stake in the evaluation process, a program will fail. A common form of failure is where participation in faculty or administrator evaluation procedures is performed as ritual—for symbolic reasons rather than for functional utility.

This gloomy prediction need not come true. We have found campuses where sincere commitment to explore together, and to develop a stake for each constituency, has led to high purpose and the beginning of substantial accomplishment. But we have become convinced that—available techniques or no available techniques—success in faculty or administrator evaluation must spring from procedures that allow each constituency to become a real and convinced beneficiary. In our experience this can best happen where each constituency is represented in the planning and implementation of the evaluation program, and in its continual renewal.

We advocate the careful involvement of faculty, students and administrators in the planning of new or improved faculty evaluation programs. During our field visits, joint discussions with faculty, students, and administrators of the possible benefits of evaluation to each constituency led to increased perceptions of potential self-benefit on the part of all constituencies. Faculty, students, and administrators recognized that they each have important perspectives which, when combined, contribute to a comprehenseive program that can benefit all.

The following chapters will expand on these potential benefits, and on procedures that can stimulate the vision of all members of the academic community to better achieve their parallel goals in education. The operating principles of mutual benefit evaluation are:

1. Multipurpose.—Given the wide variety of institutional purposes and demands, faculty and administrator evaluation programs should serve a variety of purposes for those evaluated, their constituencies, and the institution as a whole.
2. Multifaceted—In the interest of fairness and completeness, faculty and administrators should be evaluated on a broad range of their activities and responsibilities, which are weighted regarding their importance.

3. Multisource—Those affected by and informed about the actions of particular faculty and administrators should participate in the evaluation of those administrators.
4. Multimethod—Because of the range of appropriate faculty and administrative acts and styles, different methods of assessment must be combined.
5. Institutional Context-Related—The evaluation of faculty and administrators must be related to the particular purposes, needs, and stage of development of the institution.

Chapter Two

Faculty Evaluation

CHAPTER USES AND AUDIENCES

This chapter summarizes existing practice and research on faculty evaluation. It is written for college and university administrators, board members, faculty, students, and others who are interested in developing a formal program of faculty evaluation. The chapter can also serve to inform those generally interested in the topic, but not necessarily involved in the development of a formal faculty evaluation program. A variety of approaches will be discussed, and operating principles will be set forth to guide the user in developing an approach best suited to a particular institution. Because of the wide variation in the types, goals, resources, and needs of colleges and universities, this chapter will not advocate a single approach for universal application. Rather, it assumes a major investment of time and energy of those interested in translating these general guidelines into a faculty evaluation program tailored to a specific institution.

THE PURPOSES OF FACULTY EVALUATION

Evaluation of faculty has always taken place, if only by inference or casual observation. Peer review and faculty-initiated and controlled procedures are traditional methods. The academic tradition which protects faculty dignity and autonomy, and insures academic freedom and professional status must be seriously honored in any evaluation program. An understanding of the traditions of the American college or university, and in particular the faculty role in them, is a necessary precondition for the development of faculty evaluation. But it is no longer sufficient or desirable to restrict faculty evaluation to peer review. The several purposes of faculty evaluation, can benefit faculty, students, and administrators alike.

Evaluation by and for faculty, students, and administrators can provide information, and discussion of evaluation issues can stimulate its users to interpret this information within a framework that allows for informed planning and action. As institutions vary widely, the purposes for which they evaluate will also vary. Most institutions will find that it is possible to develop a system which will serve many purposes of faculty evaluation, as long as each is carefully defined. Only by addressing several purposes can they address the improvement of the quality of the whole institution. So the underlying aim of faculty evaluation for all concerned is the continuous improvement in the quality of teaching and learning, research and service. Within this broad aim lie several more specific purposes of faculty evaluation:

1. Helping faculty to improve their performance.
2. Making decisions on retention, tenure, salary, and promotion.
3. Guiding students in their selection of courses and instructors.
4. Keeping an inventory of personnel resources for reassignment and retraining.
5. Evaluating curricula, sequences, programs, departments, and units.
6. Informing external audiences on faculty performance.
7. Conducting research on factors related to faculty performance.

Helping faculty to improve their performance. This is the purpose of doing faculty evaluation that consistently comes to the top of the list of intended purposes at most colleges and universities, but typically falls short as a demonstrated accomplishment. The intention is to provide faculty members periodically with information regarding their performance in the areas of teaching, service to the institution and the community, and research and scholarly publication. When this information is fed back to faculty members, it is assumed (or hoped) that they will be sufficiently motivated and thus capable of making needed improvements. In some institutions, faculty development resources (such as a clinic, a center, an institute, or teaching specialists) are made available to help faculty members to improve. Having such services or resources available is an adjunct to evaluation for improvement that is highly recommended.

Making decisions on retention, tenure, salary, and promotion. This purpose of faculty evaluation has received heightened interest in the past several years, and has become the principal preoccupation of faculty evaluation in many institutions facing severe financial retrenchment, faculty unionization and collective bargaining, and demands for accountability and cost effectiveness. Because of these factors it is the most threatening purpose of evaluation to faculty members. Most institutions that intend to pursue this purpose, together with the purpose of helping faculty to improve their performance, have found that different procedures are required for the successful accomplishment of both results. If the same procedures are used for both purposes, the typical result is that the faculty evaluation information is used for decision-making regarding retention, tenure, salary, and promotion, but is not used for improved performance. As a result, many experts (Hildebrand, 1971; Kulik and McKeachie, 1975) recommend a separation in procedures carefully distinguishing this purpose from others.

Guiding students in their selection of courses and instructors. The increased student militancy and consumer advocacy of the 1960s gave impetus to a proliferation of programs of student ratings of courses and instructors. Typically this information is printed and distributed at the end of each semester to students as a guide in their selection of courses and instructors. It has been found that the most controversial and least useful programs are those conducted by students alone, independent of faculty or administrators. The most acceptable and useful programs tend to be those that are planned and administered jointly by students, faculty, and administrators. This purpose is also potentially threatening to faculty members, so that mechanisms to protect them by including normative or interpretive information, and providing for their own responses, is well advised.

Keeping an inventory of personnel resources for reassignment and retraining. This purpose has received little attention, but should become increasingly important as institutions are faced with financial constraints. For example, if an institution were to find that it could support only two of the three chemistry instructors currently employed, it could explore ways of reassigning or retraining them as an alternative to letting one go. Evaluation data may indicate that one instructor had experience, and would be interested in teaching food chemistry or some other applied chemistry subject. Or the three instructors could team together for teaching some subjects, and redefine their roles for other activities such as guidance and advising, work in the registrar's office, doing institutional research or recruiting, or other functions of benefit to the institution in addition to their teaching roles. Such alternatives to staff utilization would allow the retention of personnel with proven capabilities and established relationships. The successful achievement of this purpose requires a continuously updated inventory of evaluative and other information on the backgrounds, interests, and strengths of all faculty members. This may be better accomplished at a department or unit level, but typically demands attention from those at a level which commands an overview of both personnel resources and institutional needs.

Evaluating curricula, sequences, programs, departments, and units. As with the previous purpose, the place of faculty evaluation in the evaluation of curricula, sequences, programs, departments, and other units has been the subject of little exploration. Given the increasing financial crisis in higher education, this purpose may also receive further attention. Certainly an evaluation of curricula, sequences, programs, departments, and units would not be complete without an evaluation of the quality of teaching and advising within those units. In larger institutions the results of faculty evaluation can be aggregated by departments, divisions, and colleges, and similar units or courses can be compared to some degree regarding factors related to their relevance and effectiveness. In smaller institutions, less quantitative comparisons are possible, and thus more qualitative assessments are required. A faculty evaluation that includes course evaluation can provide data suggesting strategies for modifications of programs, sequences, and curricula so that faculty talents, student needs, and institutional goals are better matched.

Informing external audiences on faculty performance. This purpose has evoked horror and contempt from within institutions of higher education. The pressures for providing such information have been coming, for the most part, from outside the institutions, from consumers, legislators, advocacy groups, government officials, parents, and taxpayers. Reactive responses, such as giving out as little information as possible, may be counter-productive to long-range vision and survival. Those institutions which, on their own initiative, collect and disseminate overall effectiveness information—students served, student learning and satisfaction ratings, drop-out and matriculation rates, alumni employment and achievement patterns, community and social contributions— may in the long run be most capable of maintaining vision and surviving in the increasingly competitive environment of higher education. Information gathered in evaluation programs, and trends and changes that result, can add substance for this purpose.

Conducting research on factors related to faculty performance. This purpose has sometimes been the cause and other times the result of faculty evaluation programs. Some small research efforts have expanded into full-scale programs, while sometimes the promising results of an established program have served as the subject of further study. Since most research has taken place in an institutional rather than a laboratory setting, it can stimulate careful documentation and procedures that enhance a program. On occasion interested staff have secured outside funding when the program has promise for shared benefits. Research also implies careful review so that the program may benefit by continued focus on improving procedures.

Research efforts have typically been confined to validation of student rating scales, which, though important, can potentially distort the emphasis of a program. But many institutions have shown interest in exploring the other dimensions of the program, and efforts to establish and improve faculty evaluation may serve to assist other institutions with similar problems. These experiences can be shared through publication in professional journals. In addition, this purpose may allow for student-faculty team projects, or be related to teacher-training programs.

SOURCES AND KINDS OF INFORMATION

The kinds of information that describe faculty performance have traditionally been about teaching, research, and service. The current priority in the concern for teaching effectiveness was documented in an extensive study by Peter Seldin (1974), which compares present evaluation practices with those studied in 1967 (Astin and Lee). In the last seven years the practice of evaluating teaching has increased, while that of evaluating research and scholarly publication has declined dramatically. Attempts to define teaching effectiveness as the basis for training and hiring as well as evaluation, however, are not new; the literature has an abundance of studies that have focused on identifying the characteristics of good teachers or good teaching. Some investigators concluded that such characteristics were not definable, or that they were intangible entities that defy description.

No magic formulas were found, but over the years an amazing amount of agreement on the general characteristics of effective teachers has emerged. In a recent report, Kulik and McKeachie (1975) analyzed the findings from eleven studies done from 1943-1973, and derived from them five general dimensions that consistently characterize good teaching. These are: (1) skill; (2) rapport; (3) structure; (4) group interaction; and (5) difficulty. These or similar characteristics recur frequently enough and correlate highly enough with global or overall judgments that they have been accepted as associated with teaching effectiveness. Hildebrand (1971, pp. 46 & 47) emphatically states that we shirk our responsibility if we fail to use the information we have gathered. His study, at the University of California at Davis, established five dimensions of student ratings that discriminate between "best" and "worst" teachers.

> The first is command of the subject. It is scholarship, though not the scholarship of the specialist sequestered in a garret of the ivory tower contemplating, day after day, the ventral surface of craneflies, the crenulations of pollen grains, of fissures in figurines of the pagan god Moloch. Rather, this is scholarship that couples learning with adventure. Does this instructor analyze and show conceptual understanding? Does he contrast the implications of different theories and present the origins of ideas and concepts? Is he a participant in the quest; does he know the other explorers and have a vision of the path ahead? We call this component of effective teaching "*Analytic/Synthetic.*"
>
> The second component is ability to "put it across." It is presentation, yet it is deeper than just rhetoric, showmanship, and entertainment. It is facility at making oneself clear. It is characterized by the well-chosen example and apt analogy, the progression of ideas and gathering of interest, the placement of emphasis and timely summary. We call this component "*Organization/Clarity.*"
>
> The third component of effective teaching is rapport with the class and skill at controlling group participation and interaction. It includes the

ability of the lecturer to learn, by reading body language, if he is being heard, if he is being understood, and if he is turning minds off or on. It includes the effective use of demonstrations, students reports, question periods, and rap sessions. The instructor's concern for the quality of his teaching comes through; his personality comes through. We call this component *"Instructor-Group Interaction."*

The fourth component is one-to-one response. It can occur in the instructor's office or living room, at the coffee house, or on the lawn. It can also occur in a crowded lecture hall if the learner responds individually to the teacher. Thus: He smiled at me. He greeted me. He knows my name! He knows I'm alive and he cares. When I went to see him we just talked. He helped me, and he asked *my* advice. I value his counsel. I respect him. I want to be like him. This we call *"Instructor-Individual Student Interaction."*

The last of our components of effective teaching is the flair and infectious enthusiasm that awaken interest and stimulate response. How can one *not* respond to the instructor who is excited about his subject, radiates self-confidence, and loves to teach. He has a varied and distinctive style. He has a sense of humor. Clock-watchers forget to watch clocks. Lecture-haters forget they are hearing a lecture. He recharges everyone's mental batteries. We call this component *"Dynamism/Enthusiasm."*[a]

Students as a Source of Information

Should student ratings be included in a faculty evaluation system? This controversial issue has been the subject of many articles in the professional literature, and the majority of experts support student ratings as one source of data.

For example, Kulik and McKeachie (1975) begin their extensive review with this paragraph:

> Each sort of observer brings different strengths and liabilities to the task of rating teachers. A teacher's students are in a good position to judge his effectiveness. They are the audience for whom the teaching is intended, and they see the teacher day in and out. Many commentators feel that this daily exposure to the teacher's work more than makes up for students' lack of age and experience. In judging the food, Guthrie (1954) says, the dinner guests have an advantage both over rival chefs and the cooks.

Costin, Greenough, and Menges (1971) did a comprehensive study, the purpose of which they describe as "to review extensively and critically empirical findings concerned with the reliability, validity and usefulness of student ratings." At the end of a long and careful critique of the advantages and disadvantages of student evaluation, this same article concludes (p. 531):

[a]These five dimensions have been developed into a student rating scale, shown on p. xx.

A review of empirical studies indicates that students' ratings can provide reliable and valid information on the quality of courses and instruction. Such information can be of use to academic departments in constructing normative data for the evaluation of teaching and may aid the individual instructor in improving his teaching effectiveness. . . . In conclusion, we wish to emphasize that student ratings of undergraduate teaching fall far short of a complete assessment of an instructor's teaching contribution. . . . Nevertheless, if teaching performance is to be evaluated, either for purposes of pay and promotion or for individual improvement, a systematic measure of student attitudes, opinions and observations can hardly be ignored.

Some still question the student's capability to evaluate, but there is general agreement that with appropriate interpretive limits (such as those discussed under Situational Factors, below) student input is essential, as long as it is not the *only* source of evaluative information.

Richard I. Miller (1974, p. 30) is most emphatic about student contribution:

If one is forced to choose the most significant component of evaluating classroom teaching, it would be student evaluation, although the use of several components is preferable to any single one. The evidence clearly indicates that students can evaluate teaching fairly and preceptively. Burton (1956) points out that students are in a better position than colleagues or administrators to judge the quality of instruction they are receiving, and the American Academy of Arts and Sciences (1971) states that "student opinion . . . is crucial in identifying and rewarding successful teachers."

At present the trend is toward an increasing participation by students, and many institutions with comprehensive programs mandate student contribution as one aspect of the total program. This is true in a new statewide program in Pennsylvania, at the University of Massachusetts, and at most other colleges in Massachusetts at the institutional level. In fact, the danger now is to rely *only* on student evidence, which, as stated above, can be as great a distortion as omitting student response altogether.

Students themselves often have initiated student evaluation of faculty because they want a voice in supporting the teachers they admire, and in helping other students to avoid those whom they fault. Although there is always the possibility of a vindictive or negatively motivated student, the literature shows that composite student ratings are nearly always within a narrow range, and only between "good, very good, and excellent" (Gillmore, 1974). An awareness of this fact can sometimes alleviate faculty resistance that is based on the fear of unfavorable ratings.

It is also true that most research has found that student ratings agree remarkably well with peer and administrator ratings on teaching effectiveness (Kulik and McKeachie, 1975; and Costin, Greenough and Menges, (1971). Students, however, are only indirect observers of research and service. These subjects are often more appropriately observed by others. For most purposes that the evaluation program is serving, however, students are a valuable source of information.

If one purpose of the faculty evaluation program is to guide students in their selection of courses, the students' perspective on content, materials, text, readings, work load, level of difficulty and interest, and exams is essential. These kinds of information are distinctly useful for student course selection, but can also be helpful to the instructor for course modification. Menges (1973) differentiaties responses in this area as "reporting" rather than "evaluating." He feels this level of objective description of the course parameters is the least problematic, and often the most helpful aspect of a total program. Students are often excellent reporters and arouse little hostility while providing useful feedback when they stick to this role. When such items are interpreted within normative bounds, they are most equitable and useful. Unless the procedures are repeated too often, or forms are long and tedious, students are eager to offer information, and most of them try to be thoughtful and objective. The degree of student motivation may also depend on the degree of their understanding of the purposes, processes, and outcomes of the evaluation program, and the visible changes that offer proof of the value of their contribution.

Timing is also important to students. The nature of the class and subject matter will dictate the potential for early sampling of student response. At times students may feel lectures are "over their heads" or discussions are dominated by a few, or that readings are not appropriate; they may feel some class sessions had particular strengths, and some techniques deserve repetition. An early opportunity to assess a course offers the prospect of immediate response or change. Such responses will be more genuinely motivated because these students themselves, not future students, will benefit from any modification. Many students identify this "formative" evaluation as the most urgent and useful in a program when they participate in planning sessions. An early component may be encouraged as a voluntary component of the regular program, where instructors could use rating scales for self-improvement quarter-way or half-way through the course.

Since teaching does not occur only in the classroom, the evaluation of teaching should include a careful review of advising, supervision of field work or independent projects of students, and any other outside-of-class teaching. In some institutions these dimensions are particularly important. According to Seldin's survey (1974), student advising was the subject of evaluation in 68.8 percent of institutions queried, while only 46.8 percent had reported this subject in 1966. Educational trends toward individualization have increased the emphasis on faculty attitudes and competencies in these one-to-one relationships. Most comprehensive student scales include this area of out-of-class instruction where, again, students are the only first-hand source of information. This aspect, described by Hildebrand (1971) as "Instructor-Student Individual Interaction," has qualitative as well as quantitative dimensions. Frequency of contact is only part of the picture, and the kinds of relationships are important also. The relative importance of these dimensions should be explicitly stated in a faculty evaluation program.

On the whole, students are probably the best sources for information on teaching within and outside the classroom, and are one essential source of information about course-related materials. Although they may also be indirect observers of service and research activities, their responses are most appropriately useful as supplementary to other sources.

Interest has recently been focused on student achievement as a criterion for effective teaching. After all, many critics are saying, the real evidence of teaching is learning. Who cares if good teaching goes on; the crucial fact is whether learning is occurring. Measures of student performance have proliferated, and the challenge to inferential methods of observers is clear. Kulik and McKeachie (1975) ask: "Can performance measures replace observers in the evaluation of teachers?" They conclude that "in spite of enthusiasm about evaluating teachers through student achievement, there is little data to suggest that performance measures are really useful to do so." They cite several studies to support this contention, which point up the practical difficulties of using any results as the basis for comparison. Unless extensive norms have been developed, only instructors teaching the same course can be compared; if the same exams are not used, scores may reflect only the different standards of the teachers. In several studies where these factors were controlled, the results from all classes were so similar that any discriminations were trivial and insignificant.

When achievement levels are compared to student ratings, there have been mixed results; for example, one study shows a positive relationship for female students and no relationship for males (McKeachie, Lin, and Mann, 1971). The prevalence of negative conclusions in the literature on the use of student achievement scores to differentiate levels of effective teaching seems based more on a lack of solid methodology for conducting good studies than on a firm belief that these measures might not eventually prove useful. Or as Michael Scriven states: "In short, this is the only way to travel, but the road lies mostly ahead" (1974, p. 114).

It should be emphasized that student learning remains the underlying goal of any institution and any evaluation system. The concept that teaching and learning are two sides of the same coin is a premise in the examination of teaching. Until learning is more accessible to assessment, the teaching aspects must serve as the subject of procedures, but it should always be understood that learning is the true subject.

Orienting evaluation procedures to specific objectives as identified by the faculty member himself can constitute an entirely different approach to faculty evaluation. In conjunction with a peer or administrator, each faculty member may identify his primary objectives within the realms of teaching, research, and service. Within a defined time he and his supervisor or peer may then determine the degree of achievement of his own objectives. This approach is described in Chapter 3, and should be carefully examined in both contexts. Parallel procedures for faculty evaluation are quite possible, and can form the basis for a comprehensive program, while still allowing for input from students, administrators, and faculty themselves.

Peers as a Source of Information

Departmental peers typically witness fellow faculty members' contributions to the department, as well as service to the institution in committee work. They may also be good judges of a teacher's advisory, consulting, and supervising outside the classroom, if they are in a position to observe these activities. They can be a reliable source of information about teaching materials, syllabi, and course content. They are often the best source of information about research and professional activity. They may know something about the faculty member's teaching effectiveness, but they may only be in a position to offer indirect views on this.

Classroom Visits. A few institutions have had success with classroom visitation teams. At one small, nontraditional college, for example, teachers and students first serve as members of the peer visiting team, and then the teachers are periodically visited themselves. The visiting team first meets as a group (of 3 to 5) with the teacher to discuss current goals, problems, and personal objectives. After several visits, they meet with the teacher alone or with his class to discuss their observations. They report that the program has usually worked well and been found to be useful. Another example of systematic observation is reported by a graduate school, where interchange of individual visits has become traditional and accepted. But faculty resistance to peer visits can often be outspoken and emotional, as described in a case study at Carnegie-Mellon (Eble, 1970).

Casual visits by faculty members occur at many colleges, but systematic observation is a rare phenomenon in higher education. There is no doubt that colleagues, as well as students and administrators, could be helpful in such a setting, but there are many problems inherent in this strategy. Kulik and McKeachie (1975) question the reliability of a few visits by such a team, as compared to the daily exposure of students. They also suggest that "the act of observation itself will almost certainly influence the phenomenon observed."

Apparently in some situations this technique can be valuable, but for the majority of colleges, faculty resistance, coupled with the added burden of the time and effort needed to implement a carefully systematized procedure, will preclude it. Without an opportunity for direct observation, peers are not usually appropriate sources of information on teaching effectiveness.

Course-Related Materials. The examination of a course syllabus, texts, reading lists, and student exam questions supplemented by the teacher's description of their use offer insight into the content of a course. Other faculty members in the same department, department chairmen, and others outside the department—or even outside the institution—as well as students who have experienced the use of these materials, are appropriate sources of evaluation information. The sharing of these materials among faculty members can stimulate discussion and new ideas so that this activity can foster faculty development.

Some institutions have forms suggesting criteria for this aspect of evaluation for peers and administrators; most often these kinds of criteria are found only in student evaluation instruments. Many instruments address the usefulness of materials, the extent of innovation, and often the appropriateness of the syllabus, fairness of exams, and distribution of grades. Forms for colleagues are rarely very specific, and this information is requested in broad terms. Different features of these materials are more important at some schools; for example, at Hampshire College, the syllabus can be a significant piece of research, and as such, would be essential to the evaluation process.

Research and Scholarly Publications. The importance of scholarship and professional activity as a dimension of faculty performance to be reviewed by colleagues varies dramatically, from the faculty member who sees scholarly activities as his highest priority, to the professor whose chief concerns are classroom instruction or community service. "Professional" and "scholarly" are words subject to significantly different meanings. However, the area of scholarly or professional activity is included as a category of faculty performance subject to evaluation by fellow faculty members at most institutions. What the terms mean, and what behavioral areas are defined by this category, are dependent on the goals of individual institutions and on the individual faculty member's values. For example, at one graduate school in the East, a faculty member who elects to spend a major portion of his time in a scholarly effort, which is considered appropriate by the dean, is provided the necessary time by being excused from other responsibilities. Other institutions attempt to encourage faculty to formulate their personal goals, with scholarly pursuits as one available option. This is true in the new procedures adopted by a joint contract committee in Pennsylvania for a group of state colleges. Other colleges are attempting, on an institutional level, to identify goals and provide reward systems that are realistically based on them.

Traditionally, the criteria for research or scholarly activity have been the quantity or quality of "contribution to the field," or the number of publications accepted. They can also include reading or "keeping up with the field." Professional activity is judged from membership and degree of participation in professional organizations, or professional courses taken. Recognition by authorities in the same field may be tested by soliciting comments from others outside the teacher's home institution, but peers and administrators within the same department are more typically the sources of such judgments.

The meaning of the terms and therefore the criteria for evaluation varies considerably. In one college, where the emphasis is on nontraditional teaching, professional activity is interpreted as "creative and innovative practices." In one community college, which views its mission as serving a minority community, teachers are expected to know the professional theory and methodology related to its special student body. Some colleges regard research as the single element necessary for promotion and tenure, in the traditional "publish or perish" formula. Many colleges solicit testimony or letters from reputed experts to judge publications. Evaluation of scholarly or research activity is influenced by all these considerations, and the criteria for the effectiveness of achievement would need to be carefully determined within this context. Sources of evidence are nearly always at least colleagues, but could include students, outside experts, the administrator/supervisor, and self-ratings in the form of "activity lists," as an initial source.

Some standard forms are available for peer evaluation of this area, but they are typically in terms of broad categories of "contribution to his field," or "professional activity." The teacher being evaluated may submit evidence to his or her peers for their judgment of quality. Any useful forms would need to be based on real criteria determined for the particular school.

Service. Many institutions have been increasing the importance of and being more careful in defining the responsibilities of faculty members in community service. The responsibility to serve the immediate community is seen in varying ways, and has been increasingly demanded by the community itself. Community colleges have grown up with this philosophy, but no college is immune to the need for better community relations in contemporary society. Peers are often most aware of a colleague's activity in the community, and the community response to it.

Internal service requirements also always exist. Faculty are expected to serve on institutionwide committees on governance, discipline, promotion, or student affairs, which develop the patterns for maintenance and review of policy activities. In order to evaluate a faculty member's service, some criteria for quality and quantity must be established by each institution based on its size, organization, and perceived goals.

Some institutions specify service at all levels—department, college, and university, as well as community—as a minimal contribution. Other feel that a particular portion of a teacher's total effort should be contributed in this category; for example, 20 percent of a teacher's time should be spent in service to the college, while the direction is left to the individual. At many colleges, advising is included as service and may be essentially the only service required. Whether service is judged on the basis of time spent or diversity of contribution, is an institutional decision, but the criteria for evaluating service must parallel these decisions. Those who are in the best position to observe these activities, usually the faculty member's colleagues, are the best source of information.

Service may also include a teacher's relationship, attitudes, and behavior within a department. The instructor who is seen as supportive and positive, who may serve as catalyst to his associates or to their programs, may serve the department without spending defined periods of time in "service" activities. Service may be viewed as a willingness to carry extra work load or more of the less desirable kinds of courses in his teaching load. Therefore, in some instances, service may encompass much of a faculty member's personal behavior in the group context, and the resultant evaluation criteria could be in terms of his or her personal contribution to a more smoothly functioning organization. Other faculty and administrators in the immediate environment again are the best sources of this information.

Institutions may see service in unique terms, consonant with their goals. Service to the community, for example, may be the highest priority in a community college, and if the community has particular ethnic roots, this service may take the form of teaching ethnic culture, or creating opportunity for activities directly involving the community. In a large university, on the other hand, service as an expert on committees which are national in scope could be expected of senior faculty in some disciplines.

Since service implies that a faculty member should exert effort toward an institution's real concerns, evaluation in this category necessitates defining these concerns. Most present programs only define such areas in broad terms, and the traditional concept of committee participation is their only criterion. New emphasis on the relative importance of service, and its many dimensions, has stimulated better definition in some schools and, in turn, provided colleagues and administrators with more specific criteria with which to evaluate service.

Few rating forms except traditional kinds are available for this purpose, and, typically, administrators and peers are sources of information. In a few cases community agencies or other external sources are asked for comments. Sometimes interviews in depth about a teacher's quality of participation as well as the amount of time he or she has spent are conducted with the others with whom he or she has served. The nature of service is still controversial, and comprehensive evaluation systems are attempting to allow for a great deal of flexibility in specifying what service is and the quantity or quality criteria that may accurately assess it. The quantity and quality of direct information available to a colleague should dictate the nature of the evaluation in this area. Although forms may be devised and their specificity increased, other ways of soliciting evidence, such as interviews, should not be overlooked. The danger in using such techniques is in not providing for systematic controls. Standard interview formats and defined areas of questioning may offer better information and retain its comparability, while allowing for supplementary information on unique contributions.

Administrators as Sources of Information

College and university administrators are taking more active roles in faculty evaluation, in part because of the demands that they make more frequent and wiser decisions in the face of fiscal constraints. In the majority of institutions surveyed in this project, administrators (department chairpersons, deans, presidents) not only consider the ratings of others (students, peers, other administrators) in making final decisions regarding faculty status, but increasingly they themselves contribute evaluative input to those decisions. When other sources of evaluative information are used, administrators, and in some cases peer committees, are responsible for interpreting and weighting their evaluations.

These two roles for an administrator—that of direct observer and personal source of evaluative evidence and that of sifter and integrator of the evidence gathered from all other sources have sometimes led to confusion. Administrators at some levels may act only as sources of evidence, while the interpretive role is left to other administrators. But in many situations the demands on an administrator are dual, and these two roles must be carefully distinguished or the administrator's contribution will be ambiguous. By differentiating stages of data collection, and carefully defining (by use of specific forms, for example) the areas where the administrator may have direct access to his own information, this potential confusion may be avoided. For almost every purpose for which evaluation information is used, some administrative input is vital.

The administrator and colleagues are responsible for gathering data about the faculty member, and insuring that comprehensive evidence is considered. In the *AAUP Bulletin* (1974, p. 168) the "Statement on Teaching Evaluation" articulates this requirement:

> An important and often overlooked element of evaluating teaching is an accurate description of a professor's teaching. Such a description should include number and level and kinds of classes taught, numbers of students, and out-of-class activities related to teaching. Such data should be very carefully considered both to guard against drawing unwarranted conclusions and to increase the possibilities of fairly comparing work loads and kinds of teaching, of calrifying expectations, and of identifying particulars of minimum and maximum performance. Other useful information might include evidence of the ability of a teacher to shape new courses, to reach different levels and kinds of students, to develop effective teaching strategies, and to contribute to the effectiveness of the individual's and the institution's instruction in other ways than in the classroom.

The gathering of such data can promote a careful consideration of both the institution's and the department's values. If a department, for example, places great value upon teaching large numbers of lower level students, that value should be reflected in the judgments about teachers who perform such tasks effectively. Too often, even at the simple point of numbers and kinds of students taught, departments and institutions operate on value assumptions seldom made clear to the faculty.

Another kind of data which should be systematically gathered and examined by the teacher's colleagues includes course outlines, tests, materials, and the methods employed in instruction. Care should be taken that such scrutiny not inhibit the teacher, limit the variety of effective teaching styles, or discourage purposeful innovation. Evidence of a concern for teaching and teaching competence demonstrated in publications, attendance at meetings, delivery of lectures, and consulting should also be included among the essential information to be reviewed.

A unique administrative perspective concerns course enrollment trends, employment opportunities, and the shifting needs and interests of students. Matching faculty strengths and educational needs is an administrative function. A teacher of Greek, for example, could be rated as a brilliant teacher and scholar, but insufficient student interest in Greek could be anticipated to some degree, and other options for that faculty member considered.

Since faculty files are usually maintained in an administrator's office, the administrator responsible for those files should maintain not only old annual evaluation reports, but should analyze and summarize improvement patterns over time. Weight should be given to improved performances by faculty members, and it should be noted when declining ratings have occurred. The administrator who is in a position to view institutional needs and larger issues can also consider information suggesting trends and patterns of improvement. In this way he or she alone can be instrumental in fostering more useful development programs as well as better allocation of personnel, and information which is retained in a useful manner can help administrators base their decisions on empirical evidence gathered over time.

Self as a Source of Information

The faculty member knows the most about the amount of *effort* he or she has expended, and the *activities* pursued. The teacher may have a clear understanding of personal goals and values, and has a better chance of accurately remembering effort and activities if it has been agreed ahead of time that they will be kept track of, and some format for record-keeping is provided. He or she will also be able to articulate personal goals and values better if the institution's goals are obvious, and what is expected of the individual teacher.

Some institutions provide "activity lists" for these purposes. If additional judgmental information is desired, it is often poorly solicited. It is difficult to assess the quality of one's own efforts if no criteria are defined. In some cases the same criteria are used for self-evaluation in teaching, research, and advising as are used by students or peers. In fact, in Centra's (1973) study the most valuable information was elicited when self-evaluation and student evaluation were requested on the same instrument to reveal any discrepancies.

Any information that a faculty member gives will be influenced by the purposes for which it is to be used. According to Kulik and McKeachie (1975), and Centra (1973), when the purpose of the program is information for promotion or tenure decisions, self-evaluation is almost useless. (See Self-Evaluation, below, for Centra's full explanation.) Many investigators, including Centra, feel that self-evaluation should always be *one* component of programs.

The AAUP "Statement on Teaching Evaluation" (1974, p. 170) presents both arguments:

> The limitations of self-evaluation are obvious, and neither the teacher nor the institution should be satisfied with self-evaluation alone. However, faculty members as individuals or as members of committees can assist colleagues in making the kind of self-evaluation which constitutes a contribution to improving and evaluating teaching. Arousing an interest in self-examination, structuring self-evaluations so that they might afford more reliable data, and giving faculty members the opportunity to assess their own teaching effectiveness and to add their own interpretation of student ratings and classroom visitations can increase the usefulness of self-evaluation as a part of the review process.

If the purpose is to improve performance, the reflection stimulated by self-evaluation can be rewarding. A faculty member's views on his or her place in a total program or his assets as an institutional resource may be valuable data for administrative use.

Self-evaluation has the unique advantage of evidence from a witness, and can be useful as one source of a multisource base. Each faculty member should clearly understand what information is expected before the end of the performance period that is to be evaluated. The most important information for faculty members to contribute to their total evaluation concerns their intended objectives, and the activities and methods they have employed to attain those objectives. Where faculty goals are clear, it will be easier for students, peers, and administrators to make fair and objective assessments of performances and outcomes. In self reports, a format weighting all the kinds and sources of information which clearly outlines evidence desired, is mandatory. The self-effacing modest teacher will need encouragement to describe all of his or her relevant activity and accomplishments, while the overconfident teacher may need limits specific to the kinds of information that will be useful. Self-evaluation forms may suggest lists of activities in various categories, as well as seeking subjective judgments in particular areas. Is the teacher's personal priority classroom teaching, or is it perceived as individual counseling or advising? Such goal perceptions and their parallel in performance can provide better understanding of the fit between teacher role and departmental needs. The practice of having faculty members complete student questionnaires has also been seen as very helpful. At the University of Massachusetts' Clinic to Improve University Teaching, a questionnaire is given to students, then to the teacher, and then the teacher is asked to complete the questionnaire a second time with responses that he or she predicts the students will give. An analysis of these three response patterns helps the teacher to view objectively personal teaching skills.

Weighting the Kinds and Sources of Information

Teaching, research, and service—as defined by an institution and assessed by students, peers, administrators and the person being evaluated—are often assigned a relative priority within the context of the institution's goals. Typically this weighting is implied, or suggested, but some colleges specify weights to be applied in each category. For example, at W.R. Harper College in Palatine, Illinois, after carefully defining each area and the criteria for evaluating it, as it relates to Harper's own goals, the evaluation policy states:

These four areas to be evaluated will carry the following weights in the total evaluation:

Instruction	60%
Institutional Service	20%
Professional Growth	15%
Community Service	5%
	100%

Within the four areas the following individuals or groups will carry the following weights:

	Instruction	Institutional Service	Professional Growth	Community Service
Division Chairman	35%	60%	50%	55%
Peers	35%	35%	35%	30%
Self	0%	5%	15%	15%
Students	30%	0%	0%	0%

Such specific weighting for areas and sources of information demand careful examination of goals in the planning stages. While most evaluation committees do not see the need for a detailed weighting scheme such as this, others may feel that these concrete values enhance the legitimacy and credibility of the total program, particularly if the purpose of the program is for tenure, promotion, and retention decisions as it is at W.R. Harper College.

When the principal reason for the evaluation system is to aid in personnel decisions, accountability demands that decisions be made about the relative importance of teaching versus other categories of faculty performance, and that decisions be made about the relative weight to be given to the evidence gathered from each source. These decisions can be translated into quantitative procedures as they are at Harper, or broad categorical priorities depending on the nature of the institution and, perhaps, the climate of acceptance or resistance to the evaluation program. At Harper these weights were assigned only in a revision stage, which suggests that specific delineation had been an issue in initial program trials.

At Sangamon State University in Springfield, Illinois, weighting is also applied; student evaluation of teaching is given 60 percent and colleague and administrator evaluation of service 40 percent of the total weight in promotional decisions.

At Kansas State University, each faculty member assigns weights consonant with his or her individual goals to student ratings of teaching before they are administered. Items are grouped in major categories, and the faculty member selects the group or groups which are: (1) of no more than minor importance; (2) important; and (3) essential. Those the teacher places in the first group are given no weight, and disregarded; those in the second group are given single weight; while those rated essential are double weighted. In this way the teacher sets the objectives, and the evaluation is geared to his or her own values.

Whatever the relative weight assigned to each area, it is most important that all areas are included and that each is carefully defined as to meaning, criteria, and relative importance for the unique setting at that institution. If classroom teaching is considered very important, then this emphasis should be translated into relative weight in the total program. If a faculty member is to set individual goals, then this, too, can be part of the evaluation design.

Many sources of information on the different areas of performance of faculty members can increase the scope, perspective, and potential benefit of an evaluation program. Interpreting and melding these sources of evidence into practical usefulness will be eased by the consensus of those involved on the relative contribution of each source and of each area.

RATING SCALES

Student Rating Scales
Since the student component of faculty evaluation has become so important, methods of eliciting student ratings have, in turn, been increasingly emphasized. The research literature includes a myriad of studies on student rating scales, with factor analyses and validity studies conducted over many years. The findings from other studies have been translated into rating scales for students evaluating faculty, and these are presented at the end of this chapter under

Sample Rating Scales. For example, Hildebrand's identification of five areas of characteristics, culled from his "best and worst" teacher study, is the basis of the Wilson and Dienst scale (see Rating Scale 2-1). McKeachie's findings are the basis for the McKeachie scale (see RS 2-3). Similarly, extensive studies have produced standardized rating scales at Princeton University (see RS 2-4). The Purdue Rating Scale, the earliest to be published, has had many years of reliability studies, and a recent modification (see RS 2-6). Educational Testing Services produced the Student Instructional Report, which grew out of work that John Centra began at Michigan (see RS 2-8). Hoyt's work at Kansas State University was the basis for his forms (see RS 2-9). From the use of this form, Hoyt has developed extensive norms. At Kansas State each faculty member weights items he or she feels are priority objectives, and these weights are translated into the scoring procedures. This work was the basis of a faculty evaluation system called the "Instructional Development and Effectiveness Assessment" system (IDEA), which is available through the Center for Faculty Evaluation and Development at Kansas State University. The Endeavor Instructional Rating Form (RS 2-11), based on studies by Frey (1973) at Northwestern University, comprises twenty-one items but identifies seven primary attributes, each of which is represented by three items. Therefore, results are reported in terms of the seven primary factors, supported by three student responses for each item. The Instructional Assessment System (RS 2-12) from the University of Washington is discussed below under "Flexibility."

Ronan's scale (RS 2-13) based on the Critical Incident Technique, suggests a different approach, both in the development of the scale, which was empirical in nature, and in the responses, which are also empirical and require only yes or no as answers. Inquiring about concrete incidents has been quite productive, according to Ronan's study, in eliciting constructive information for many benefits.

One other form is included (RS 2-14) because it is an example of a scale designed for a specific purpose. That is the TABS form developed by the Clinic to Improve University Teaching at the University of Massachusetts at Amherst, using Hildebrand, Dienst, and Wilson's work as a base, and identifying significant and "treatable" teaching skills and behaviors. It is not intended as evaluative but as diagnostic so that a faculty member and consultant specialist can localize significant strengths and weaknesses as targets of improvement procedures. The clinic's approach is to use this scale three ways in each cycle. The students in class complete it, the teacher completes it, and the teacher predicts how students will respond to each item. The comparison of these three sets of results are a major portion of the diagnostic study for the teacher. This is supplemented by interviewing the teacher and by videotaping and observing his or her classroom performance.

These forms are all available, some on a cost basis, some for a fee. They may not be reproduced or copied by any means. *Please note* details on each sample form which specify restrictions on the use of these instruments. The names and addresses of people to contact for further information about these and other rating forms are given in the Resources section at the end of the chapter, along with a further explanation of their uses.

So there are presently available a number of research-based or carefully validated student rating scales. Any institution in the process of developing evaluation programs should be aware of these when selecting an instrument. It would be like reinventing the wheel to set out from scratch when there are carefully researched instruments readily available.

However, many colleges find only pieces of these scales to be appropriate, and prefer to modify or supplement an assortment of devices before evolving the instrument they feel is most attuned to their particular situation.

As the AAUP "Statement on Teaching Evaluation" (1974, p. 169) states:

> There is no one questionnaire or method suitable to every department or institution. Different kinds of questionnaires can be useful in assessing different kinds of courses and subject matters and to meet the need for information of a particular kind. However, a common instrument covering a range of teachers, departments, and subject matter areas has the great advantage of affording meaningful comparative data. The important consideration is to obtain reliable data over a range of teaching assignments and over a period of time.

As you will see by examining the sample instruments included below, there has been a concerted effort to develop one that is applicable generally, and a variety of methods have been tried to meet diverse needs with a single form.

Flexibility. There are many features that have been identified as essential in student rating scales. The first is the flexibility to allow for a variety of teaching styles and different disciplines to be appropriately addressed. This feature has been addressed the University of Washington, by asking faculty members to select one of five versions of a student instrument which best reflects the type of course given (see RS 2-12). These forms serve three purposes. Section 1 is used by administrators as one input into their decisions regarding retention, salary, and promotion. Section 2 is used for the faculty member's self-improvement. Section 3 is used to inform students regarding their selection of courses and instructors. They therefore allow for flexibility by serving three purposes on a one-sheet scale, and more important, by providing five alternative forms for different kinds of teaching techniques. Yet in all five they retain a core of comparable items.

Other institutions have used core items from standard instruments, therefore having national or other norms available, but have expanded the forms to include items uniquely suited to their own situations. Texas Christian University, for example, modified Hildebrand's research-based scale. The Purdue Scale has a new form called "The Cafeteria System" (see RS 2-6), which extends a group of core items by the addition of other items that a teacher, department, or college may select from a catalog of possible items. In this way normative information and interpretation are applicable on the core items, but the flexibility to meet differing needs is still provided by self-selected additional items.

Other institutions have preferred to create their own instruments from scratch, and some have expended great time and effort establishing the reliability and validity of their scales. Sangamon State University, for example, spent a year developing an instrument, with repeated review and revision by representatives of all factions of the college. The result is a brief three-question scale.

It is perhaps most important to remember that faculty evaluation program must avoid advocating uniform styles. Menges (1973, pp. 68-69) describes this possibility:

> I believe that the consequences of a responsible program of student evaluation of teaching are overwhelmingly positive. Of the possible negative consequences, I am most concerned about a leveling effect on creative teaching. If evaluations are built from a narrow empiricist tradition, they are likely to be severely inhibiting. The most "useful" empirical results are sometimes the most dehumanizing. Imposing uniform rating procedures on a diverse faculty can only raise the cry, "All teachers are exceptional. By virtue of being human, they are bound to be highly individual" (Kossoff 1971-72, p. 85).
>
> Some of the most innovative teachers, probably the source of the most significant educational reforms, are highly individualistic teachers. Characteristics of these "new teachers" include styles and techniques which do not fit most rating forms. "His teaching style is a life style, and life styles are highly individualistic and depend on make-up and background and often vary from situation to situation. . . . The New Teacher is learning, often the hard way, that not all students still see a need to intellectualize everything (Flournoy, 1972, pp. 2, 4)." Teachers who are growing and experimenting may not fare well under conventional student ratings. That possibility does not make them less accountable for providing some evidence of their impact as teachers, but it does suggest that institutions must take special care to ensure that a variety of evidence is acceptable.

If teaching goals include encouragement of creative and innovative styles, then student instruments must have the flexibility to provide for a variety of sources of evidence to equitably assess widely differing teaching styles. Evaluation can encourage creativity, and certainly must be careful not to discourage it.

Length. If a questionnaire is too brief it may not produce enough information, but if it is too long it may cause resentment among students who fill it out, and also may present logistics problems in tabulating results. Some standard devices have long, medium, and short forms available, and others are flexible enough to abbreviate. Ten to twenty minutes is about the length of time students will concentrate on completing questionnaires. Ten to thirty item scales on one or two pages is an optimal length.

Format. Students are more likely to complete a questionnaire that has clear, simple instructions, and easy to check answers. The purpose of the program, uses which are to be made of the results, and nature of the confidentiality of responses should be explicitly stated on every form. An attractive yet business-like appearance is more motivating to students, and conveys the importance and seriousness of the need for student participation.

Scale Range. Most student rating scales have quantitative answers. For example, the student is asked to answer on a scale of 1, excellent, to 5, poor. The points may range from 1 to 3, or 1 to 7, or more. The University of Washington, for instance, uses a 1 to 6 span, which they explain in this way (Gilmore 1974, pp. 3-4):

> We have chosen the following six response categories for use for these and all other items: Excellent, Very Good, Good, Fair, Poor, Very Poor. These categories were chosen rather than the more common Likert-categories, Strongly Agree to Strongly Disagree (at the expense of greater difficulty in writing coherent items), for two reasons. First, actual responses to these categories, and class means, are more readily interpretable. It is easier to understand that on the average you are "good" than you are "agree." Secondly, student ratings have a tendency to bunch up at the favorable end. There is evidence that use of both an Excellent and a Very Good category at the favorable end yield more between class variance, i.e., discrimination, than a four or five point Likert scale.

Some committees have preferred using terms such as "fascinating" to "boring" as the Osgood Semantic Differential does. In general, a minimum of 5 points and a maximum of 7 points as a range has been optimal for student ratings. The characteristics, such as point span, of a variety of instruments, are listed in a manual by Hodgkinson (1974).

Validity.[b] The validity of an instrument, or whether it measures what it purports to measure, has been studied extensively for some instruments. Other institutions pilot test their own instruments, and may test the validity by re-

[b]This book does not treat issues of instrument validity or reliability in depth because of the abundance of literature on these topics. Also, such technical information on the instruments shown herein are not included because we assume that readers interested in using them will communicate with those sources, listed under Resources at the end of the chapter.

questing the same information in a variety of ways on different items, and then seeing if the answers are statistically consistent. In Chapter 3, two instruments displayed from Texas Christian University—a trial run and a rerun based on their own factor analysis—illustrate the dramatic change that a validity check can produce (pp. 154-157). Validity is often measured by comparing a test instrument with one that has already established its validity. Many committees decide that face validity is acceptable; that is, the instrument logically appears to be valid.

Reliability. Reliability is a similar problem that has been studied extensively in the literature. Reliability in student ratings has been seen in two ways: (1) as stability over time, or whether the students' ratings remain the same over time (in one study [Drucker and Remmers, 1950], alumni ten years out of school remained consistent in their ratings); or (2) as consistency among raters of the same teacher (Kulik and McKeachie, 1975). The latter is most easily obtained for one teacher over several sections, or several courses. Many other variables affect these ratings, so it is difficult to establish that it is really validity and reliability that one is identifying. A large sample and repeated trials give more confidence in results.

Situational Factors. Other sources of variation in student responses should be noted, understood, and considered when selecting, modifying, or constructing student rating scales. It might seem obvious that a good teacher will get good ratings from students, and that a poor teacher will receive poor ratings, but many factors besides teaching influence the student's view of the teacher.

Student Characteristics. Many investigators have tried to identify the specific student characteristics that influence ratings of teachers. Rating sheets typically ask for sex, major or minor, and college year, and these have been found to account for some of the variation, but not much. The most important characteristic is probably the general disposition of the student toward instructors and courses in general. Questions that attempt to identify these attitudes are sometimes included in student scales; for example, at Kansas State University (see RS 2-9), this kind of information is asked directly. Sex, age, previous experience, or the grade a student expects to receive do not appear to affect ratings significantly.

Teacher Characteristics and Teaching Conditions. The teacher's characteristics and the conditions under which he or she teaches also contribute predictable variation. Research indicates that lower-level courses, moderate-sized rather than very small or very large classes, on-campus instead of off-campus locations, and required versus elective courses tend to receive less favorable ratings from students. Requesting this information on rating scales can allow for more equitable interpretation.

The teacher's age, rank, and experience are also related positively to students' ratings, but other teacher characteristics seem more important. The teacher who is called "effective" by students and by peers as well is often called "enthusiastic." Another common trait most often appearing to discriminate between those called effective and noneffective is the ability to "communicate." Being verbally fluent, expressive, and enthusiastic are essential to drawing high ratings (Kulik and McKeachie. (1975); and Hildebrand (1971). Many scales now include items that not only cover competency and skill, but also communications or teacher presentation.

One study in California (Naftulin *et al.* 1973) illustrated this point dramatically. These authors instructed an actor, totally ignorant of the topic, to lecture "charismatically and nonsubstantively" to a sophisticated group of psychiatrists, psychologists, social workers, educators, and administrators. All fifty-five subjects who served as students rated the lecture and lecturer favorably. The authors conclude that ratings of teachers are more influenced by his style than by his substance. Or, as McKeachie says, "the good teacher is a good talker."

Interaction Effects. One of the reasons that student characteristics and teacher characteristics do not account for all of the variation in student evaluation is that interaction between different students and different teachers produces its own effects. This chemistry between students and teachers has been studied. Remmers, in 1928, in his original work for the Purdue Rating Scale, examined the relationship between student ratings and student course grades. He noted the overall correlations were zero, but there were individual variations for some instructors from highly positive to highly negative. Subsequent investigators with similar findings suggested that some instructors were teaching to the bright students and some to the slower students. Therefore teaching styles are perceived differently, and this interaction may explain some of the variation in findings.

Measures of the degree of structure of a class style when interacting with students of differing achievement orientations produced differences both in student satisfaction and achievement. Some students who preferred more highly structured classes evidenced better achievement and satisfaction when class styles were matched to their preferences. Therefore, when classes are highly structured or completely nonstructured, some variation will be due to student attitudes and orientation.

Acceptance. Acceptance or nonacceptance of a rating scale may be influenced by all the other features. If students, faculty members, and administrators do not have confidence in the relevance and usefulness of the questionnaire, as well as the seriousness of purpose of the program itself, all the preparatory work may be wasted.

Several procedures may contribute to a state of acceptance. One factor that seems to be crucial is complete openness of the planning and adoption of instruments and procedures from the very beginning of the program. A second is the concrete participation of each constituency in the academic community. If students, faculty, and administrators—or at least representatives of each—have actively contributed to the planning of each step, they will "own" the program that emerges. Only this perceived ownership can lend real acceptance in the implementation stages. Students who have helped select rating scales and are informed about the uses to which their responses are to be put will remain motivated to complete questionnaires thoughtfully. Faculty members whose opinions about the real issues of performance have been respected and truly incorporated into the program will subsequently consider the results as meaningful and equitable. Administrators who feel the program is necessary and useful because their judgement has been consulted along the way are much more likely to use the evidence collected as the basis for the uses for which the program is intended.

Three other factors may contribute to this acceptance: (1) the clarity of directions for filling out the form; (2) the explicit statement of the purpose of the evaluation of the intended use of the results of the questionnaire on the form itself (McKeachie's scale does this better than most); and, perhaps most important, (3) room for comments, or prose responses provided somewhere on the forms. Many students feel restricted by quantitative instruments and are more comfortable and free to express real concerns in an open-ended format.

The mechanics for keeping planning and procedures visible and open to constant question and suggestion are often different at each institution. However, incorporating presentations about the program into student orientation meetings, or regular campus publications and posted "news items" are some possibilities. Insuring that teachers inform students in initial class sessions may reinforce teacher as well as student awareness. Suggestions of early, formative procedures for teacher use may pave the way for later evaluation, as well as prove to be helpful immediately.

Timing and Procedures. On most campuses, student rating scales are given at the last possible moment (e.g. at the last class session), and in a rushed and casual manner that is anticlimactic. The students fill out their questionnaires casually and hastily, yielding results that miss the fine points of their true feelings. A student who (on a 1–5 scale) checks all 5's, all 1's, all 4's and 5's, all 1's and 2's, etc., is probably indicating only a generalized attitude (favorable or unfavorable) toward the course and the instructor. If all items on the questionnaire are more or less answered as if they were the same item, the purpose of a differentiated-item questionnaire is defeated.

We recommend a practice that appears to work well on several campuses surveyed in this project. Students fill out their rating scales of instructors one to two weeks before the class ends, and before final exams are taken. The questionnaires are collected and put into sealed envelopes in view of the students; they are locked up in a known, trusted, and secure place, to be processed immediately *after* final grades are issued. Students need to have confidence that anonymity will be preserved, that their questionnaire responses will not affect their grade in the course, and that those involved convey a sense of seriousness and importance in this activity (these points are further elaborated below).

Some faculty and students may object to giving a questionnaire one to two weeks before the class is over on the grounds that "they haven't seen the whole show yet," or that "it will take away precious class time needed especially near the end of a course." But taking that precious time near the end attests to the seriousness and importance of the questionnaire, and to the entire faculty evaluation program. As for the issue of incompleteness, it has been found that student ratings remain stable after courses are about half over, given no dramatic change in the instructor's performance.

If student questionnaires are given in every course, every semester, a staggered schedule should be worked out, to span a one- to two-week period, where questionnaires are filled out in certain assigned classes on particular days, so that no student will be asked to fill out several questionnaires on one day.

Peer Rating Scales

In contrast to the proliferation of research-based student evaluation scales there are few instruments derived from research for the use of peer evaluation of faculty. Forms for use in classroom visitation, and for systematic observation of classroom instruction or student-teacher interactions are also rare in higher education, as mentioned previously. There are no research-based instruments used in faculty evaluation programs for rating course content, texts, exams, or reading lists, or in judging research or service areas of performance. In the absence of research-based instruments, many faculty members use checklists, questions, or broad criteria of performance derived from practice as guides in evaluating peers.

The one exception is the Colleague Description of Teachers (RS 2-15) developed by Wilson and Dienst, which results from research on the distinguishing characteristics of effective teachers as reported by colleagues (other aspects of this study were reported also under Student Rating Scales, above). The 27 items on this instrument, derived from a pool of 67 items, were those significantly related to effective teaching.

The Greenfield Community College's Peer Evaluation Form (RS 2-16) and Class Observation Report (RS 2-17) are typical of the types of broad areas used in instruments derived from practice.

More standardized and specific peer instruments are needed, and the paucity of such forms presently should not be interpreted as an indication of their lack of importance. On the other hand the use of standardized interviews, testimonials solicited in a uniform format, and other kinds of information should not be overlooked.

Some features of a peer instrument are essential if the instrument is to be useful and equitable. Some of the dimensions are equally applicable to other forms of data that might be collected.

Format. The form should include specific questions so that some comparative information is elicited. Some effective instruments use a point range scale as in student scales, while others use well-defined guidelines. There should also be space for open-ended comments. The purpose for which responses are to be used should be stated explicitly on the form. Clear directions and an easy response format increases motivation.

Flexibility. Colleagues may feel that a faculty member has a particular talent or makes a unique contribution to the department or school. The instrument should have the flexibility to allow them to describe these facets. One may also want to indicate a priority or importance of the faculty member's contribution in one area—for example, service—which that person feels outweighs the weakness of some other area. Since it is difficult to include particular items that cover every situation, the form should be flexible enough to allow individual additional comments within the structure, which also provides some uniformity. A balance between quantitative and qualitative responses is difficult to achieve in colleague forms, but is particularly important to many teachers.

Appropriateness. Every area evaluated by a colleague should be one that the colleague has had an opportunity to observe directly. Peers are typically asked to judge course-related materials, research and service, and sometimes teaching. If items request information about the quantity and quality of course syllabi, reading lists, exams, and grade distributions, then careful procedures that allow for thorough examination of these materials must be provided. If research and service are to be evaluated, procedures to insure that good evidence is available should also be provided. Some peer instruments include questions asking the evaluator to indicate to what extent he or she has observed each area.

Some programs allow the faculty member to select the most appropriate sources of information for different aspects of his or her performance. For example, one may choose five from a list of ten potential evaluators, or identify a colleague who served with him on a committee or with whom he has consulted on a research project. Only peers who are qualified by having carefully reviewed or directly observed an area should be asked to evaluate a colleague in that area.

Acceptance. As described in the student ratings section, acceptance of the instrument and procedures that accompany it are vital to program success. Colleagues must have confidence in the forms and the uses to which results are to be put, to motivate them to participate thoughtfully and seriously. If they have participated in the planning, selection, or development of the instrument, and all the other features have been considered, they are more likely to accept their own task and contribution. Since faculty members are apt to be evaluator and evaluatee at some time, their stake in the program is very great, and their acceptance of the fairness and legitimacy of what is done is essential.

Administrator Rating Scales

Instruments that have been developed for administrators to use in evaluating faculty essentially fall into the same category as those developed for peer evaluation—few are research-based, many identify broad areas of concern, or specific factors deemed important to particular situations. Most administrative evaluation is done without forms and can be very inadequate and noncomparable. Using forms that at least suggest guidelines and at most *specify* real criteria is more equitable.

The first sample form shown (RS 2-18) is an instrument derived from research on faculty performance at the Institute of Technology at Southern Methodist University in Dallas. There are three dimensions (personal qualities, research production, teaching), each of which has several related items. The relative values of all items are rated and ratings are adjusted and combined to give item scores, dimension scores, and an overall performance score (the numbers in the boxes are hypothetical ratings and scores for purposes of illustration). Administrators use this instrument to evaluate all faculty every year, and the overall performance score is used as the basis for determining faculty salaries for the subsequent year (a ratio between score and salary has been established for this purpose).

The second example shown (RS 2-19) is an instrument that typifies those derived from practice, rather than from research (RS 2-18). It identifies broad areas of concern, or specific factors deemed important to particular situations.

The same features of an instrument that are essential for peers are necessary for administrators or supervisors. Since this heading may include department chairmen, deans, or presidents, it may require differentiation in forms. The specific substance which is appropriate may vary, and different perspectives may cause the focus of the instrument to differ. However, these factors remain important. (They are explained in greater detail in the preceding section on peer instruments).

Format. Both quantitative and qualitative information should be included. If an instrument is not used, but letters or testimonials are preferred for some administrators, some standardization in format can still be obtained. Evidence can be categorized into areas of research, teaching, etc., or topics such as personal characteristics and departmental or college contributions. Questions that limit or guide responses into useful and comparable formats are very helpful to the evaluator, and provide better information, as well.

Flexibility. Instruments should be flexible enough to include special talents or contributions, often through the inclusion of open-ended sections.

Appropriateness. Only information the administrator has observed or reviewed directly is requested. For example, if an administrator who has not directly observed teaching cannot be expected to assess it. If he or she is to be asked to rate classroom teaching, then the opportunity to observe it with a systematic listing of those aspects to be evaluated must be provided.

Acceptance. Administrators must understand and have confidence in the instrument, procedures, and purposes of the program if they are to contribute them thoughtfully and seriously. Often a department head, for example, is expected to be the primary source of information about those within his department, and he may find this acceptable only if he can involve others in his final assessment. Eble (1973, p. 64) comments:

> Since departments and department chairmen are so important in the practices of evaluating faculty, the department chairman should involve all members of the department in frequent review and written formulation of the criteria and procedures for promotion and tenure.

Such a process contributes to the visibility and acceptance of administrator evaluation, because it shelters the sensitivity of all concerned by sharing the burden. It can lend an equitable balance to the evidence, which is fairer to the faculty member.

Overview. In addition, the administrator has the responsibility of viewing the faculty member from a unique perspective, that of the department, college, or university. Therefore, an added dimension is faculty contribution to the needs of these contexts. This meshing of performance with needs is a high priority for an administrator.

Since administrators at every level have traditionally been responsible for evaluation of faculty, programs that now incorporate student and colleague evaluation as well must be careful to define the contribution still expected of the administrators. By empowering a group representative of all constituencies to discuss and select all instruments and procedures the most appropriate areas and the specific demands on each can be equitably allocated, without unnecessary overlap, but offering legitimate input from each perspective. The administrator's additional task of sifting and interpreting the evidence of others also needs to be considered by the group.

Self-Evaluation

As described in a previous section, the bulk of research evidence indicates that most faculty consistently rate themselves very highly. As Centra (1972, p. 14-15) has concluded:

> Can teachers really be expected to see themselves *realistically?* The results of a study recently completed by the writer demonstrate a clear discrepancy between the way most teachers described their instruction, and the way students described it (Centra, 1972).[c]

> Not surprisingly, most teachers in that study viewed themselves in more favorable terms, particularly on such matters as whether they stimulated student interest, the extent to which the course objectives were met, and whether the instructor seemed open to other viewpoints. Of course there were some teachers who viewed themselves very much as their students viewed them, and even a few who had more negative perceptions. Nevertheless, the majority saw themselves in rather glowing terms—this in spite of the well-known tendency for students' ratings of teaching to be rather lenient and skewed in a positive direction. . . .
> Previously, studies at the college level that investigated faculty self-ratings employed a single overall measure of teaching (instead of many specific items relating to instructional practices), and they too produced similar findings. In fact, not only were faculty and student ratings of "overall teacher effectiveness" only modestly correlated, but so were faculty-administrator and faculty-colleague ratings (Clark and Blackburn, 1971; Choy, 1969). In other words, there seems to be ample evidence that most teachers do *not* view their teaching as their students, their colleagues, or administrators at their college view it. On the other hand, these same researchers report fairly substantial agreement among colleagues, students, and administrators in their ratings of teachers, so it might justifiably be concluded that teacher self-ratings miss the mark by a good deal. Self-analysis alone would seem to have little promise for improving instruction (Remmers, 1963, pp. 14–15).

It should not be concluded from this rather gloomy picture, however, that self-evaluation is entirely without use. In another study, Centra (1973) demonstrated that where self-evaluation and the evaluation of others were largely discrepant, improvement was most likely to take place. So having faculty evalu-

---

[c]Items from a student evaluation-of-teaching form were reworded slightly for instructor responses. Instructors were asked, for example, whether they thought they had made objectives clear, whether they were encouraging students to think for themselves, and so on.

ate themselves using the same forms as students, peers, and administrators would allow for comparison and the identification of large discrepancies. Questions can be added that cover situtional or other factors not covered in the instruments used by others.

Because research has been unable to relate self-evaluation factors to faculty effectiveness, no research-based instruments for self-evaluation are available. Rating Scale 2–20 is typical of those derived from practice, and it does combine questions asked of others (for comparative purposes) with questions of special interest. Other self-evaluation forms are often activity-list requests, where no particular judgments are asked. Some features that should be considered in developing self-evaluation "instruments" are:

Activities. Only the individual faculty member can list all personal activities in research, service, teaching, advising, and supervision. There should be provision for enumeration of all of these efforts. Some guidelines should be included to insure the inclusion of all pertinent activities, like courses taught and at what level, or independent projects supervised or students advised. His or her service to the college or community can be described explicitly.

Goals. In addition to this activity list, the faculty member should explain his or her own priorities, or why he or she has exerted efforts in some direction at the expense of other areas. Some self-evaluation forms request more specific goals or future objectives, so that future evaluations can focus on achievement of these goals.

Purpose. Questions to be included in the self-evaluation instrument should be consonant with the purposes of the evaluation program. As suggested above, if the program is for improvement of teaching, then items such as strengths and weaknesses or preferred styles and techniques should be included.

Acceptance. As with student and peer instruments, the faculty member's confidence in contributing his or her own evidence will affect the thoughtfulness or seriousness of his or her participation. If the instrument and use of the evidence are understood as legitimate, and relevant, responses are more likely to be full and honest.

Format. As with other instruments, the format should be specific enough to elicit comparative and valid information, yet flexible enough to allow the faculty member to describe special talents or unique contributions. Particularly in self-evaluation forms, requests should be specific because of the sensitive nature of this area. Some members will expound too much while others will be hesitant to give enough information. Open-ended comments should be requested but other parts of the form should request explicit statements.

THE RECIPIENTS OF FEEDBACK

Just as different sources are appropriate for soliciting varying kinds of information, different recipients may make use of different kinds of information. Since some of the evidence collected is usually intended as confidential, the decision about who has access to it becomes a sensitive one.

Recipients of Information

Self. If the purpose of the program is improvement of faculty performance, the faculty member must receive feedback, and must receive it first, before anyone else. Whether this feedback has any effect on performance has been the topic of numerous investigations. Teachers do use the information for course redesign, but there is some conflicting evidence about its use for the improvement of teaching effectiveness. Several studies found no significant improvement in teacher effectiveness at the end of the semester after mid-semester feedback sessions. In Centra's (1973) study of this topic, at first the results seemed to agree with these earlier studies, but further analysis showed that some of the faculty members did improve significantly. He concluded that three specific conditions were met in the improved cases: the information in the feedback (1) provided new or discrepant information; (2) increased the teacher's motivation; or (3) gave prescription and resources for change and improvement. These three conditions are consonant with learning theory. Centra also found that the evidence of improvement increased over time; one-half semester was too limited a period for teachers to modify their teaching; when post-tests were repeated at the end of a year, changes and improvements had occurred. Students who hope to provide the teacher with information early enough to allow for immediate changes in the course may be discouraged, because they are more likely to be providing the basis for course improvement for later students. But, sometimes, short-term goals are also served. Teachers who discover new or startling information, discrepant from their own beliefs; or are offered positive support that increases their motivation; or find constructive suggestions that are easily attained (the three conditions that Centra found), may show immediate change.

For long-term teaching improvement, Hoyt (1973) and McKeachie (1973) both urge that results be viewed over several evaluation periods, not as one-shot programs, because trends are far more meaningful. If the purpose of a program is faculty improvement, both diagnostic and prescriptive information must be included. Perhaps a teacher will learn to identify personal weaknesses but will not know how to change them. A boring lecturer needs to know how to try discussion-style classes, or to add new materials. Either a development program or consultative assistance associated with evaluation procedures tend to offer the teacher resources, allow him or her to seek help, yet protect feelings of professionalism.

If the information gathered is to be used in personnel decisions, faculty members need to see enough data to have confidence that reasonable and equitable evidence was available for those decisions.

If information was gathered by students for course selection guides, teachers are often allowed to preview the results and add comments if these are appropriate. At Amherst College, for example, the teacher of each course writes a descriptive paragraph in the student guide to courses, about changes planned for the following semester.

If the purpose of the program is to improve curricula or programs, to inform external audiences, to conduct research or take an inventory of resources, the faculty member should receive at least a summary of the data. His or her self-evaluation is another component, and if discrepancies are apparent, he or she may want to clarify them. A faculty member, as the subject of the evaluation, should always see the results in some form.

Students. If student ratings have been used, the students should see the results. Students in field visits frequently observed that, "We spend a lot of time filling out forms, but never know what happens." Summaries of the results, frequency distributions, or interpreted narratives may be adequate. More information can be furnished for student use in course selection guides including any local or collegewide norms available. When students publish the results, they might consider some of the things suggested under Format in this section.

The kind of student feedback most appropriate when the program is for more administrative purposes, such as personnel decisions, program or external audiences, is partially dependent on institutional philosophy and organization. In a few institutions students participate on committees that involve them directly in these processes, so that student representatives receive the same feedback that other sources get. In others, teachers discuss the results with their classes, perhaps in a summarized form. No matter what mechanism is selected, students should see the results of their efforts and should be well informed of their use. For example, when student endorsement has been instrumental in supporting a tenure or promotion decision for a teacher, the public acknowledgment of this fact may serve as highly motivating to students and faculty.

Peers. If peers or colleagues have contributed to the evaluation information, they should get a summary of the results to maintain motivation, allay resentment, and expand their view of the process. The format should be carefully planned to display information in an understandable way. If the purpose of the program is to improve faculty performance, peers may play a consultative role in the process, so that more diagnostic information can be provided. For example, colleagues who learn that a teacher received high ratings on presentation may want to visit that teacher's class for their own improvement. If peers receive diagnostic feedback, cooperative efforts like team-teaching or the sharing of visual aids can be encouraged. If a systematic approach to understanding the interpretation or relative meaning of the evidence is offered, more visibility and confidence in the program will result. Departmental discussions about strengths and weaknesses, and balance of styles, can be both informative and useful. Since all faculty members are usually both evaluators and the subjects of evaluation at some time, the faculty as a group should make the decision about what feedback is appropriate and relevant.

Administrators/Supervisors. As the details of the process for using the information are determined, the kinds and form of the information needed will be decided. For example, if the purpose of the program is improvement of performance, and the administrator is not a source of information, then he or she will not necessarily need or use feedback. Some supervisory administrators, on the other hand, could have a direct role in teacher improvement. For all other purposes, except student course selection, the administrator usually has a direct role in the operation of the system; at least receiving summaries of the information. In the case of personnel decisions, the administrator may need as much evidence as possible for legitimate results. In large institutions where administrators need information on many faculty members, often the feedback needs to be interpreted and arranged for comparison. More reasonable use can be made of a quantity of feedback when it is displayed in context, with constraints or special considerations, as well as normative interpretation, carefully specified.

Others. In some cases, feedback is furnished to evaluation, promotion, or tenure committees. In other cases results may go to a group responsible for follow-up activities like tutorial or consultation sessions, or training workshops. This type of organization, where the audience is independent, intended only for personal support, is often very useful when the purpose of the program is improvement of faculty performance.

GENERAL CONDITIONS OF FEEDBACK

Disclosure
The AAUP "Statement on Teaching Evaluation" (1974, p. 169) succinctly states:

> Evaluations in which results go only to the individual professor may be of use in improving an individual teacher's performance, but they contribute little to the process of faculty review.

Although the purposes of an evaluation program usually dictate the recipients of the information, there are still conflicting opinions about the usefulness of providing feedback to some sources. Determining whether an audience can make direct use of the results is not the only criterion. For example, if students have invested time and energy in providing ratings, they deserve to see the results in some form. This is true for every source of information. If the program is to be maintained, and data is to be solicited periodically, the motivation for contributing thoughtfully will not persist if these sources know little of the eventual outcomes. So all sources of information in a program should receive feedback in some form. Balancing this general rule is the principle of privacy and confidentiality. Faculty resistance, based on the perception of evaluation programs as an intrusion into academic freedom and the right to privacy, has slowed the adoption of many evaluation programs.

Many institutions have found ways to protect faculty privacy and also to meet the need for feedback. Hoyt (1973) describes a turbulent process at Kansas State University which led to allowing each faculty member the privilege of signing release forms that identify the audiences who will receive results, before the program is administered. A faculty member then has control of the information, though it is important that this control is exerted before rating scales are administered and not after he or she has seen the results.

At the University of Washington another solution has been successful. Students complete a one-page questionnaire, which is divided into three sections. The first section answers global questions that are used for promotional and tenure decisions and provide feedback for administrators. The second section seeks detailed, diagnostic information for the faculty member themselves, and only they see the results. The third section contains questions about content, materials, and workload, and the results are published for student use in course selection. To add to its usefulness to the faculty member (who sees all three sections), the second section has space for the addition of eight items, which individual faculty members may create to suit their own needs. A final flexibility device is built in by having five forms of this second part available for the faculty member to choose from. These five choices are keyed to instructional goals and techniques; for example, large lectures with little interaction, or small seminar, discussion-type courses (See Rating Scales 2-12A-E).

At William Rainey Harper College in Palatine, Illinois, a student scale consists of twenty-three items for diagnostic purposes, and one overall item for administrative use in personnel decisions. Only the faculty member sees the entire result. Harper College also provides space on colleague and administrative forms for the faculty member to comment on the ratings he or she receives. The practice of having a faculty members review and critique their own evaluation is becoming more common.

All of these are possible ways of dealing with the issue of privacy and protection of rights, while insuring the usefulness of the information collected. Most solutions to the problem will be keyed to purposes of the program. For example, if a program is to provide information for guidance in student course selection, student must at least receive summarized, pertinent results. If the purpose of the program is to identify resources for reallocation or program modification, Harper's one-item evaluation would not suffice.

The issue of confidentiality has become increasingly controversial, and institutional decisions addressing this issue and establishing an explicit policy are essential. Since the Buckley amendment (Education Amendments of 1974) was passed, allowing students access to their own files, institutions have had to adjust some of their thinking. Public pressures at this time have tended to create a climate where few documents are remaining confidential, and legislative actions and court procedures have supported personal access to one's own files. Many collective bargaining contracts specify that faculty members should review their own recommendations before they are collected for others to review. In some cases, faculty members even retain the right to release data or not.

Whether faculty control is exerted over the release of information (as at Kansas State), or over the kinds of information given to different audiences (as at the University of Washington), the fact that faculty members have some control over the recipients of the feedback will increase the legitimacy and acceptance of the program.

Timing

Not only who receives what feedback, but when, or in what order, may be an issue. Sometimes an administrator may gather all information first to sift it, add normative evidence and arrange the format before others receive it. This function is most usefully performed by an independent office or development center, if one is available. Some faculty members feel strongly that they have the perogative to see their own raw data before it goes to anyone else. Some institutions not only submit the whole package to the evaluatee first, but provide him the opportunity to add his own remarks or comments at that point before data is assimilated or supplemented by final norms or tabulations. Explicit timing procedures and sequences are vital and must be decided in the planning phase of a program, and written into procedures from the beginning.

Format

The range of possibilities for the display of results runs from publishing all raw data to composite tabulations to interpreted summaries. Composites can include frequency distributions of the mean factor ratings, or item frequencies or narrative descriptions. If computer facilities are available, numerous displays are possible. If mean ratings are given, across classes, the mass of figures, often to two decimal places, may be quite formidable. Several institutions use graphic presentations such as a histogram or bar graph, which can simplify and clarify the evaluation data. Composites of frequencies are more legitimate presentations because they allow for a balance of extremes. Using appropriate norms that compare courses or teachers in which some situational factors are equally influential is essential. For example, comparing lecture-style courses, or comparing small, or introductory courses, can eliminate predictable variation that is not due to teaching. Therefore if a teacher of a large introductory required English course gets mediocre ratings, he will understand that this is typical and that higher ratings are outstanding for that type of course.

Graphic displays or simple numerical formats are preferable to small decimal numbers. Planning the format of the feedback when instruments are selected can help avoid complex results. McKeachie (1974) recommends the use of "ranges" of numbers rather than precise quantification. As he says, "This is measurement, too. Don't use a micrometer when a yardstick will do."

INDICATORS OF SUCCESS

Acceptance

The climate of acceptance of the faculty evaluation program has a profound effect on ratings and the uses to which they are put. If participants fully understand both the procedures and the real purposes of the program, motivation and participation are strengthened. Students who know how their ratings will be used are far more inclined to give thoughtful answers. Again, representative participation at every stage contributes to eventual acceptance.

Constant monitoring and evaluation of the evaluation program itself is required in order to identify what is useful and worth maintaining, and what is not useful and should either be dropped or improved.

Visibility

Sometimes acceptance is more a problem of visibility; open presentations and well-defined objectives that are publicized usually enhance acceptance. Faculty and administrators as well as students must agree to the rationale and purposes of a program, and see the role that each contribution plays in a total system for full support. Presentations in student orientation programs, periodic descriptions in student or campus newspapers, and publicized open meetings are often useful in disseminating information about evaluation programs. Questions and suggestions can be solicited in similar fashion. At Texas Christian University the success of the evaluation program was attributed to the long process of development, with open meetings where meaningful input and change occurred.

Program Administration

Whether the administrative responsibility for an evaluation program lies with an individual, an office, or a committee, this authority must be explicit and agreed to by all participants. In some institutions a central office provides computer service and technical assistance, in others one faculty member is designated by a faculty committee to administer the total program; typically this is a committee in which the faculty, students, and administrators participate and administer the program. In large universities these duties may be subdivided into smaller units within the university, but overall responsibility or coordination is more successful if it is centrally assigned. Another advantage of a centralized administration is the ability to utilize uniform procedures so that burdens are equitably distributed and norms may be established.

Usually there are standard guidelines so that procedures are applied uniformly. For example, forms and instructions are distributed at an appointed date and time of day, week, and year, by a specified person, and then collected in a particular fashion. If this is not possible, differences in the details of the administration process will be reflected in the results, and may distort any subsequent comparison across instructors. Miller (1974, p. 36) has written, for instance:

> The subtle but important factors related to how the rating system is administered often are given inadequate attention. For example, Kirchner (1969) found that student ratings were significantly higher when the instructor being rated was in the room than when he was absent. And Colliver (1972) found that students who do not sign the evaluation forms give significantly lower evaluations than those who do. Whether the instructor is in or out of the room when the students are completing the rating scale is not important, but consistency in how the ratings are administered is, if comparable results are expected or desired. And even if no comparison is sought, the teacher is unknowingly penalized by leaving the room when students are completing the form.

Uniformity is the key to fairness in the results.

Other small details, such as collection of student questionnaires, can be substantial roadblocks. At several institutions these forms are gathered by a student, sealed in an envelope which is signed by the instructor on the outside, and deposited in a department office to be opened by the instructor (or other designated person) only after final grades are given. Mechanical techniques like these may seem overly fussy, yet the research suggests that both instructor and student are more comfortable with assured procedures (Menges, 1973; McKeachie, 1973).

The establishment of a central office with overall responsibility for all evaluation procedures across an institution greatly enhances both standardization and protection of participants. Sometimes a Vice President, Dean of Faculty, Registrar, counseling unit or independent group concerned with a development process can best serve this function. In larger universities this central office may act as coordinator for specified administrative personnel in smaller units. Who fulfills this responsibility may depend on the purpose of the program. When programs are multipurpose, and information is gathered from many sources, central administration is most necessary. There is no reason why this central-izing of the administration of the system should interfere with an individualized focus for each college, section, or department if a desire for such autonomy has been expressed. Methods such as including core items on instruments allow cross-college comparisons to be made, while providing great flexibility for the unique demands of individual units. In such cases, standard procedures, plus centralized administration, allows for several levels of comparison. Intra- and interdepartmental, as well as institutional and even national norms, can be established for a set of core items, while other information is available for an individual's own needs. The Purdue Cafeteria System (Rating Scale 2-6) exem-plifies this kind of procedure.

Another important feature of central administration is the provision for explicit uniform policy. Evaluation procedures are, ideally, used with tenured as well as nontenured faculty, and with faculty at all ranks and in all disciplines. Only if the process has comprehensive and uniform participation will it be viewed as legitimate and fair. One department cannot be expected to expend its efforts if members feel that other departments are only superficially or routinely involved. If practices are to differ for nontenured staff, this, too, should be uniform. As a rule most faculties feel that performance evaluation should occur at least annually for all staff. Additional procedures are added when the faculty member is being considered for tenure. The tenure process is usually timed to start during the fall before the decision is due, so that an entire school year is available for data collection and interpretation.

If early evaluation for course and teacher improvement is planned, this may occur approximately one month after class begins. Other procedures can occur at the end of each semester, or each year, as the participants choose. Student course guides usually prefer input each semester, but teacher evaluation may be annual. Other policy decisions, such as requiring information from all students (or at least 80 percent of every class) must be uniformly enforced. Some com-mittees rule that student responses are not considered unless such standards of participation are adhered to.

Overcoming Resistance

Any new program may bring out imagined as well as real objections from faculty, students, and administrators. A number of forces against evaluation are natural and may serve as safeguards and eventual supports to a program, but others are destructive. The balance of weight in these forces for and against adoption of a program may determine the very survival of a program. The experience of others in identifying and dealing with resistances to the progress of development may help prepare those presently concerned with similar problems. Donald Hoyt from Kansas State University has described some of the situations that arose there, and we paraphrase them here:

Resistance: The faculty said we assumed a model of "good teacher," when there are a variety of styles and differences among disciplines.

Result: Student rating scales were revised so that each instructor could *weight* the set of items that he felt were his highest priority within his own objectives.

Resistance: Students said the administration was not committed to the program; they demanded that results be published.

Result: The faculty senate ruled that each faculty member would participate only voluntarily, but they must sign the release before the questionnaires were administered. The faculty senate also ruled that there *must* be student input and it *must* be representative of all students for each instructor.

Resistance: Students complained about filling out forms four or five times a year without seeing changes.

Result: Rules for timing were discussed but not changed. Some attempts were made to better publicize changes due to program.

Resistance: Faculty complained that only department heads benefited from the program. They also called it a popularity contest, and said it couldn't help good teachers because they are already good. They said it would increase frictions; faculty members are busy and it would add more work load and that grievances and legal factors would multiply.

Results: After the first run of the program, some teachers were surprised by good ratings. Some commented that they never knew some teaching devices had been so successful. Another said, "Oh, is that what they want. No one ever told me what they wanted before." Some new complaints arose, and some old ones did not disappear.[d]

A small core of supportive people in an institution who are convinced of the real benefits possible from the program can be the weight in this balance of forces that serves to support the survival and renewal of the program. Open planning sessions allowing these resistances (from students, faculty, and administrators) to be expressed early in planning stages may allow healthy complaints to turn into positive forces.

Grievance Procedures and Legal Factors

Any evaluation program must include specific mechanisms for faculty grievance procedures. In collective bargaining agreements these are carefully spelled

[d]Video Tape 206, The KSU Instructional Effectiveness Assessment Program: A case Study (paraphrased).

out, and usually allow the faculty member several layers of appeal in case of perceived injustices at any stage. Some of these procedures may serve as models for institutions in which the faculty has not organized. The American Association of University Professors, in its "Statement on Teaching Evaluation" (1974, p. 170), specifies some grievance procedures guidelines:

> Those being evaluated should be invited to supply information and materials relevant to that evaluation. If the department has not constituted final authority, the faculty's considered judgment should constitute the basic recommendation to the next level of responsibility, which may be a college-wide or university-wide faculty committee. If the chairman's recommendation is contrary to that of the faculty, the faculty should be informed of the chairman's reasons prior to the chairman's submitting his and the faculty's recommendations and should be given an opportunity to respond to the chairman's views.
>
> The dean's function, where separate from a department chairman's or division head's, is typically that of review and recommendation either in the dean's own person or through an official review body at that level. If the recommendation at this level is contrary to that of the department chairman or faculty, opportunity should be provided for discussion with the chairman or faculty, before a formal recommendation is made.

In practice, one community college, for example, has formed two separate committees; one to hear procedural grievances and one to hear substantive grievances. These committees are representative of administration, faculty, and students, but they could be all-faculty committees. A device that allows for a review of all procedures and evidence, and a method for making final decisions, must be incorporated from the beginning. Some institutions provide a second and third layer of appeals in case these committees fail to agree. These could involve staff from larger networks, such as the Regional Board for Community Colleges in Massachusetts, or the trustees of private institutions. A group decision always lessens the burden on an individual, and is often more acceptable to faculty members. In the case of a decision not to grant tenure, humane practices that reassign, retrain, or assist in placing faculty in more suitable positions are also increasingly common.

The purpose of tenure was to insure academic freedom, which is the heart of the educational process. In its original statement on "Academic Freedom and Tenure," codified and endorsed in 1940 by the AAUP and the Association of American Colleges, the nature of precise procedures mandated for termination of tenure or appointments were defined. These procedures, expanded upon in later AAUP statements (as above in 1974), have nevertheless been classic and enduring guidelines, supported by the courts in subsequent years, and still pertinent today. Nearly all present personnel policy and therefore grievance procedures are based on this document (AAUP, 1940, p. 2):

Termination for cause of a continuous appointment, or the dismissal for cause of a teacher previous to the expiration of a term appointment, should, if possible, be considered by both a faculty committee and the governing board of the institution. In all cases where the facts are in dispute, the accused teacher should be informed before the hearing in writing of the charges against him and should have the opportunity to be heard in his own defense by all bodies that pass judgement upon his case. He should be permitted to have with him an advisor of his own choosing who may act as counsel. There should be a full stenographic record of the hearing available to the parties concerned. In the hearing of charges of incompetence the testimony should include that of teachers and other scholars, either from his own or from other institutions. Teachers on continuous appointment who are dismissed for reasons not involving moral turpitude should receive their salaries for at least a year from the date of notification of dismissal whether or not they are continued in their duties at the institution.

Affirmative Action

James Cass (1975, p. 45), Education Editor of the Saturday Review, describes this sensitive issue as it affects universities today:

The federal government's active effort to eliminate racial, religious, and sexual discrimination in employment through affirmative action programs is a major concern on many campuses today. Much has been written about the subject, and the debate goes on. Certainly discrimination of any kind is unjust, immoral, and indefensible—it must be eliminated from the American academic scene. But in the process of requiring institutions to submit affirmative action plans for seeking out capable women and minority faculty, many educators have come to believe that the government is threatening the very integrity of the academy. They contend that the government, on threat of witholding federal funds, is imposing quotas that force institutions to make employment decisions on criteria other than pure merit.

He goes on to describe the confusion between goals and quotas. Imposing numerical quotas on institutions to insure minority representation is seen by some as discriminatory as past efforts to restrict by these same quotas. He quotes President Derek C. Bok of Harvard University in an address before an NAACP Legal Defense and Educational Fund dinner in defining the real role of affirmative action:

In essence, affirmative action simply requires that institutions make special efforts to identify candidates from underrepresented groups and that the ultimate choice among candidates be made without regard to race or sex. These obligations do not weaken the quality of personnel; they enhance the quality by forcing institutions to look at a wider range of candidates.

Although affirmative action programs have chiefly addressed hiring procedures, their influence has been evidence in evaluation programs as well. When these programs provide the criteria and evidence for personnel decisions for promotion, salary, tenure, and retention, the whole issue is crucial. Should minority candidates be exempt from the performance demands exacted from others? Should they be given special consideration if past injustices have impaired their backgrounds and left them less qualified? Professor Sidney Hook of New York University is quoted by Cass as firmly stating: "Where persons are evaluated for fitness to fill specific posts, one standard for all must prevail." While no one can contest the need in higher education to attempt to be true to this doctrine, it does not seem impossible to support special consideration for minority candidates. Jeffrey L. Sammons in the *Yale Alumni Magazine* (February 1975, p. 16) states it succinctly:

> There are certain disciplines in which the human experience of women and minorities makes a special contribution to the integrity of learning and understanding. Of course there are women archaeologists and black medievalists; but a woman in psychology, and a black in urban studies, a Chicano in Spanish literature—such a person brings out of his or her own life a perspective without which the discipline cannot remain true to its object, just as a German department without any Germans would risk parochial distortion and imprecise vision.

One criterion that a peer or administrative perspective must apply to faculty performance is the degree of contribution of that member to a department, college, or university. An awareness that a teacher's background, sex, or ethnic membership may provide him or her with a special competence, allowing an extra dimension to teaching skills or to the fullness of the departmental instruction, is basically within the scope of objective criteria. The hypersensitivity in the current competitive climate, where advancement and even survival are daily questions, presses this issue into the forefront of evaluation systems. Open discussions and overt policy decisions in this context are vital to program success.

Stages of Development

Some institutions prefer to adopt programs in stages. Research studies may serve as small-scale pilot programs, or student ratings alone may be introduced first. Sometimes psychology departments, engineering schools, or schools of business administration develop the first efforts and then attempt to interest other departments. At some point, word may come from the top down to explore the feasibility of a uniform program using developmental clinics or training. In some places, several disconnected pieces have started simultaneously, so that often a first major problem has been to identify the fragments already present to tie them together. If a central office or committee is established with administrative backing, this is facilitated, but a long and gradual process may be required before any institutional purposes are identified and addressed. Open committees, representative of students, faculty, and administrators from all disciplines and departments, work long hours to achieve such goals.

At Kansas State University a first stage of the program was introduced to serve only the purpose of faculty improvement in teaching effectiveness. After the first year this was viewed as less threatening. The additional purpose of promotion and tenure decisions was added without too much difficulty in a second year of operation. Unique institutional organizations and climates are conducive to different approaches. The important consideration is that a program can begin anywhere for any purpose, but the ultimate goal for effective systems, which provide benefits to all the members of the academic community, is a multipurpose program, centrally governed.

Maintenance and Renewal

Reviewing the program is essential if it is to remain functional and more than mere ritual. In initial planning stages the procedures for a systematic review must be specified, and the timing and mechanisms for these procedures spelled out. The use of assessment inventories and priority or goal-setting teachniques included in this book may be useful in this area.

A major factor in the maintenance and renewal of a faculty evaluation program is *sponsorship.* Those who make policy, supply resources, influence opinion, and establish rewards, must continually advocate and support the faculty evaluation program. Even within the best of faculty evaluation programs, grievances will arise, agreements will inadvertently be violated, some will be threatened, and others will occasionally misuse evaluation results. The problem is not that imperfections will always exist; the problem is to build and maintain moral and financial support necessary to withstand and deal constructively with them when they occur.

SELECTED BIBLIOGRAPHY

AAUP. "Statement on Teaching Evaluation," *AAUP Bulletin* 60 (Summer 1974): 168–170.

Astin, A., and Lee, C.B.T. "Current Practices in the Evaluation and Training of College Teachers," in *Improving College Teaching,* ed. Calvin B.T. Lee. Washington, D.C.: American Council on Education, 1967.

Astin, A.W. et al. *Faculty Development in a Time of Retrenchment.* New Rochelle: Change Publication, 1974.

Cass, James. "Affirmative Action in the Academy," *Saturday Review,* Feb. 8, 1975, p. 45.

Centra, J.A. "Effectiveness of Student Feedback in Modifying College Instruction," *Journal of Educational Psychology* 65 (1973): 395–401.

——. *Strategies for Improving College Teaching.* ERIC Report No. 8, Washington, D.C.: American Association of Higher Education, 1972.

Costin, F., Greenough, W.T., and Menges, R.J. "Student Ratings of College Teaching: Reliability, Validity, and Usefulness," *Review of Educational Research* 41 (1971): 511–535.

Drucker, A.J., and Remmers, H.H. "Do Alumni and Students Differ in Their Attitudes toward Instructors?" *Purdue University Studies in Higher Education* 70 (1950): 62–74.

Eastman, A. "How Visitation Came to Carnegie-Mellon University," in K.E. Eble, ed., *The Recognition and Evaluation of Teaching.* Salt Lake City, Utah: Project to Improve College Teaching, 1970.

Eble, K.E., ed. *The Recognition and Evaluation of Teaching* (Salt Lake City, Utah: Project to Improve College Teaching, 1970).

——. *Professors as Teachers.* San Francisco: Jossey-Bass, 1973.

Flanagan, J.C. "The Critical Incident Technique," *Psychological Bulletin* 51 (1954): 327–358.

Frey, P.W. "The Endeavor Instructional Rating Form" Evanston, Illinois: Department of Psychology, Northwestern University, 1973.

——. "The Ongoing Debate: Student Evaluation of Teaching," *Change* (Feb. 1974), pp. 47–48.

Gilmore, G.M. "A Brief Preliminary Description of the Student Rating Forms of the University of Washington Instructional Assessment System" Educational Assessment Center Project 276, July 1974.

Hildebrand, M., Wilson R.C., Dienst, E.R. *Evaluating University Teaching.* Center for Research and Development in Higher Education, University of California, Berkeley, 1971.

Hildebrand, M. "How to Recommend Promotion for a Mediocre Teacher without Actually Lying," *Experiment and Innovation: New Directions in Education at the University of California* (1971): 1–21.

Hodgkinson, H., Hurst, J., Levine, H., Brint, S. *A Manual for the Evaluation of Innovative Programs and Practices in Higher Education.* University of California, Berkeley, 1974.

Hoyt, Donald P. Video Tape #207, "Implementing Faculty Evaluation and Development Programs." Kansas State University, Division of Continuing Education, Manhattan, Kansas, 1973.

Kulik, J.A., and McKeachie, W.J. "The Evaluation of Teachers in Higher Education," in F.N. Kerlinger, ed., *Review of Research in Education,* Vol. 3. Itasca: Peacock Publishers, 1975.

Menges, R.J., "The New Reporters: Students Rate Instruction," in C.R. Pace, ed., *Evaluating Learning and Teaching: New Directions in Higher Education.* San Francisco: Jossey-Bass, 1973.

McKeachie, W.J., Lin, Y., Mann, W. "Student Ratings of Teacher Effectiveness: Validity Studies," *American Educational Research Journal* 8 (1971): 435–445.

McKeachie, W.J. "Resistances to Evaluation of Teaching, Occasional Paper Number Two." Center for the Teaching Professions, Northwestern University, Evanston, Illinois, 1973.

Miller, R.I. *Evaluating Faculty Performance* San Francisco: Jossey-Bass 1972.

——. *Developing Programs for Faculty Evaluation: A Source Book.* San Francisco: Jossey-Bass, 1974.

Naftulin, D.H., Ware, J.E., Jr., and Donnelly, F.A. "The Doctor Fox Lecture: A Paradigm of Educational Seduction," *Journal of Medical Education* 48 (1973): 630–635.

Remmers, H.H. "The Relationship between Students' Marks and Students' Attitudes toward Instruction," *School and Society* 28 (1928): 759–760.

Ronan, W.W. "Evaluating College Classroom Teaching Effectiveness." PREP Report No. 34, HEW Publication No. (OE) 72-9, 1972.

Sammons, J.L. *Yale Alumni Magazine,* February, 1975.

Scriven, M. "The Evaluation of Teachers and Teaching," *California Journal of Educational Research* 25 (1974): 109–115.

Seldin, P. "A Study to Determine the Current Policies and Practices Used in Liberal Arts Colleges to Evaluate Classroom Teaching Performance of Members of the Faculty." 1974, Fordham University; part published: "How Deans Evaluate Teachers," *Change* 6 (1974): 48–49.

Walberg, H.J., ed. *Evaluating Educational Performance: A Sourcebook of Methods, Instruments, and Examples.* Berkeley, California: McCutchan Publishing Corp., 1974.

Sample Rating Scales: Student

Rating Scale 2-1. Student Description of Teachers: Short Form

Instructor _____ Department _____ (1-3)

(4-6)

Course number or title _____ (7-9)

I. The following items reflect some of the ways teachers can be described in and out of the classroom. For the instructor named above, please circle the number which indicates the degree to which you feel each item is descriptive of him or her. In some cases, the statement may not apply to this individual. In these cases, check *Does not apply or don't know* for that item.

	Not at all descriptive	*Very descriptive*	*Doesn't apply or don't know*	
1. Has command of the subject, presents material in an analytic way, contrasts various points of view, discusses current developments, and relates topics to other areas of knowledge.	1 2 3 4 5 6 7		( )	(10)
2. Makes himself clear, states objectives, summarizes major points, presents material in an organized manner, and provides emphasis.	1 2 3 4 5 6 7		( )	
3. Is sensitive to the response of the class, encourages student participation, and				

(continued)

Rating Scale 2-1 continued

	Not at all descriptive	Very descriptive	Doesn't apply or don't know	
welcomes questions and discussion.	1 2 3 4 5 6 7		( )	
4. Is available to and friendly towards students, is interested in students as individuals, is himself respected as a person, and is valued for advice not directly related to the course.	1 2 3 4 5 6 7		( )	
5. Enjoys teaching, is enthusiastic about his subject, makes the course exciting, and has self-confidence.	1 2 3 4 5 6 7		( )	(14)

(Additional items may be presented by instructor and/or department)

6.	1 2 3 4 5 6 7		( )	(15)
7.	1 2 3 4 5 6 7		( )	
8.	1 2 3 4 5 6 7		( )	
9.	1 2 3 4 5 6 7		( )	
10.	1 2 3 4 5 6 7		( )	(19)

II. 1. How does the instructor of this course compare with other teachers you have had at *this school?*

	Among the very worst		About average			Among the very best	
	1	2	3	4	5	6	7	(20)

2. How does the instructor of this course compare with other teachers you have had in *this department?*

	Among the very worst		About average			Among the very best	
	1	2	3	4	5	6	7	(21)

You are invited to comment further on the course and/or effectiveness of this instructor especially in areas not covered by the questions.

Developed by Robert C. Wilson and Evelyn R. Dienst, Center for Research and Development in Higher Education, University of California, Berkeley. Form SSF-3. Used by permission. See Resources, p. 124, for further information and restrictions.

Rating Scale 2-2. Student Description of Teachers: Long Form

Instructor _____   Department _____   (1-3)

                                                                                  (4-6)

Course number or title _____   (7-9)

I. The following items reflect some of the ways teachers can be described. For the instructor named above, please circle the number which indicates the degree to which you fell each item is descriptive of him or her. In some cases, the statement may not apply to this individual. In these cases, check *Does not apply or don't know* for that item.

	Not at all descriptive		Very descriptive	Doesn't apply or don't know	
1. Discusses points of view other than his own	1 2 3 4 5			( )	(10)
2. Contrasts implications of various theories	1 2 3 4 5			( )	
3. Discusses recent developments in the field	1 2 3 4 5			( )	
4. Presents origins of ideas and concepts	1 2 3 4 5			( )	
5. Gives references for more interesting and involved points	1 2 3 4 5			( )	
6. Presents facts and concepts from related fields	1 2 3 4 5			( )	
7. Emphasizes conceptual understanding	1 2 3 4 5			( )	
8. Explains clearly	1 2 3 4 5			( )	
9. Is well prepared	1 2 3 4 5			( )	
10. Gives lectures that are easy to outline	1 2 3 4 5			( )	
11. Is careful and precise in answering questions	1 2 3 4 5			( )	
12. Summarizes major points	1 2 3 4 5			( )	
13. States objectives for each class session	1 2 3 4 5			( )	
14. Identifies what he considers important	1 2 3 4 5			( )	
15. Encourages class discussion	1 2 3 4 5			( )	
16. Invites students to share their knowledge and experiences	1 2 3 4 5			( )	
17. Clarifies thinking by identifying reasons for questions	1 2 3 4 5			( )	(26)
18. Invites criticism of his own ideas	1 2 3 4 5			( )	(27)

(continued)

Rating Scale 2-2 continued

	Not at all descriptive	*Very descriptive*	*Doesn't apply or don't know*
19. Knows if the class in understanding him or not	1 2 3 4 5		( )
20. Knows when students are bored or confused	1 2 3 4 5		( )
21. Has interest in and concern for the quality of his teaching	1 2 3 4 5		( )
22. Has students apply concepts to demonstrate understanding	1 2 3 4 5		( )
23. Has a genuine interest in students	1 2 3 4 5		( )
24. Is friendly toward students	1 2 3 4 5		( )
25. Relates to students as individuals	1 2 3 4 5		( )
26. Recognizes and greets students out of class	1 2 3 4 5		( )
27. Is accessible to students out of class	1 2 3 4 5		( )
28. Is valued for advice not directly related to the course	1 2 3 4 5		( )
29. Respects students as persons	1 2 3 4 5		( )
30. Is a dynamic and energetic person	1 2 3 4 5		( )
31. Has an interesting style of presentation	1 2 3 4 5		( )
32. Seems to enjoy teaching	1 2 3 4 5		( )
33. Is enthusiastic about his subject	1 2 3 4 5		( )
34. Seems to have self-confidence	1 2 3 4 5		( )
35. Varies the speed and tone of his voice	1 2 3 4 5		( )
36. Has a sense of humor	1 2 3 4 5		( ) (45)

(Additional items may be presented by the instructor and/or department)

37.	1 2 3 4 5		( )
38.	1 2 3 4 5		( )
39.	1 2 3 4 5		( )
40.	1 2 3 4 5		( )
41.	1 2 3 4 5		( )
42.	1 2 3 4 5		( )
43.	1 2 3 4 5		( )
44.	1 2 3 4 5		( )
45.	1 2 3 4 5		( )
46.	1 2 3 4 5		( ) (55)

(continued)

Rating Scale 2-2 continued

	Not at all descriptive	Very descriptive	Doesn't apply or don't know

II. 1. How does the instructor of this course compare with other teachers you have had at *this school?*

Among the very worst			About average			Among the very best	(56)
1	2	3	4	5	6	7	

2. How does the instructor of this course compare with other teachers you have had in *this department?*

Among the very worst			About average			Among the very best	(57)
1	2	3	4	5	6	7	

You are invited to comment further on the course and/or effectiveness of this instructor especially in areas not covered by the questions.

Developed by Robert C. Wilson and Evelyn R. Dienst, Center for Research and Development in Higher Education, University of California, Berkeley. Form SSF-3. Used by permission. See Resources, p. 124, for further information and restrictions.

Rating Scale 2–3. Student Perception of Learning and Teaching

W.J. McKeachie, University of Michigan

Please put your *SECTION NUMBER* and *TF's NAME* at the top of the IBM answer sheet as well as in the spaces provided on this sheet.

Course _____   U-of-M GPA _____

Section _____   Instructor _____

Sex M ___ F ___ Class Standing FR ___ SOPH ___ JUN ___ SR ___ GRAD _____

For each question, choose a numerical answer from the scale at the top of each page, and mark it on the separate IBM answer sheet. Your teacher will appreciate it if you *also* make comments in the spaces provided.

The questionnaire has nine brief parts. The first part is intended to assess your perception of your own learning; the second part is your perception of characteristics related to instructor effectiveness; the remaining parts are not evaluative but are intended to assess aspects of teacher style. For example, either a high or low degree of structure can be effective.

The results of this course evaluation will not be given to your teacher until grades have been turned in.

Thank you for taking the time to fill this form out thoughtfully. Your answers and comments will help improve the course for next year.

If not applicable, leave blank	3 = occasionally or moderate
1 = almost never or almost nothing	4 = often or much
2 = seldom or little	5 = almost always or a great deal

(Circle One)

Impact on Students

1. My intellectual curiosity has been stimulated by this course.   1 2 3 4 5
   Comments:

2. I am learning how to think more clearly about this area of this
   course.   1 2 3 4 5
   Comments:

3. I am learning how to read materials in this area more effectively.   1 2 3 4 5
   Comments:

4. The instructor is effective in conveying the larger human context
   within which this subject lies.   1 2 3 4 5
   Comments:

5. I am acquiring a good deal of knowledge about the subject.   1 2 3 4 5
   Comments:

6. The course is making a significant contribution to my self-
   understanding.   1 2 3 4 5
   Comments:

7. The course is increasing my interest in learning more about this
   area.   1 2 3 4 5
   Comments:

Instructor Effectiveness

8. The instructor is enthusiastic.   1 2 3 4 5
   Comments:

(continued)

Rating Scale 2–3 continued

	(Circle One)

Instructor Effectiveness

9. The instructor gives good examples of the concepts.   1 2 3 4 5
Comments:

10. The definitions and concepts the instructor gives in class are
generally clear.   1 2 3 4 5
Comments:

11. The instructor goes into too much detail.   1 2 3 4 5
Comments:

12. The instructor is able to tell when students are confused.   1 2 3 4 5
Comments:

13. The instructor is helpful when students are confused.   1 2 3 4 5
Comments:

14. The instructor seems knowledgeable in many areas besides
psychology.   1 2 3 4 5
Comments:

Rapport

15. The instructor is permissive.   1 2 3 4 5
Comments:

16. The instructor is friendly.   1 2 3 4 5
Comments:

17. The instructor invites criticism of his/her acts.   1 2 3 4 5
Comments:

Low Standards

18. The class is more pleasant than productive.   1 2 3 4 5
Comments:

19. The instructor spends so much time being "one of the gang"
that we don't learn as much as we could.   1 2 3 4 5
Comments:

Group Interaction

20. Students volunteer their own opinions.   1 2 3 4 5
Comments:

21. Students argue with one another. (Not necessarily with hostility).   1 2 3 4 5
Comments:

22. Students feel free to argue with the instructor.   1 2 3 4 5
Comments:

Difficulty

23. The instructor assigns very difficult reading.   1 2 3 4 5
Comments:

24. The instructor asks for more than students can get done in the
time available.   1 2 3 4 5
Comments:

Structure

25. The instructor plans class activities in detail.   1 2 3 4 5
Comments:

26. The instructor follows an outline closely.   1 2 3 4 5
Comments:

(continued)

Rating Scale 2-3 continued

	(Circle One)

Feedback

27. The instructor keeps students informed of their progress. 1 2 3 4 5
Comments:

28. The instructor tells students when they have done a particularly good job. 1 2 3 4 5
Comments:

29. Tests and papers are graded and returned promptly. 1 2 3 4 5
Comments:

Indicate your evaluation of characteristics below, using numbers based on the following scale:

1. Excellent 2. Very good 3. Good 4. Fair 5. Poor

30. Rate the instructor's general teaching effectiveness for you. 1 2 3 4 5
Comments:

31. Rate the value of the course as a whole to you. 1 2 3 4 5
Comments:

If not applicable, leave blank   3 = in-between
1 = definitely false   4 = more true than false
2 = more false than true   5 = definitely true

NOTICE! THIS SCALE IS DIFFERENT!

	(Circle One)

Student Responsibility

32. I come to class prepared to contribute to building a positive learning environment. 1 2 3 4 5
Comments:

33. I had a strong desire to take this course. 1 2 3 4 5
Comments:

34. I actively participate in class discussions. 1 2 3 4 5
Comments:

35. I consciously try to make a tie-in between what I am learning in the course and my own experience. 1 2 3 4 5
Comments:

36. I attend class regularly. 1 2 3 4 5
Comments:

37. I utilize all the learning opportunities provided in the course. 1 2 3 4 5
Comments:

38. I have created learning experiences for myself in connection with the course. 1 2 3 4 5
Comments:

Added Comments Below:

Developed by W.J. McKeachie, University of Michigan, Ann Arbor, Michigan. Used by permission. See Resources, p. 124, for further information and restrictions.

Rating Scale 2–4.

COURSE EVALUATION—PRINCETON UNIVERSITY
QUESTIONNAIRE COPYRIGHT BY PRINCETON UNIVERSITY, 1971. ALL RIGHTS RESERVED.

DEPT. NO.   COURSE NO.   COURSE LEAVE BLANK

RATINGS KEY

0 = NOT APPLICABLE
1 = UNACCEPTABLE
2 = POOR
3 = FAIR
4 = GOOD
5 = EXCELLENT

CLASS INSTRUCTOR —   DRILL OR LAB INSTRUCTOR —   LECTURER —   PRECEPTOR —

LECTURES

1. Rate the general quality of lectures as a whole

Rate the quality of lectures in terms of the degree to which they:

2. Covered the material at an appropriate intellectual level—neither too complicated nor too simple
3. Clearly presented the relevant subject matter
4. Stimulated your intellectual curiosity and provoked independent thinking

READINGS

5. Rate the general quality of readings as a whole

Rate the quality of readings in terms of the degree to which they:

6. Were of the right level of difficulty—neither too complicated nor too simple
7. Clearly presented the relevant subject matter
8. Stimulated your intellectual curiosity and provoked independent thinking
9. Were coordinated with other parts of the course

PRECEPTS OR CLASSES

10. Rate the general quality of precepts or classes as a whole

Rate the quality of precepts or classes on each of the following items

11. The instructor's responsiveness to students' concerns and questions
12. The instructor's ability to encourage broad student participation
13. The instructor's ability to help clarify readings and lectures
14. The instructor's ability to raise challenging questions

PAPERS, REPORTS AND PROBLEM SETS

Rate each of the following aspects of papers, reports, problem sets and other exercises in this course

15. The overall value of the papers, reports, problem sets and other exercises to this course
16. The helpfulness of the instructor's comments in response to your written work
17. The quality of guidance given by the instructor in choice of topics and suggestions for relevant research

LABORATORIES

18. Rate the quality of laboratories as a whole

Rate the quality of laboratories in terms of the degree to which they:

19. Were useful to you as a supplement to the lectures and readings—added significantly to the course
20. Contained the right amount of structure and guidance by the instructor

SEMINARS

21. Rate the quality of seminars as a whole

Rate the quality of seminars on each of the following items:

22. The degree to which you felt part of a continuing scholarly discussion
23. The degree to which you felt a sense of challenge, insight and discovery
24. The instructor's ability to conduct discussions
25. The instructor's ability to encourage broad student participation
26. The instructor's ability to raise stimulating, provocative questions

LANGUAGE COURSES

Rate the quality of language instruction in terms of the degree to which you found that it:

27. Helped you to read the language
28. Helped you to understand the language
29. Helped you to speak the language
30. Helped you to write the language

Rate the utility of each of the following in assisting you to master the language

31. Classes
32. Drills
33. Textbooks
34. Tests
35. Laboratories
36. Rate the general quality of the course as a whole

OVERALL RATINGS

37. How would you rate the overall quality of teaching in this course?

In relation to your objectives in this course and compared to other courses you have taken at Princeton, how would you rate it in terms of its contribution to each of the following:

38. Your capacity for critical evaluation of the subject matter
39. Your increased interest in the field
40. Rate the overall effectiveness of quizzes or examinations in this course as educational devices
41. Overall, how well integrated were the various parts of this course?

Educational Testing Service.
Princeton, N. J. 08540

INSTRUCTIONS ON REVERSE SIDE

698893P35M

(continued)

Rating Scale 2-4 continued

INSTRUCTIONS

This course evaluation questionnaire has been designed to benefit both students and faculty. The responses provided by you and other students in this course will be analyzed by the Office of the Registrar, reported back to the faculty, and made available for student use. Please read and follow these directions:

1. This is a combination questionnaire and machine-processable answer sheet. Mark it in pencil with care. Because this answer sheet will be processed by optical scanning equipment, a No. 2 pencil is provided and is required.

2. Do not write on this side of the questionnaire. When you begin, turn this sheet to the other side and to a horizontal position. Indicate in the top right-hand corner the department (or program number) and course number for this course. A list of department code numbers is given below. Religion 204, for example, has department number 72 and course number 204. Print these department and course numbers at the top in the appropriate columns, then blacken the boxes below corresponding to these digits. In a student initiated seminar such as Politics Seminar 1, code the department in the usual way and the course number by only its numeric part—in this instance as 65bb1 (where bb represents two blanks).

3. In the spaces provided at the margin write in the names of all your teachers in the course you are evaluating: each and every lecturer, class instructor, preceptor, and drill or lab instructor. This is essential to assure that all your instructors will receive the ratings applicable to them in any course with more than one teacher.

4. Do not write your name on this answer sheet. There is no need for you to identify yourself. Please be candid and honest in your judgments without utilizing anonymity to be unfair. Do not make comments on this form. Another form is provided for all your comments.

5. Now return the answer sheet to its vertical position. Since this questionnaire is being used for all courses, some sections will be applicable while others are not. Please respond to only those sections of the questionnaire which are applicable to this course. For each item indicate your choice of one rating (the alternatives are 0=Not Applicable, 1=Unacceptable, 2=Poor, 3=Fair, 4=Good, 5=Excellent) and mark the corresponding box adjacent to the question being answered. Be sure to fill in completely the boxed space you choose.

6. If you wish to change a response on the answer sheet, be sure to erase the incorrect mark. Do not cross out responses to delete them or make other stray marks, since the machinery will interpret any marks as responses.

Your frank and thoughtful answers to these questions will be appreciated.

COURSE CODES

Code Number	Program or Department	Code Number	Program or Department
88	African Studies	*37	Germanic Languages and Literatures
00	Afro-American Studies	41	History
02	American Studies Program	42	History and Philosophy of Science
03	Anthropology	43	Humanistic Studies
04	Architecture and Urban Planning	53	Latin American Studies
06	Art and Archaeology	51	Linguistics
07	Astrophysical Sciences	48	Literature (only Lit. 121, 122, 131, 132, 141, 142, 151)
10	Biochemical Science	50	Mathematics
08	Biology	54	Music
11	Chemistry	57	Near Eastern Studies
13	Classics (courses not requiring use of Greek or Latin)	05	Arabic
39	Greek	59	Persian
47	Latin	83	Turkish
49	Comparative Literature	40	Hebrew
15	Creative Writing and Theater	61	Philosophy
16	East Asian Studies	63	Physics
12	Chinese	65	Politics
46	Japanese	69	Psychology
44	Korean	72	Religion
74	Sanskrit	*	Romance Languages and Literatures
18	Economics	34	French
20	Engineering & Applied Science Divisional courses	45	Italian
21	Aerospace and Mechanical	67	Portuguese
22	Basic Engineering	77	Spanish
23	Chemical		Slavic Languages and Literatures
24	Civil and Geological	75	Russian
25	Electrical	76	Sociology
32	English	81	Statistics
78	European Civilization	99	Teacher Preparation
33	European Literature	85	Visual Arts
35	Geological and Geophysical Sciences	82	Western Cultural and Historical Studies
36	Geophysical Fluid Dynamics	79	Woodrow Wilson School

* Please note that European Literature and European Civilization are listed separately.

Used by permission. See Resources, p. 124, for further information and restrictions.

Rating Scale 2–5. Princeton University Course Evaluation Written Comment Form

Name of Course	Lecturer	Preceptor, Class Instructor or Seminar Leader	Drill or Laboratory Instructor

Your comments and suggestions will help to improve this course.

1. *Lectures:*

2. *Precepts, Classes, Laboratories, Drills, Seminars:*

3. *Readings, Textbooks:*

4. *Papers, Problem Sets, Reports, Tests:*

5. *Other Comments or Suggestions:*

Rating Scale 2-6.   The Purdue "Cafeteria System"

Recognizing that unique instructional strategies often transcend the facility of standard methods to evaluate them, the staff of the Measurement and Research Center, in the spring of 1972, created a computer-assisted system for building tailor-made rating instruments and for analyzing responses to them. From a catalog of rating scale items, each instructor selects those that fit his needs. Alternatives to this procedure include item selection by students or by faculty and student committee. To each selected set, a standardized and non-optional "core" of five items is automatically added. These serve both for comparisons across and between individuals and they assure that each of five recurring factors, facets or dimensions of teaching are represented.

Traditional rating instruments can never satisfy everyone, but unlike most traditional approaches, cafeteria encourages and requires considerable faculty participation. The applicability and fairness of each cataloged item becomes a faculty decision. Quite literally, each instructor shops for a match between characteristics of his course—its focus, content style and goals—and of the questions by which the course is then evaluated. Procedures that the system uses are relatively new, although the concept and its application were suggested by McKeachie, who wrote: "It may be desirable for instructors to devise different specific questions for their own use while only a few broad questions are used for the entire faculty." He also wrote that: "an important principle here is that one is most likely to use information one wants. Thus, if we want professors to use information from students ratings, our purpose is most likely to be achieved if we use items he has asked to include."* This prediction seems amply supported by experience in the early semesters of cafeteria's use. The majority of users are purely voluntary and their numbers grow steadily. They exceed all expectations and any prior experience with the more restrictive standardized systems.

In designing cafeteria, the staff of the Measurement and Research Center has sought to meet the three requirements for program integration previously discussed: the system should be *flexible, diagnostic* and *standardized.* It meets these in the following ways:

1. Flexible. An important virtue of an evaluation system is its ability to accommodate differences in instructional strategies. Cafeteria achieves flexibility through its *Catalog,* a listing of rating scale items which is printed and in computer storage. The instructor selects items from the catalog to meet his needs by checking the item numbers on a request form. This form instructs a computer, which in turn prints the tailor-made rating instrument in the quantity desired. These rating instruments are later returned to MRC for scoring, an instructor report is generated and group data are stored for use in building and updating norms.

2. Diagnostic. In addition to scale relevance, effective diagnosis depends on an absence of cross-purposes. If diagnostic functions are to be satisfied, instruc-

(continued)

*W.J. McKeachie, "Student Ratings of Faculty," *AAUP Bulletin* 55 (1969); 439–443.

Rating Scale 2-6 continued

tors should be free of unnecessary threat and free to search out weaknesses as well as strengths. Then when instructional techniques or strategies have been found unsuccessful or falling short of instructor goals, he must be free to explore and invent alternatives without unreasonable pressure from either students or administrators. What is unreasonable can best be decided in terms of assumptions or implications accompanying evaluation. To the extent that we pretend to know precisely what good teaching is and evaluate faculty according to that standard, or to the extent that we hold teachers absolutely accountable for student learning, unreasonable pressure exists. To avoid pressuring faculty unreasonably, we must be prepared to believe that effective teaching varies along several dimensions and in several different combinations of these. Moreover, we must not act as if we believed teachers omniscient about student learning processes. Rather, we should believe that in teaching, as in other things, intelligent people functioning under relevant incentives are adaptive and self-correcting. In other words, they improve when they are motivated and when they have learned what is wrong.

3. Standardized. Standardization aids in diagnosis and is crucial to the informed interpretation of results. Simply put, this is because evaluation items may *seem* on the surface to be the same but frequently result in varied judgments. Thus, without standardization and without norms that accompany standardization, the variations are unknown and the possible interpretations are crude, at best. Through Cafeteria, evaluations representing all participating faculty are first stored (in a form that protects anonymity), then periodically these are retrieved and analyzed to create published norms. As a result, faculty can compare ratings, item-by-item, with those sharing similar teaching circumstances, of the same academic rank or other ranks, etc. The evaluation *core* provides for comparisons with ratings received by all participating faculty; items from the catalog will, of course, have less frequent use. Nevertheless, the continuing refinement and revisions of the Catalog will delete the marginal items and will in time insure that retained items have had an ample range of uses and have developed a "pedigree."

Faculty acceptance and adoptions of the Cafeteria system during its few semesters of availability have been much greater than expected, almost certainly because of the system's adaptability to most course contents and the opportunity it affords faculty to shape and select contents in ways they individually prefer. The system dictates little; essentially, it dictates only the format of questions and responses, plus the contents of the five *core* items. In return, it provides free choice from the 200 item catalog, freedom to author and include other new items, the processing and summarizing of ratings received, and increasingly useful norms and interpretative information. These must be things that account for adoptions by faculty in about 1000 classrooms this fall, 1973. Since some faculty clusters who share specific teaching responsibilities have adopted Cafeteria *en bloc,* these cannot be described as purely

(continued)

Rating Scale 2-6 continued

voluntary participants, but others, contributing the majority, have been. These facts, plus the several refinements and system additions now planned, make it likely that the Cafeteria program will serve more faculty, and better, for several years to come.

Uses of Cafeteria at Other Colleges

From its first conception, Cafeteria was envisioned as an evaluation system with applications for many other colleges, whatever their size. Recent advancement in computer technology, especially the increased availability of inexpensive mini-computers, make Cafeteria system adoptions feasible and likely at other institutions. Accordingly, MRC is currently working toward publication of a systems manual which contains a detailed description of Cafeteria operations, a listing of each computer program and complete item response characteristics for the catalog. These manuals are available at a moninal cost and will provide sufficient information for relatively easy implementation at other institutions. As part of the general licensing agreement, schools are asked to participate in a cooperative data exchange. In this manner, norms for Cafeteria can be established for a wide range of instructor and course characteristics and hence each Cafeteria user benefits from the experience of others.

In addition, other manuals describing systems pertaining to instruction and instructional development are planned. These could include complete test scoring packages, programs for generating documents, including final examinations, and/or information retrieval systems. Announcements of additional developments will be made separately.

Persons interested in obtaining the manual for Cafeteria are invited to write the Measurement and Research Center, ENAD 402, Purdue University, West Lafayett 47906.

Figure 2. Sample Instructor Report (Program EVAL)

		Response Frequencies				
		A	B	C	D	E
	1. Classification (FR = A, SO = B, JR = C, SR = D, GRAD = E)	39	2			
	2. Sex (FEMALE = A, MALE = B)	4	37			
	3. School (AGR = A, ENGR = B, HOME EC = C, HSSE = D)	0	29	0	0	
	4. School Con't (IM = A, PHARM = B, SCI = C, TECH = D, VSCI = E)	0	2	10	0	0
	5. Expected Grade (A/PASS = A, B = B, C = C, D = D, F/FAIL = E)	2	17	19	3	0
	6. Course Required? (YES = A, NO = B)	38	3			

1973 Catalog Number		*Response Frequencies*					
		SA (5)	A (4)	U (3)	D (2)	SD (1)	University Median
1	7. I am impressed with the knowledge of my instructor...	40	1	0	0	0	5.0
2	8. My instructor is a competent resource person.	41	0	0	0	0	5.0
16	9. My instructor is able to simplify difficult materials.	27	5	2	7	0	4.7
40	10. Mutual respect is a concept practiced in this course.	0	7	0	34	0	2.1
50	11. My instructor respects divergent viewpoints.	0	2	32	7	0	2.9
70	17. My instructor stimulates my thinking.	0	41	0	0	0	4.0
90	18. My instructor uses novel teaching methods...	1	0	40	0	0	3.0
105	19. This course gives me an excellent background for study.	0	40	1	0	0	4.0
120	20. Exams helps students find their strengths and weaknesses.	1	1	38	1	0	3.0
195	21. The content of recitation sessions is worthwhile.	13	23	4	1	0	4.2
210	22. This course should include a field trip.	1	0	0	38	2	2.0
215	23. In this course students proceed at their own pace.	0	0	0	0	41	1.0

(continued)

Figure 2 continued

1973 Catalog Number		Response Frequencies					University Median
		SA (5)	A (4)	U (3)	D (2)	SD (1)	
24.	My instructor motivates me to do my best work.	1	0	40	0	0	3.0
25.	Course assignments are interesting and stimulating.	2	37	0	2	0	4.0
26.	This instructor explains difficult material clearly.	22	4	9	6	0	4.6
27.	Overall, this course is among the best I have taken	4	0	36	1	0	3.0
28.	Overall, this instructor is among the best teachers. . .	0	2	32	7	0	2.9

Number of Students = 41

Copyright 1973 Purdue Research Foundation
5 = high rating
1 = low rating

Figure 4. Sample from the University Research Report (Program EVALPLOT)

University Core Item Number 5
Overall, this instructor is among the best teachers I have known.

Range of Scores	*Freq*	*Pct*	*5 10 15 20 25 30 35 40 45 50*
1.00–1.19	0	0	
1.20–1.39	1	1	x
1.40–1.59	1	1	x
1.60–1.79	2	1	x
1.80–1.99	3	2	xx
2.00–2.19	5	3	xxx
2.20–2.39	12	7	xxxxxx
2.40–2.59	6	4	xxxx
2.60–2.79	14	9	xxxxxxxx
2.80–2.99	14	9	xxxxxxxx
3.00–3.19	32	20	xxxxxxxxxxxxxxxx
3.20–3.39	17	10	xxxxxxxxx
3.40–3.59	21	13	xxxxxxxxxxx
3.60–3.79	15	9	xxxxxxxx
3.80–3.99	11	7	xxxxxx
4.00–4.19	5	3	xxx
4.20–4.39	1	1	x
4.40–4.59	1	1	x
4.60–4.79	1	1	x
4.80–5.00	0	0	

Note: Program EVALPLOT prints a distribution of instructor medians, ranging from 1.0 to 5.0 at .20 intervals. The purpose of this report is to provide a graphic display of item response characteristics. In the example above, the item produces a normal-appearing distribution. A copy of the Research Report can be seen at the Measurement and Research Center, ENAD 402.

 See Resources, p. 124, for further information and restrictions.

Rating Scale 2-7.

INSTRUCTOR'S COVER SHEET
STUDENT INSTRUCTIONAL REPORT
INSTITUTIONAL RESEARCH PROGRAM FOR HIGHER EDUCATION

A. From the subjects listed on the back, record at the right the two digit number representing the field to which this course most appropriately belongs. Blacken the corresponding oval in each column. If the most appropriate fine category is not listed, indicate the most similar general category. Only one category should be chosen.

B. Indicate your academic rank.
- ① Teaching Assistant
- ② Instructor
- ③ Assistant Professor
- ④ Associate Professor
- ⑤ Professor
- ⑥ Other

C. Indicate number of years you have been teaching.
- ① Less than 1 full year
- ② 1 or 2 years
- ③ 3 to 6 years
- ④ 7 to 12 years
- ⑤ More than 12 years

D. Indicate your credit-hour teaching load this term.
- ① 3 or fewer credit-hours
- ② 4 to 6
- ③ 7 to 9
- ④ 10 to 12
- ⑤ 13 or more

E. In general, how was this class conducted?
- ① Lecture- little or no discussion
- ② Lecture and discussion combined
- ③ Discussion mainly
- ④ Lecture and laboratory
- ⑤ Laboratory
- ⑥ Other

F. Indicate approximate level of course.
- ① Freshman-Sophomore
- ② Junior-Senior
- ③ Graduate
- ④ Other

G. Have there been major revisions in the teaching methods used for this course during the last
- ① 1 year
- ② 2 years
- ③ 3 years
- ④ 4 or more years
- ⑤ There have been no changes

H. Where did students complete the questionnaire?
- ① In the classroom
- ② Out of the classroom
- ③ Some in and some out of the classroom
- ④ Other

I. When was the questionnaire completed?
- ① At or around the midpoint of the course
- ② Toward the end of the course

SIR REPORT NUMBER **49089**

COLLEGE CODE

NUMBER of ANSWER SHEETS RETURNED

CLASS ENROLLMENT

ADMIN. DATE MONTH YEAR

FIRST DIGIT
SECOND DIGIT

College Name _____

Instructor's Name _____

Department Name _____

Course Name _____

Course Number _____

Section Number _____

The section below should be used by instructor to specify summary report heading. See *Instructions* for further information.

Report Heading-Alphabetical   Report Heading-Numerical

(continued)

Rating Scale 2-7 continued

RESPONSE CATEGORIES FOR QUESTION A.
SELECT MOST APPROPRIATE SUBJECT

First Digit ↓ Second Digit ↓

1 0 AGRICULTURE or FORESTRY	4 4 HOME ECONOMICS
1 1 ARCHITECTURE or DESIGN	4 5 HUMANITIES
1 2 BIOLOGICAL SCIENCES	4 6 English Language and Literature
1 3 Bacteriology, Molecular biology, Virology, Microbiology	4 7 History
	4 8 Philosophy
1 4 Biochemistry	4 9 Religion or Theology
1 5 General Botany	5 0 Other Humanities fields
1 6 Physiology, Anatomy	5 1 INDUSTRIAL ARTS
1 7 General Zoology	5 2 JOURNALISM
1 8 General Biology	5 3 LAW
1 9 BUSINESS, COMMERCE, or MANAGEMENT	5 4 LIBRARY SCIENCE
2 0 Secretarial	5 5 MATHEMATICS or STATISTICS
2 1 EDUCATION	5 6 MILITARY SCIENCE
2 2 ENGINEERING or ENGINEERING TECHNOLOGY	5 7 PHYSICAL and HEALTH EDUCATION
2 3 Chemical	5 8 PHYSICAL SCIENCES
2 4 Civil	5 9 Chemistry
2 5 Electrical	6 0 Earth Sciences or Geology
2 6 Mechanical	6 1 Physics
2 7 Other Engineering fields	6 2 Other Physical Sciences
2 8 FINE ARTS	6 3 PSYCHOLOGY
2 9 Art	6 4 Clinical
3 0 Dramatics and Speech	6 5 Experimental
3 1 Music	6 6 Educational
3 2 Other Fine Arts	6 7 Industrial
3 3 FOREIGN LANGUAGES and LITERATURE	6 8 Counseling and Guidance
3 4 French	6 9 Other Psychology fields
3 5 German	7 0 SOCIAL SCIENCES
3 6 Spanish	7 1 Anthropology or Archeology
3 7 Other Foreign Languages	7 2 Economics
3 8 GEOGRAPHY	7 3 Political Science, Government
3 9 HEALTH FIELDS	7 4 Sociology
4 0 Medicine	7 5 Social Work, Social Welfare
4 1 Medical Technology	7 6 Other Social Sciences
4 2 Nursing	7 7 TRADE or INDUSTRIAL
4 3 Physical Therapy	7 8 ALL OTHER FIELDS

Developed by Educational Testing Service, Princeton, N. J. 08540

Rating Scale 2-8.

STUDENT INSTRUCTIONAL REPORT

This questionnaire gives you an opportunity to express anonymously your views of this course and the way it has been taught. Indicate the response closest to your view by blackening the appropriate oval. Use a soft lead pencil (preferably No. 2) for all responses to the questionnaire. Do not use an ink or ball point pen.

SIR Report Number

SECTION I. Items 1-20. Blacken one response number for each question.

NA (0) = **Not Applicable or don't know.** The statement does not apply to this course or instructor, or you simply are not able to give a knowledgeable response.

SA (4) = **Strongly Agree.** You strongly agree with the statement as it applies to this course or instructor.

A (3) = **Agree.** You agree more than you disagree with the statement as it applies to this course or instructor.

D (2) = **Disagree.** You disagree more than you agree with the statement as it applies to this course or instructor.

SD (1) = **Strongly Disagree.** You strongly disagree with the statement as it applies to this course or instructor.

		NA	SA	A	D	SD
1.	The instructor's objectives for the course have been made clear	⓪	④	③	②	①
2.	There was considerable agreement between the announced objectives of the course and what was actually taught	⓪	④	③	②	①
3.	The instructor used class time well	⓪	④	③	②	①
4.	The instructor was readily available for consultation with students	⓪	④	③	②	①
5.	The instructor seemed to know when students didn't understand the material	⓪	④	③	②	①
6.	Lectures were too repetitive of what was in the textbook(s)	⓪	④	③	②	①
7.	The instructor encouraged students to think for themselves	⓪	④	③	②	①
8.	The instructor seemed genuinely concerned with students' progress and was actively helpful	⓪	④	③	②	①
9.	The instructor made helpful comments on papers or exams	⓪	④	③	②	①
10.	The instructor raised challenging questions or problems for discussion	⓪	④	③	②	①
11.	In this class I felt free to ask questions or express my opinions	⓪	④	③	②	①
12.	The instructor was well-prepared for each class	⓪	④	③	②	①
13.	The instructor told students how they would be evaluated in the course	⓪	④	③	②	①
14.	The instructor summarized or emphasized major points in lectures or discussions	⓪	④	③	②	①
15.	My interest in the subject area has been stimulated by this course	⓪	④	③	②	①
16.	The scope of the course has been too limited; not enough material has been covered	⓪	④	③	②	①
17.	Examinations reflected the important aspects of the course	⓪	④	③	②	①
18.	I have been putting a good deal of effort into this course	⓪	④	③	②	①
19.	The instructor was open to other viewpoints	⓪	④	③	②	①
20.	In my opinion, the instructor has accomplished (is accomplishing) his objectives for the course	⓪	④	③	②	①

SECTION II. Items 21-31. Blacken one response number for each question.

21. For my preparation and ability, the level of difficulty of this course was:
- ① Very elementary
- ④ Somewhat difficult
- ② Somewhat elementary
- ⑤ Very difficult
- ③ About right

22. The work load for this course in relation to other courses of equal credit was:
- ① Much lighter
- ④ Heavier
- ② Lighter
- ⑤ Much heavier
- ③ About the same

23. For me, the pace at which the instructor covered the material during the term was:
- ① Very slow
- ④ Somewhat fast
- ② Somewhat slow
- ⑤ Very fast
- ③ Just about right

24. To what extent did the instructor use examples or illustrations to help clarify the material?
- ④ Frequently
- ② Seldom
- ③ Occasionally
- ① Never

Questionnaire continued on the other side.

FORM NO. 3068

(continued)

Rating Scale 2-8 continued

25. Was class size satisfactory for the method of conducting the class?

① Yes, most of the time ③ No, class was too small
② No, class was too large ④ It didn't make any difference one way or the other

26. Which one of the following best describes this course for you?

① Major requirement or elective within major field
② Minor requirement or required elective outside major field
③ College requirement but not part of my major or minor field
④ Elective not required in any way
⑤ Other

27. Which one of the following was your most important reason for selecting this course?

① Friend(s) recommended
② Faculty advisor's recommendation
③ Teacher's excellent reputation
④ Thought I could make a good grade
⑤ Could use pass/no credit option
⑥ It was required
⑦ Subject was of interest
⑧ Other

28. What grade do you expect to receive in this course?

① A ⑤ Fail
② B ⑥ Pass
③ C ⑦ No credit
④ D ⑧ Other

29. What is your approximate cumulative grade-point average?

① 3.50-4.00 ⑥ 1.00-1.49
② 3.00-3.49 ⑦ Less than 1.00
③ 2.50-2.99 ⑧ None yet--freshman or transfer
④ 2.00-2.49
⑤ 1.50-1.99

30. What is your class level?

① Freshman ④ Senior
② Sophomore ⑤ Graduate
③ Junior ⑥ Other

31. Sex:

① Female
② Male

SECTION III Items 32-39. Blacken one response number for each question.

	Not applicable, don't know, or there were none.	Excellent	Good	Satisfactory	Fair	Poor
32. Overall, I would rate the textbook(s)	⓪	⑤	④	③	②	①
33. Overall, I would rate the supplementary readings	⓪	⑤	④	③	②	①
34. Overall, I would rate the quality of the exams	⓪	⑤	④	③	②	①
35. I would rate the general quality of the lectures	⓪	⑤	④	③	②	①
36. I would rate the overall value of class discussion	⓪	⑤	④	③	②	①
37. Overall, I would rate the laboratories	⓪	⑤	④	③	②	①
38. I would rate the overall value of this course to me as	⓪	⑤	④	③	②	①

39. Compared to other instructors you have had (secondary school and college), how effective has the instructor been in this course? (Blacken one response number.)

One of the most effective (among the top 10%)	More effective than most (among the top 30%)	About average	Not as effective as most (in the lowest 30%)	One of the least effective (in the lowest 10%)
⑤	④	③	②	①

SECTION IV Items 40-49. If the instructor provided supplementary questions and response options, use this section for responding. Blacken only one response number for each question.

NA
40. ⓪ ① ② ③ ④ ⑤ ⑥ ⑦ ⑧ ⑨
41. ⓪ ① ② ③ ④ ⑤ ⑥ ⑦ ⑧ ⑨
42. ⓪ ① ② ③ ④ ⑤ ⑥ ⑦ ⑧ ⑨
43. ⓪ ① ② ③ ④ ⑤ ⑥ ⑦ ⑧ ⑨
44. ⓪ ① ② ③ ④ ⑤ ⑥ ⑦ ⑧ ⑨

NA
45. ⓪ ① ② ③ ④ ⑤ ⑥ ⑦ ⑧ ⑨
46. ⓪ ① ② ③ ④ ⑤ ⑥ ⑦ ⑧ ⑨
47. ⓪ ① ② ③ ④ ⑤ ⑥ ⑦ ⑧ ⑨
48. ⓪ ① ② ③ ④ ⑤ ⑥ ⑦ ⑧ ⑨
49. ⓪ ① ② ③ ④ ⑤ ⑥ ⑦ ⑧ ⑨

If you would like to make additional comments about the course or instruction, use a separate sheet of paper. You might elaborate on the particular aspects you liked most as well as those you liked least. Also, how can the course or the way it was taught be improved? PLEASE GIVE THESE COMMENTS TO THE INSTRUCTOR.

If you have any comments or suggestions about this questionnaire (for example, the content or responses available), please send them to: Student Instructional Report, Educational Testing Service, Princeton, New Jersey 08540.

SURVEY FORM -- STUDENT REACTIONS TO INSTRUCTION AND COURSES

Your thoughtful answers to these questions will provide helpful information to your instructor.

● Describe the frequency of your instructor's teaching procedures, using the following code:

1 — Hardly Ever	3 — Sometimes
2 — Occasionally	4 — Frequently 5 — Almost Always

The Instructor:

1. Promoted teacher-student discussion (as opposed to mere responses to questions).
2. Found ways to help students answer their own questions.
3. Encouraged students to express themselves freely and openly.
4. Seemed enthusiastic about the subject matter.
5. Changed approaches to meet new situations.
6. Gave examinations which stressed unnecessary memorization.
7. Spoke with expressiveness and variety in tone of voice.
8. Demonstrated the importance and significance of the subject matter.
9. Made presentations which were dry and dull.
10. Made it clear how each topic fit into the course.
11. Explained the reasons for criticisms of students' academic performance.
12. Gave examination questions which were unclear.
13. Encouraged student comments even when they turned out to be incorrect or irrelevant.
14. Summarized material in a manner which aided retention.
15. Stimulated students to intellectual effort beyond that required by most courses.
16. Clearly stated the objectives of the course.
17. Explained course material clearly, and explanations were to the point.
18. Related course material to real life situations.
19. Gave examination questions which were unreasonably detailed (picky).
20. Introduced stimulating ideas about the subject.

● On each of the objectives listed below, rate the progress you have made in this course compared with that made in other courses you have taken at this college or university. In this course my progress was:

1 — Low (lowest 10 per cent of courses I have taken here)
2 — Low Average (next 20 per cent of courses)
3 — Average (middle 40 per cent of courses)
4 — High Average (next 20 percent of courses)
5 — High (highest 10 per cent of courses)

Progress on:

21. Gaining factual knowledge (terminology, classifications, methods, trends).
22. Learning fundamental principles, generalizations, or theories.
23. Learning to apply course material to improve rational thinking, problem-solving and decision making.
24. Developing specific skills, competencies and points of view needed by professionals in the field most closely related to this course.
25. Learning how professionals in this field go about the process of gaining new knowledge.
26. Developing creative capacities.
27. Developing a sense of personal responsibility (self-reliance, self-discipline).
28. Gaining a broader understanding and appreciation of intellectual-cultural activity (music, science, literature, etc.).
29. Developing skill in expressing myself orally or in writing.
30. Discovering the implications of the course material for understanding myself (interests, talents, values, etc.).

● On the next four questions, compare this course with others you have taken at this institution, using the following code:

1 — Much Less than Most Courses
2 — Less than Most
3 — About Average
4 — More than Most
5 — Much More than Most

The Course:

31. Amount of reading
32. Amount of work in other (non-reading) assignments
33. Difficulty of subject matter
34. Degree to which the course hung together (various topics and class activities were related to each other)

● Describe your attitudes toward and behavior in this course, using the following code:

1 — Definitely False	
2 — More False than True	4 — More True than False
3 — In Between	5 — Definitely True

Self-rating:

35. I worked harder on this course than on most courses I have taken.
36. I had a strong desire to take this course.
37. I would like to take another course from this instructor.
38. As a result of taking this course, I have more positive feelings toward this field of study.
39. I have given thoughtful consideration to the questions on this form.

● Describe your status on the following by blackening the appropriate space on the Response Card.

A. To which sex-age group do you belong?

1 — Female, under 25	3 — Female, 25 or over
2 — Male, under 25	4 — Male, 25 or over

B. Do you consider yourself to be a full-time or a part-time student?

1 — Full-time
2 — Part-time

C. Counting the present term, for how many terms have you attended this college or university?

1 — 1 term	3 — 4 or 5
2 — 2 or 3	4 — 6 or more

D. What grade do you expect to receive in this course?

1 — A	3 — C	
2 — B	4 — D or F	5 — Other

E. What is your classification?

1 — Freshman	3 — Junior or Senior	
2 — Sophomore	4 — Graduate	5 — Other

F. For how many courses have you filled out this form during the present term?

1 — This is the first course	
2 — 2 or 3 courses	3 — 4 or more courses

G. How well did the questions on this form permit you to describe your impressions of this instructor and course?

1 — Very well	3 — Not very well
2 — Quite well	4 — Poorly

If your instructor has extra questions, answer them in the space designated on the Response Card.

Your comments are invited on how the instructor might improve this course or teaching procedures. Use the back of the Response Card (unless otherwise directed).

Rating Scale 2–10.

FACULTY INFORMATION FORM

FOR USE WITH THE IDEA SURVEY FORM

Fill out one form for each **course** which is to be rated. If you are teaching two or more sections (classes) of the same course and want ratings on each, you need **not** fill out separate forms unless they are taught by different methods. However, it is necessary that you list the hour and days each section meets, the number of students enrolled in each, and the date these forms will be administered. (Please Print)

(1-20) NAME _____ COURSE NAME _____
                Last   Initials

(32-37) COURSE NUMBER _____ NUMBER OF SECTIONS TO RATED _____

(38) ACADEMIC RANK _____ (39-40) YRS. TEACHING IN HIGHER ED. _____
                                                                (exclude current year)

(41) How many times (prior to this term) have you taught this course? _____

(42) If you have taught this course previously, was your approach this term significantly different?
     ____ (1) Yes   ____ (2) No

(43) How did you feel about teaching this course?
     ____ (1) Wanted to.   ____ (2) Didn't care.   ____ (3) Didn't want to.

(44) Did you make the decisions which defined major features of this course (objectives, assignments, examinations, etc.)?
     ____ (1) Yes.   ____ (2) Partially.   ____ (3) No.

(45) Would you like to teach this course again?
     ____ (1) Unqualified "Yes."   ____ (2) It depends upon whether changes can be made.   ____ (3) No.

(46) Please estimate the percentage of students in this course who were well motivated.
     ____ (1) Over 75%   ____ (2) 25-75%   ____ (3) Less than 25%

CLASS SCHEDULE (e.g., 10:30 MWF)		NUMBER OF STUDENTS ENROLLED	DATE TO BE ADMINISTERED
HOUR	DAYS		
SECTION 1			
SECTION 2			
SECTION 3			
SECTION 4			
(47-50)	(51-55)	(56-5ථ)	

> CIRCLE THE NUMBER WHICH DESCRIBES THE RELATIVE IMPORTANCE OF EACH OF THE FOLLOWING AS AN OBJECTIVE FOR THIS COURSE:
>
> 1 = Of No More Than Minor Importance   2 = Important   3 = Essential

                                                                   IMPORTANCE

21. Gaining factual knowledge (terminology, classifications, methods, trends) 21.   1   2   3
22. Learning fundamental principles, generalizations, or theories 22.   1   2   3
23. Learning to apply course material to improve rational thinking, problem-solving and decision-making 23.   1   2   3
24. Developing specific skills, competencies and points of view needed by professionals in the field most closely related to this course 24.   1   2   3
25. Learning how professionals in this field go about the process of gaining new knowledge 25.   1   2   3
26. Developing creative capacities 26.   1   2   3
27. Developing a sense of personal responsibility (self-reliance, self-discipline) 27.   1   2   3
28. Gaining a broader understanding and appreciation of intellectual-cultural activity (music, science, literature, etc.) 28.   1   2   3
29. Developing skill in expressing oneself orally or in writing 29.   1   2   3
30. Discovering the implications of the course material for understanding oneself (interests, talents, values, etc.) 30.   1   2   3

Do you intend to add extra questions of your own to those printed on the form?   ____ Yes (*) (80)   ____ No ($)

YOUR DEPARTMENT _____ YOUR OFFICE _____
                                                                      Number   Building

ENDEAVOR INSTRUCTIONAL RATING FORM

Copyright by Endeavor Information Systems, Inc., 1973

COMPLETELY DARKEN THE APPROPRIATE BOXES

USE NO. 2
PENCIL ONLY

Student I.D. Number

Course Code Number

Instructor I.D. Number

FOR EACH ITEM, DARKEN THE BOX WHICH MOST CLOSELY INDICATES YOUR ASSESSMENT OF THIS COURSE.

	1	2	3	4	5	6	7
1. The students had to work hard in this course.	NEVER	SELDOM	SOMETIMES		OFTEN		ALWAYS
2. Each class period was carefully planned in advance.	NEVER	SELDOM	SOMETIMES		OFTEN		ALWAYS
3. The instructor listened to each student's problems and was willing to help.	NEVER	SELDOM	SOMETIMES		OFTEN		ALWAYS
4. It is now easier for me to understand advanced material on this subject.	DEFINITELY NO		NO		YES		DEFINITELY YES
5. The grading system in this course was fair and impartial.	DEFINITELY NO		NO		YES		DEFINITELY YES
6. Class discussion was welcome in this course.	NEVER	SELDOM	SOMETIMES		OFTEN		ALWAYS
7. The instructor's presentations helped to clarify the course material.	NEVER	SELDOM	SOMETIMES		OFTEN		ALWAYS
8. This course has developed my ability to analyze issues in this field.	DEFINITELY NO		NO		YES		DEFINITELY YES
9. The student was able to get personal help in this course.	NEVER	SELDOM	SOMETIMES		OFTEN		ALWAYS
10. This course required a lot of time.	NEVER	SELDOM	SOMETIMES		OFTEN		ALWAYS
11. The instructor presentated material clearly and summarized major points.	NEVER	SELDOM	SOMETIMES		OFTEN		ALWAYS
12. The grading accurately reflected the student's performance.	DEFINITELY NO		NO		YES		DEFINITELY YES
13. Students were actively encouraged to participate in class discussions.	NEVER	SELDOM	SOMETIMES		OFTEN		ALWAYS
14. The instructor organized the course schedule in a detailed fashion.	DEFINITELY NO		NO		YES		DEFINITELY YES
15. The grading procedure fairly indicated each student's accomplishments.	DEFINITELY NO		NO		YES		DEFINITELY YES
16. The instructor made good use of examples and illustrations.	NEVER	SELDOM	SOMETIMES		OFTEN		ALWAYS
17. Class activities were scheduled in an orderly way.	NEVER	SELDOM	SOMETIMES		OFTEN		ALWAYS
18. Students were encouraged to openly express ideas.	NEVER	SELDOM	SOMETIMES		OFTEN		ALWAYS
19. This course has increased my knowledge and competence in this area.	DEFINITELY NO		NO		YES		DEFINITELY YES
20. This course had a heavy work load.	NEVER	SELDOM	SOMETIMES		OFTEN		ALWAYS
21. The instructor was genuinely concerned about each student's difficulties.	NEVER	SELDOM	SOMETIMES		OFTEN		ALWAYS

(continued)

FACTOR STRUCTURE OF THE
ENDEAVOR INSTRUCTIONAL RATING FORM
COPYRIGHT, 1973, BY
ENDEAVOR INFORMATION SYSTEMS, INC.

I. CLARITY OF PRESENTATIONS

7. The instructor's presentations helped to clarify the course material.
11. The instructor presented material clearly and summarized major points.
16. The instructor made good use of examples and illustrations.

II. WORK LOAD

1. The students had to work hard in this course.
10. This course required a lot of time.
20. This course had a heavy work load.

III. PERSONAL ATTENTION

3. The teacher listened to each student's problems and was willing to help.
9. The student was able to get personal help in this course.
21. The teacher was genuinely concerned about each student's difficulties.

IV. CLASS DISCUSSION

6. Class discussion was welcome in this course.
13. Students were actively encouraged to participate in class discussions.
18. Students were encouraged to openly express ideas.

V. ORGANIZATION-PLANNING

2. Each class period was carefully planned in advance.
14. The instructor organized the course schedule in a detailed fashion.
17. Class activities were scheduled in an orderly way.

VI. GRADING

5. The grading system in this course was fair and impartial.
12. The grading accurately reflected the student's performance.
15. The grading procedure fairly indicated each student's accomplishments.

VII. STUDENT ACCOMPLISHMENT

4. It is now easier for me to understand advanced material on this subject.
8. This course has developed my ability to analyze issues in this field.
19. This course has increased my knowledge and competence in this area.

Used by permission. See Resources, p. 124, for further information and restrictions.

Rating Scale 2-12A

INSTRUCTIONAL ASSESSMENT SYSTEM

INSTRUCTOR_____

EDUCATIONAL ASSESSMENT CENTER
UNIVERSITY OF WASHINGTON

COURSE_____ SECTION_____

DIRECTIONS: YOU MAY RETURN THIS QUESTIONNAIRE COMPLETELY OR PARTIALLY UNANSWERED WITHOUT PENALTY. USE A NO. 2 PENCIL AND MAKE MARKS FIRM BUT NOT SHINY. DO NOT CROSS OUT GRIDS. DO NOT MAKE STRAY MARKS. ERASE CLEANLY IF YOU CHANGE AN ANSWER.

	STUDENT RATING FORM
WHEN REGISTERING, WAS THIS A COURSE YOU WANTED TO TAKE? ▯ YES ▯ NO ▯ NEUTRAL	
IS THIS COURSE: ▯ IN YOUR MAJOR ▯ IN YOUR MINOR OR PROGRAM REQUIREMENT ▯ A DISTRIBUTION REQUIREMENT ▯ AN ELECTIVE ▯ OTHER	**A**
YOUR CLASS: ▯ FRESHMAN ▯ SOPHOMORE ▯ JUNIOR ▯ SENIOR ▯ GRADUATE ▯ OTHER	
GRADE YOU EXPECT TO RECEIVE: ▯ A ▯ B—• ▯ C ▯ D ▯ E ▯ PASS	

IMPORTANT: IN RATING THIS COURSE, RESPOND TO EACH ITEM CAREFULLY AND THOUGHTFULLY. AVOID LETTING YOUR RESPONSES TO SOME ITEMS INFLUENCE YOUR RESPONSES TO OTHERS. KEEP THE PURPOSE OF EACH SECTION IN MIND AS YOU RATE THE COURSE.

E—EXCELLENT
VG—VERY GOOD
G—GOOD
F—FAIR
P—POOR
VP—VERY POOR

SECTION 1:
TO PROVIDE A GENERAL EVALUATION.
1. THE COURSE AS A WHOLE WAS:
2. THE COURSE CONTENT WAS:
3. THE INSTRUCTOR'S CONTRIBUTION TO THE COURSE WAS:
4. THE INSTRUCTOR'S EFFECTIVENESS IN TEACHING THE SUBJECT MATTER WAS:

SECTION 2:
TO PROVIDE DIAGNOSTIC FEEDBACK TO THE INSTRUCTOR.
5. COURSE ORGANIZATION WAS:
6. CLARITY OF INSTRUCTOR'S VOICE WAS:
7. EXPLANATIONS BY INSTRUCTOR WERE:
8. INSTRUCTOR'S ABILITY TO PRESENT ALTERNATIVE EXPLANATIONS WHEN NEEDED WAS:
9. INSTRUCTOR'S USE OF EXAMPLES AND ILLUSTRATIONS WAS:
10. QUALITY OF QUESTIONS OR PROBLEMS RAISED BY INSTRUCTOR WAS:
11. STUDENT CONFIDENCE IN INSTRUCTOR'S KNOWLEDGE WAS:
12. INSTRUCTOR'S ENTHUSIASM WAS:
13. ENCOURAGEMENT GIVEN STUDENTS TO EXPRESS THEMSELVES WAS:
14. ANSWERS TO STUDENT QUESTIONS WERE:
15. AVAILABILITY OF EXTRA HELP WHEN NEEDED WAS:

SECTION 3:
TO PROVIDE INFORMATION ABOUT THE COURSE TO OTHER STUDENTS.
16. USE OF CLASS TIME WAS:
17. INSTRUCTOR'S INTEREST IN WHETHER STUDENTS LEARNED WAS:
18. AMOUNT YOU LEARNED IN THE COURSE WAS:
19. RELEVANCE AND USEFULNESS OF COURSE CONTENT IS:
20. EVALUATIVE AND GRADING TECHNIQUES (TESTS, PAPERS, PROJECTS, ETC.) WERE:
21. REASONABLENESS OF ASSIGNED WORK WAS:
22. CLARITY OF STUDENT RESPONSIBILITIES AND REQUIREMENTS WAS:

SECTION 4:
OPTIONAL ITEMS—USE ONLY AS DIRECTED.
27.
28.
29.
30.

23.
24.
25.
26.

78

Rating Scale 2-12B

INSTRUCTIONAL ASSESSMENT SYSTEM

INSTRUCTOR_____

COURSE_____ SECTION_____

EDUCATIONAL ASSESSMENT CENTER
UNIVERSITY OF WASHINGTON

DIRECTIONS: YOU MAY RETURN THIS QUESTIONNAIRE COMPLETELY OR PARTIALLY UNANSWERED WITHOUT PENALTY. USE A NO. 2 PENCIL AND MAKE MARKS FIRM BUT NOT SHINY. DO NOT CROSS OUT GRIDS. DO NOT MAKE STRAY MARKS. ERASE CLEANLY IF YOU CHANGE AN ANSWER.

WHEN REGISTERING, WAS THIS A COURSE YOU WANTED TO TAKE? YES NO NEUTRAL

IS THIS COURSE: IN YOUR MAJOR | IN YOUR MINOR OR PROGRAM REQUIREMENT | A DISTRIBUTION REQUIREMENT | AN ELECTIVE | OTHER

YOUR CLASS: FRESHMAN | SOPHOMORE | JUNIOR | SENIOR | GRADUATE | OTHER

GRADE YOU EXPECT TO RECEIVE: A | B | C | D | E | PASS

STUDENT RATING FORM

B

IMPORTANT: IN RATING THIS COURSE, RESPOND TO EACH ITEM CAREFULLY AND THOUGHTFULLY. AVOID LETTING YOUR RESPONSES TO SOME ITEMS INFLUENCE YOUR RESPONSES TO OTHERS. KEEP THE PURPOSE OF EACH SECTION IN MIND AS YOU RATE THE COURSE.

E—EXCELLENT
VG—VERY GOOD
G—GOOD
F—FAIR
P—POOR
VP—VERY POOR

SECTION 1:
TO PROVIDE A GENERAL EVALUATION.
1. THE COURSE AS A WHOLE WAS:
2. THE COURSE CONTENT WAS:
3. THE INSTRUCTOR'S CONTRIBUTION TO THE COURSE WAS:
4. THE INSTRUCTOR'S EFFECTIVENESS IN TEACHING THE SUBJECT MATTER WAS:

SECTION 2:
TO PROVIDE DIAGNOSTIC FEEDBACK TO THE INSTRUCTOR.
5. COURSE ORGANIZATION WAS:
6. SEQUENTIAL PRESENTATION OF CONCEPTS WAS:
7. EXPLANATIONS BY INSTRUCTOR WERE:
8. INSTRUCTOR'S ABILITY TO PRESENT ALTERNATIVE EXPLANATIONS WHEN NEEDED WAS:
9. INSTRUCTOR'S USE OF EXAMPLES AND ILLUSTRATIONS WAS:
10. INSTRUCTOR'S ENHANCEMENT OF STUDENT INTEREST IN THE MATERIAL WAS:
11. STUDENT CONFIDENCE IN INSTRUCTOR'S KNOWLEDGE WAS:
12. INSTRUCTOR'S ENTHUSIASM WAS:
13. CLARITY OF COURSE OBJECTIVES WAS:
14. INTEREST LEVEL OF CLASS SESSIONS WAS:
15. AVAILABILITY OF EXTRA HELP WHEN NEEDED WAS:

SECTION 3:
TO PROVIDE INFORMATION ABOUT THE COURSE TO OTHER STUDENTS.
16. USE OF CLASS TIME WAS:
17. INSTRUCTOR'S INTEREST IN WHETHER STUDENTS LEARNED WAS:
18. AMOUNT YOU LEARNED IN THE COURSE WAS:
19. RELEVANCE AND USEFULNESS OF COURSE CONTENT IS:
20. EVALUATIVE AND GRADING TECHNIQUES (TESTS, PAPERS, PROJECTS, ETC.) WERE:
21. REASONABLENESS OF ASSIGNED WORK WAS:
22. CLARITY OF STUDENT RESPONSIBILITIES AND REQUIREMENTS WAS:

SECTION 4:
OPTIONAL ITEMS—USE ONLY AS DIRECTED.

27.
28.
29.
30.

23.
24.
25.
26.

Rating Scale 2-12C

INSTRUCTIONAL ASSESSMENT SYSTEM

INSTRUCTOR_____

EDUCATIONAL ASSESSMENT CENTER
UNIVERSITY OF WASHINGTON

COURSE_____ SECTION_____

DIRECTIONS: YOU MAY RETURN THIS QUESTIONNAIRE COMPLETELY OR PARTIALLY UNANSWERED WITHOUT PENALTY. USE A NO. 2 PENCIL AND MAKE MARKS FIRM BUT NOT SHINY. DO NOT CROSS OUT GRIDS. DO NOT MAKE STRAY MARKS. ERASE CLEANLY IF YOU CHANGE AN ANSWER.

WHEN REGISTERING, WAS THIS A COURSE YOU WANTED TO TAKE? ⬚ YES ⬚ NO ⬚ NEUTRAL

IS THIS COURSE: ⬚ IN YOUR MAJOR ⬚ IN YOUR MINOR OR PROGRAM REQUIREMENT ⬚ A DISTRIBUTION REQUIREMENT ⬚ AN ELECTIVE ⬚ OTHER

YOUR CLASS: ⬚ FRESHMAN ⬚ SOPHOMORE ⬚ JUNIOR ⬚ SENIOR ⬚ GRADUATE ⬚ OTHER

GRADE YOU EXPECT TO RECEIVE: ⬚ A ⬚ B ⬚ C ⬚ D ⬚ E ⬚ PASS

STUDENT RATING FORM

C

IMPORTANT: IN RATING THIS COURSE, RESPOND TO EACH ITEM CAREFULLY AND THOUGHTFULLY. AVOID LETTING YOUR RESPONSES TO SOME ITEMS INFLUENCE YOUR RESPONSES TO OTHERS. KEEP THE PURPOSE OF EACH SECTION IN MIND AS YOU RATE THE COURSE.

E—EXCELLENT
VG—VERY GOOD
G—GOOD
F—FAIR
P—POOR
VP—VERY POOR

SECTION 1:
TO PROVIDE A GENERAL EVALUATION.
1. THE COURSE AS A WHOLE WAS:
2. THE COURSE CONTENT WAS:
3. THE INSTRUCTOR'S CONTRIBUTION TO THE COURSE WAS:
4. THE INSTRUCTOR'S EFFECTIVENESS IN TEACHING THE SUBJECT MATTER WAS:

SECTION 2:
TO PROVIDE DIAGNOSTIC FEEDBACK TO THE INSTRUCTOR.
5. COURSE ORGANIZATION WAS:
6. INSTRUCTOR'S PREPARATION FOR CLASS WAS:
7. INSTRUCTOR AS A DISCUSSION LEADER WAS:
8. INSTRUCTOR'S CONTRIBUTION TO DISCUSSIONS WAS:
9. CONDUCIVENESS OF CLASS ATMOSPHERE TO STUDENT LEARNING WAS:
10. QUALITY OF QUESTIONS OR PROBLEMS RAISED WAS:
11. STUDENT CONFIDENCE IN INSTRUCTOR'S KNOWLEDGE WAS:
12. INSTRUCTOR'S ENTHUSIASM WAS:
13. ENCOURAGEMENT GIVEN STUDENTS TO EXPRESS THEMSELVES WAS:
14. INSTRUCTOR'S OPENNESS TO STUDENT VIEWS WAS:
15. INTEREST LEVEL OF CLASS SESSIONS WAS:

SECTION 3:
TO PROVIDE INFORMATION ABOUT THE COURSE TO OTHER STUDENTS.
16. USE OF CLASS TIME WAS:
17. INSTRUCTOR'S INTEREST IN WHETHER STUDENTS LEARNED WAS:
18. AMOUNT YOU LEARNED IN THE COURSE WAS:
19. RELEVANCE AND USEFULNESS OF COURSE CONTENT IS:
20. EVALUATIVE AND GRADING TECHNIQUES (TESTS, PAPERS, PROJECTS, ETC.) WERE:
21. REASONABLENESS OF ASSIGNED WORK WAS:
22. CLARITY OF STUDENT RESPONSIBILITIES AND REQUIREMENTS WAS:

SECTION 4:
OPTIONAL ITEMS—USE ONLY AS DIRECTED.

27. 0 1 2 3 4 5 6 7 8 9
28. 0 1 2 3 4 5 6 7 8 9
29. 0 1 2 3 4 5 6 7 8 9
30. 0 1 2 3 4 5 6 7 8 9

23.
24.
25.
26.

© University of Washington 1974. Reprinted by permission. See Resources, p. 124, for further information and restrictions.

Rating Scale 2–12D

INSTRUCTIONAL ASSESSMENT SYSTEM

INSTRUCTOR_____

COURSE_____ SECTION_____

EDUCATIONAL ASSESSMENT CENTER
UNIVERSITY OF WASHINGTON

DIRECTIONS: YOU MAY RETURN THIS QUESTIONNAIRE COMPLETELY OR PARTIALLY UNANSWERED WITHOUT PENALTY.
USE A NO. 2 PENCIL AND MAKE MARKS FIRM BUT NOT SHINY. DO NOT CROSS OUT GRIDS.
DO NOT MAKE STRAY MARKS. ERASE CLEANLY IF YOU CHANGE AN ANSWER.

WHEN REGISTERING, WAS THIS A COURSE YOU WANTED TO TAKE?   YES   NO   NEUTRAL

IS THIS COURSE: IN YOUR MAJOR   IN YOUR MINOR OR PROGRAM REQUIREMENT   A DISTRIBUTION REQUIREMENT   AN ELECTIVE   OTHER

YOUR CLASS: FRESHMAN   SOPHOMORE   JUNIOR   SENIOR   GRADUATE   OTHER

GRADE YOU EXPECT TO RECEIVE: A   B   C   D   E   PASS

STUDENT RATING FORM

D

IMPORTANT: IN RATING THIS COURSE, RESPOND TO EACH ITEM CAREFULLY AND THOUGHTFULLY. AVOID LETTING YOUR RESPONSES TO SOME ITEMS INFLUENCE YOUR RESPONSES TO OTHERS. KEEP THE PURPOSE OF EACH SECTION IN MIND AS YOU RATE THE COURSE.

E—EXCELLENT
VG—VERY GOOD
G—GOOD
F—FAIR
P—POOR
VP—VERY POOR

SECTION 1:
TO PROVIDE A GENERAL EVALUATION.
1. THE COURSE AS A WHOLE WAS:
2. THE COURSE CONTENT WAS:
3. THE INSTRUCTOR'S CONTRIBUTION TO THE COURSE WAS:
4. THE INSTRUCTOR'S EFFECTIVENESS IN TEACHING THE SUBJECT MATTER WAS:

SECTION 2:
TO PROVIDE DIAGNOSTIC FEEDBACK TO THE INSTRUCTOR.
5. COURSE ORGANIZATION WAS:
6. SEQUENTIAL PRESENTATION OF CONCEPTS WAS:
7. EXPLANATIONS BY INSTRUCTOR WERE:
8. INSTRUCTOR'S ABILITY TO PRESENT ALTERNATIVE EXPLANATIONS WHEN NEEDED WAS:
9. INSTRUCTOR'S USE OF EXAMPLES AND ILLUSTRATIONS WAS:
10. QUALITY OF QUESTIONS OR PROBLEMS RAISED BY INSTRUCTOR WAS:
11. CONTRIBUTION OF ASSIGNMENTS TO UNDERSTANDING COURSE CONTENT WAS:
12. INSTRUCTOR'S ENTHUSIASM WAS:
13. INSTRUCTOR'S ABILITY TO DEAL WITH STUDENT DIFFICULTIES WAS:
14. ANSWERS TO STUDENT QUESTIONS WERE:
15. AVAILABILITY OF EXTRA HELP WHEN NEEDED WAS:

SECTION 3:
TO PROVIDE INFORMATION ABOUT THE COURSE TO OTHER STUDENTS.
16. USE OF CLASS TIME WAS:
17. INSTRUCTOR'S INTEREST IN WHETHER STUDENTS LEARNED WAS:
18. AMOUNT YOU LEARNED IN THE COURSE WAS:
19. RELEVANCE AND USEFULNESS OF COURSE CONTENT IS:
20. EVALUATIVE AND GRADING TECHNIQUES (TESTS, PAPERS, PROJECTS, ETC.) WERE:
21. REASONABLENESS OF ASSIGNED WORK WAS:
22. CLARITY OF STUDENT RESPONSIBILITIES AND REQUIREMENTS WAS:

SECTION 4:
OPTIONAL ITEMS—USE ONLY AS DIRECTED.
27. 28. 29. 30.
23. 24. 25. 26.

Rating Scale 2–12E

INSTRUCTIONAL ASSESSMENT SYSTEM

INSTRUCTOR_____

EDUCATIONAL ASSESSMENT CENTER
UNIVERSITY OF WASHINGTON

COURSE_____ SECTION_____

DIRECTIONS: YOU MAY RETURN THIS QUESTIONNAIRE COMPLETELY OR PARTIALLY UNANSWERED WITHOUT PENALTY. USE A NO. 2 PENCIL AND MAKE MARKS FIRM BUT NOT SHINY. DO NOT CROSS OUT GRIDS. DO NOT MAKE STRAY MARKS. ERASE CLEANLY IF YOU CHANGE AN ANSWER.

WHEN REGISTERING, WAS THIS A COURSE YOU WANTED TO TAKE? ▯ YES ▯ NO ▯ NEUTRAL	**STUDENT RATING FORM**
IS THIS COURSE: ▯ IN YOUR MAJOR ▯ IN YOUR MINOR OR PROGRAM REQUIREMENT ▯ A DISTRIBUTION REQUIREMENT ▯ AN ELECTIVE ▯ OTHER	
YOUR CLASS: ▯ FRESHMAN ▯ SOPHOMORE ▯ JUNIOR ▯ SENIOR ▯ GRADUATE ▯ OTHER	**E**
GRADE YOU EXPECT TO RECEIVE: ▯ A ▯ B ▯ C ▯ D ▯ E ▯ PASS	

IMPORTANT: IN RATING THIS COURSE, RESPOND TO EACH ITEM CAREFULLY AND THOUGHTFULLY. AVOID LETTING YOUR RESPONSES TO SOME ITEMS INFLUENCE YOUR RESPONSES TO OTHERS. KEEP THE PURPOSE OF EACH SECTION IN MIND AS YOU RATE THE COURSE.

E—EXCELLENT
VG—VERY GOOD
G—GOOD
F—FAIR
P—POOR
VP—VERY POOR

SECTION 1:
TO PROVIDE A GENERAL EVALUATION.
1. THE COURSE AS A WHOLE WAS:
2. THE COURSE CONTENT WAS:
3. THE INSTRUCTOR'S CONTRIBUTION TO THE COURSE WAS:
4. THE INSTRUCTOR'S EFFECTIVENESS IN TEACHING THE SUBJECT MATTER WAS:

SECTION 2:
TO PROVIDE DIAGNOSTIC FEEDBACK TO THE INSTRUCTOR.
5. OPPORTUNITY FOR PRACTICING WHAT WAS LEARNED WAS:
6. SEQUENTIAL DEVELOPMENT OF SKILLS WAS:
7. EXPLANATIONS OF UNDERLYING RATIONALES FOR NEW TECHNIQUES OR SKILLS WERE:
8. DEMONSTRATIONS OF EXPECTED SKILLS WERE:
9. INSTRUCTOR'S CONFIDENCE IN STUDENTS' ABILITY WAS:
10. RECOGNITION OF STUDENT PROGRESS BY INSTRUCTOR WAS:
11. STUDENT CONFIDENCE IN INSTRUCTOR'S KNOWLEDGE WAS:
12. FREEDOM ALLOWED STUDENTS TO DEVELOP OWN SKILLS AND IDEAS WAS:
13. INSTRUCTOR'S ABILITY TO DEAL WITH STUDENT DIFFICULTIES WAS:
14. TAILORING OF INSTRUCTION TO VARYING STUDENT SKILL LEVELS WAS:
15. AVAILABILITY OF EXTRA HELP WHEN NEEDED WAS:

SECTION 3:
TO PROVIDE INFORMATION ABOUT THE COURSE TO OTHER STUDENTS.
16. USE OF CLASS TIME WAS:
17. INSTRUCTOR'S INTEREST IN WHETHER STUDENTS LEARNED WAS:
18. AMOUNT YOU LEARNED IN THE COURSE WAS:
19. RELEVANCE AND USEFULNESS OF COURSE CONTENT IS:
20. EVALUATIVE AND GRADING TECHNIQUES (TESTS, PAPERS, PROJECTS, ETC.) WERE:
21. REASONABLENESS OF ASSIGNED WORK WAS:
22. CLARITY OF STUDENT RESPONSIBILITIES AND REQUIREMENTS WAS:

SECTION 4:
OPTIONAL ITEMS—USE ONLY AS DIRECTED.

27. 28. 29. 30.   23. 24. 25. 26.

Rating Scale 2-13.   Critical Incident Technique Instructor Evaluation

Instructor _____   Course _____

Quarter and Year _____   Day and Time _____

INSTRUCTIONS: Please answer yes or no to each of the following questions.

1. Know or attempt to know student's names?
2. Talk with students before and/or after class?
3. Hold social events for his students?
4. Refuse to give advice or assistance on student request (class or office) with personal problems?
5. Discuss (answer questions on) extra-class issues?

6. Encourage (answer) *all* questions in class?
7. Treat all students equally (regardless of sex, major, etc.)?
8. Ridicule, "ride," or otherwise embarrass students (either on questions or their performance)?
9. Give or offer individual help with course material (class or office)?
10. Lose control of himself in class (shout, curse, anger, etc.)?

11. Bother (harrass) students during recitation, quizzes, etc.?
12. Make threats concerning class work or personal behavior?
13. Accept your excuse, explanation (as for missing quiz)?
14. Refuse to listen to or recognize other viewpoints in class?
15. Say or indicate in some way that students are inferior?

16. Miss more than two scheduled (rescheduled) classes?
17. On time for all classes?
18. Arrange quiz dates or deadlines for student convenience?
19. End lectures at end of class time?
20. Distribute a course outline or study plan (course objectives)?

21. Follow course outline or study plan?
22. Give examples of quiz items?
23. Require *and* grade homework?
24. Return papers and quizzes promptly?
25. Permit classroom distrubances (as students talking to each other)?

26. Make false statements concerning course requirements (number of cuts, grading, etc.)?
27. Give excessive work?
28. Ask student preference as to topics covered?
29. Ask for student suggestions on his teaching?
30. Encourage (ask for) discussion, questions, or student opinions?

31. Appear well-groomed?
32. Speak clearly and distinctly?

(continued)

Rating Scale 2–13 continued

33. Use humor in lecture to illustrate points?
34. Read lectures from notes or book?
35. Appear nervous, ill-at-ease during lecture?

36. Talk or present material too rapidly?
37. Give rambling, dis-organized lecture?
38. Look at students during lecture?
39. Use language students understand?
40. Use profane language excessively?

41. Stress, in some way, important points in the material?
42. Use current, pertinent, or personal examples to illustrate points?
43. Show usefulness of material in "real world"?
44. Admit not knowing answer to a question?
45. Use outside references to supplement course?

46. Distribute hand-outs/notes to supplement lecture?
47. Use visual aids to (including blackboard) supplement lecture?
48. Have full command of the subject matter?
49. Usually lectures from text?
50. Cover all course requirements?

51. Avoid trivial detail?
52. Answer questions; work problems if requested?
53. Lecture over student's heads?
54. Give erroneous information about course material?
55. Refuses to or does not explain course material?

56. Follow course schedule?
57. Prepared for class?
58. Base tests on relevant (important) material?
59. Base test on emphasized material?
60. Make tests too difficult?

61. Schedule quizzes at regular intervals?
62. Make tests too long?
63. Comment on (correct) returned papers, quizzes, etc.?
64. Excuse high average students from final?
65. Permit extra work to improve grade?

66. Disregard lowest test score in grading?
67. Refuse to explain grading system?
68. Tell how students are to be graded?
69. Curve grades?
70. Return all papers and quizzes?

71. Grade all quizzes and assignments?
72. Give make-up tests at individual convenience?
73. Grade on such things as major, sex, athlete, etc?

(continued)

Rating Scale 2-13 continued

74. Grade on class attendance?
75. Grade on final exam only?

76. Pass-fail a predetermined percentage of the class?
77. Willing to discuss grades?
78. Make derogatory comments about teaching?
79. Make derogatory comments about the course?
80. Indicate he would rather consult and/or do research than teach?

81. Make personal criticisms of fellow teachers?
82. Was this professor less interesting than the average professor?
83. Was this professor a poorer than average teacher?
84. Would you advise a friend to take this course under this professor?
85. Do you desire to learn more about this subject because of taking this course under this professor?

III. Written Evaluation of Instructor and Course

INSTRUCTIONS: Please answer the following questions in the space provided below.

1. What has your instructor done especially well in his teaching of this course?
2. What should your instructor do to improve his teaching of this course?
3. In what way or ways did this course meet or fail to meet your expectations for it?

Developed at Georgia Institute of Technology, School of Psychology, Atlanta, Georgia 30302. Used by permission. See Resources, p. 124, for further information and restrictions.

Rating Scale 2-14.   Teaching Analysis by Students (TABS)

The Clinic to Improve University Teaching is working with instructors to improve the quality of teaching which they offer to their students. The Clinic is designed to help instructors identify and effectively use their particular teaching strengths, to isolate their specific teaching problems, and to develop improvement strategies directed at these problems.

In order to identify these strengths and problems, we are collecting information about teaching in this course by discussing course objectives and teaching patterns with your instructor, by observing and video-taping some classes, and by asking for student opinions about performance on some specific teaching skills and behaviors. The information will be used to obtain a clearer understanding of specific teaching strengths and weaknesses so that your instructor can work toward improvement. Thus, your responses will be of most value to your instructor if they are thoughtful and honest. Your cooperation will be very much appreciated.

CLINIC TO IMPROVE UNIVERSITY TEACHING
School of Education
University of Massachusetts at Amherst

SECTION I—TEACHING SKILLS AND BEHAVIORS

In this questionnaire there are some statements concerning a variety of specific teaching skills and behaviors. Please read each statement carefully and then indicate the extent to which you feel your instructor needs improvement. Respond to each statement by selecting one of the following:

1. No improvement is needed (very good or excellent performance).
2. Little improvement is needed (generally good performance).
3. Improvement is needed (generally mediocre performance).
4. Considerable improvement is needed (generally poor performance).
5. Not a necessary skill or behavior for this course.

Please make your decisions about the degree of improvement needed on the basis of what you think would be best for this particular course and your learning style. Try to consider each statement separately, rather than let your overall feelings about the instructor determine all the responses.

1. The instructor's explanation of *course* objectives.
2. The instructor's explanation of the objectives for each class session and learning activity.
3. The instructor's ability to arouse my interest when introducing an instructional activity.
4. The instructor's explanation of the work expected from each student.
5. The instructor's ability to maintain a clear relationship between the course content and the course objectives.

(continued)

Rating Scale 2–14 continued

6. The instructor's skill in clarifying the relationships among the various topics treated in the course.
7. The instructor's skill in making clear the distinction between major and minor topics.
8. The instructor's skill in adjusting the rate at which new ideas are covered so that the material can be followed and understood.
9. The instructor's ability to clarify material which needs elaboration.
10. The instructor's speaking skills.
11. The instructor's ability to ask easily understood questions.
12. The instructor's ability to ask thought-provoking questions.
13. The instructor's ability to answer questions clearly and concisely.
14. The instructor's overall effectiveness as a discussion leader.
15. The instructor's ability to get students to participate in class discussions.
16. The instructor's skill in facilitating discussions *among students* as opposed to discussions only between the instructor and students
17. The instructor's ability to wrap things up before moving on to a new topic.
18. The instructor's ability to tie things together at the end of a class.
19. The instructor's explanation of precisely how my performance is to be evaluated.
20. The instructor's ability to design evaluation procedures which are consistent with course objectives.
21. The instructor's performance in periodically informing me of my progress.
22. The instructor's selection of materials and activities which are thought-provoking.
23. The instructor's ability to select materials and activities which are not too difficult.
24. The instructor's provision of *variety* in materials and activities.
25. The instructor's ability to use a variety of teaching techniques.
26. The instructor's demonstration of creativity in teaching methods.
27. The instructor's management of day-to-day administrative details.
28. The instructor's flexibility in offering options for individual students.
29. The instructor's ability to take appropriate action when students appear to be bored.
30. The instructor's availability for personal consultation.
31. The instructor's ability to relate to people in ways which promote mutual respect.
32. The instructor's maintenance of an atmosphere which actively encourages learning.
33. The instructor's ability to inspire excitement or interest in the content of the course.
34. The instructor's ability to relate the subject matter to other academic disciplines and real world situations.
35. The instructor's willingness to explore a variety of points of view.
36. The instructor's ability to get students to challenge points of view raised in the course.

(continued)

Rating Scale 2-14 continued

37. The instructor's performance in helping me to explore the relationship between my personal values and the course content.
38. The instructor's performance in making me aware of value issues within the subject matter.

SECTION II—OTHER INFORMATION

Please mark the appropriate response for each of the following items beside the correct statement number on the answer sheet.

39. Class:
    (1) freshman
    (2) sophomore
    (3) junior
    (4) senior
    (5) graduate student

41. Grade point average:
    (1) less than 1.50 (lowest)
    (2) 1.50–2.49
    (3) 2.50–2.99
    (4) 3.00–3.49
    (5) 3.50–4.00 (highest)

43. In this course I am learning:
    (1) a great deal
    (2) a fair amount
    (3) very little
    (4) I am unsure

40. Sex:
    (1) male
    (2) female

42. In terms of the directions my life is taking, this course is:
    (1) relevant
    (2) somewhat relevant
    (3) irrelevant
    (4) I am unsure

44. As a result of this course, my attitude toward the instructor is:
    (1) becoming more positive
    (2) becoming more negative
    (3) unchanged

45. As a consequence of participating in this course, my attitude toward the subject matter is:
    (1) becoming more positive
    (2) becoming more negative
    (3) unchanged

46. I would prefer that this course:
    (1) become more structured or organized
    (2) become less structured or organized
    (3) maintain about the present level of structure

47. Which of the following descriptions of student learning styles most nearly approximates your own?
    (1) I like to think for myself, work alone, and focus on learning personally relevant content.
    (2) I prefer highly structured courses and will focus on learning what is required.

(continued)

Rating Scale 2-14 continued

(3) I try to get the "most out of classes," and like sharing my ideas with others and getting involved in class activities.

(4) I am competitive, concerned about getting good grades, and try to learn material so that I can perform better than others.

(5) I am generally turned off as a student, uninterested in class activities, and don't care to work with teachers or other students.

48. About how much time and effort have you put into this course compared to other courses of equal credit?
    (1) much more
    (2) somewhat more
    (3) about the same amount
    (4) somewhat less
    (5) much less

49. Generally, how valuable have you found the assigned readings in terms of their contribution to your learning in this course?
    (1) very valuable
    (2) fairly valuable
    (3) not very valuable
    (4) there have been no assigned readings

50. Overall, I would rate this course as:
    (1) excellent
    (2) good
    (3) mediocre
    (4) poor

Sample Rating Scales: Peer

Rating Scale 2-15. Colleague Description of Teachers

Instructor _____ Department _____ (1–3)

(4–6)

I. The following items reflect some of the ways teachers can be described. For the instructor named above, please circle the number which indicates the degree to which you feel each item is descriptive of him or her. In some cases, the statement may not apply to this individual. In these cases, check *Does not apply or don't know* for that item.

	Not at all descriptive	Very descriptive	Doesn't apply or don't know
SCALE 1–Research Activity and Recognition			
1. Does work that receives serious attention from others	1 2 3 4 5	( )	(7)
2. Corresponds with others about his research	1 2 3 4 5	( )	
3. Does original and creative work	1 2 3 4 5	( )	
4. Expresses interest in the research of his colleagues	1 2 3 4 5	( )	
5. Gives many papers at conferences	1 2 3 4 5	( )	
6. Keeps current with developments in his field	1 2 3 4 5	( )	
7. Has done work to which I refer in teaching	1 2 3 4 5	( )	
8. Has talked with me about his research	1 2 3 4 5	( )	

(continued)

Rating Scale 2-15 continued

	Not at all descriptive	Very descriptive	Doesn't apply or don't know	
SCALE 2—Intellectual Breadth				
9. Seems well read beyond the subject he teaches	1 2 3 4 5		( )	
10. Is sought by others for advice on research	1 2 3 4 5		( )	
11. Can suggest reading in any area of his general field	1 2 3 4 5		( )	
12. Knows about developments in fields other than his own	1 2 3 4 5		( )	
13. Is sought by colleagues for advice on academic matters	1 2 3 4 5		( )	
SCALE 3—Participation in the Academic Community				
14. Encourages students to talk with him on matters of concern	1 2 3 4 5		( )	
15. Is involved in campus activities that affect students	1 2 3 4 5		( )	
16. Attends many lectures and other events on campus	1 2 3 4 5		( )	(22)
17. Has a congenial relationship with colleagues	1 2 3 4 5		( )	(23)
SCALE 4—Relations with Students				
18. Meets with students informally out of class	1 2 3 4 5		( )	
19. Is conscientious about keeping appointments with students	1 2 3 4 5		( )	
20. Meets with students out of regular office hours	1 2 3 4 5		( )	
21. Encourages students to talk with him on matters of concern	1 2 3 4 5		( )	
22. Recognizes and greets students out of class	1 2 3 4 5		( )	
SCALE 5—Concern for Teaching				
23. Seeks advice from others about the courses he teaches	1 2 3 4 5		( )	
24. Discusses teaching in general with colleagues	1 2 3 4 5		( )	

(continued)

Rating Scale 2–15 continued

	Not at all descrip- tive	*Very descrip- tive*	*Doesn't apply or don't know*	
25. Is someone with whom I have discussed my teaching	1 2 3 4 5		( )	
26. Is interested in and informed about the work of colleagues	1 2 3 4 5		( )	
27. Expresses interest and concern about the quality of his teaching	1 2 3 4 5		( )	(33)

(Additional items may be presented by instructor and/or department)

28.	1 2 3 4 5		( )	(34)
29.	1 2 3 4 5		( )	
30.	1 2 3 4 5		( )	
31.	1 2 3 4 5		( )	
32.	1 2 3 4 5		( )	
33.	1 2 3 4 5		( )	
34.	1 2 3 4 5		( )	
35.	1 2 3 4 5		( )	
36.	1 2 3 4 5		( )	
37.	1 2 3 4 5		( )	
38.	1 2 3 4 5		( )	(44)

II. 1. How does this instructor compare with other teachers at *this school?*

Among the very worst			About average			Among the very best	
1	2	3	4	5	6	7	(45)

2. How does this instructor compare with other teachers in *this department?*

Among the very worst			About average			Among the very best	
1	2	3	4	5	6	7	(46)

You are invited to comment further on the effectiveness of this instructor especially in areas not covered by the questions.

Developed by Robert C. Wilson and Evelyn R. Dienst, Center for Research and Development in Higher Education, University of California, Berkeley. Form CMF. Used by permission. See Resources, p. 124, for further information and restrictions.

Rating Scale 2–16.   Greenfield Community College Faculty Committee

Peer Evaluation Form For The File Of _____

One part of the Faculty Professional Improvement Program at Greenfield Community College involves the professional judgment and insight of one's peers. You are among those who have been selected as one whose experience and close association with the individual named above may provide a useful source of first-hand information regarding professional performance.

Please answer the questions as candidly as possible, responding only to those areas wherein you feel especially knowledgeable. Your thoughtful assistance is appreciated.

1. From your particular point of view, and observation, what is/are this individual's greatest asset(s) as a community college instructor?

2. What areas of professional activity or responsibility, if any, do you see as needing attention, evaluation, improvement, change?

3. In your judgment, what are this individual's shortcomings?

(continued)

Rating Scale 2-6 continued

4. Additional insights or comments. (Use reverse side if necessary).

_____   _____
(Signature of Respondent)   Date

Developed by Greenfield Community College, Greenfield, MA 01301. Form 3. Used by permission. See Resources, p. 124, for further information and restrictions.

Rating Scale 2-17.   Greenfield Community College Faculty Committee

Class Observation Report For The File Of _____

Instructor _____   Observer _____

Subject _____   Topic of the Day _____   No. in class _____

Approach(es) Used: Lecture ___ Exposition___ Demonstration___ Discussion ___

Other_____

To the Observer: Please respond specifically to every part of the following
questions. Where the question is not appropriate to the
particular class, please so indicate.

1. Comment on the instructor's clarity in a) exposition b) questioning of students and c) responding to questions.

2. Did the students seem involved in the learning process? How was this involvement manifested?

3. What, if any, teaching devices were used? Could this particular class have been more effective if others were used?

(continued)

Rating Scale 2-17 continued

4. What impressed you most about this class?

5. Every instructor has a characteristic manner toward his students. Try to describe this attitude as you perceived it.

6. Offer comments or suggestions for improvement; please try to offer at least one specific suggestion.

Developed by Greenfield Community College, Greenfield, MA 01301. Form 2. Used by permission. See Resources, p. 124, for further information and restrictions.

Sample Rating Scales: Administrator

Rating Scale 2-18. Southern Methodist University

Name of Rater _____   Name of Person Rated _____   Date _____

Personal Qualities	Unsatisfactory Lower 10% (0 1 2)	Fair 20% (3)	Good 40% (4 5 6)	Superior 20% (7 8)	Outstanding Upper 10% (9 10)	Rating	Score Rating X Factor	Adjust Score by	Job Points = Score + Adjust
INITIATIVE 1 Extent to which he sees what needs to be done and gets it done.	Must be told; no personal initiative.	Needs close, frequent supervision.	Requires average supervision.	Independent; resourceful acts.	Highly resourceful and agressive.	7.66	7.66	±3 / 0	7.66
EFFORT FOR UNIT 1 Motivation to achieve unit goals, without regard to effectiveness	Exerts effort only when forced.	Could do much better than he does. Low effort.	Satisfactory; average motivation.	Hard worker; above average.	Intense motivation; maximum effort.	7.94	7.94	±3 / 0	7.94
RESPONSIBILITY 1 Dependability, reliability, trustworthiness, persistence.	Unreliable, or gives up easily, or evades normal authority lines.	"Gets by," avoids responsibility.	Trustworthy, reliable, average persistence.	Persists in spite of problems.	Completely reliable; always finishes job at any cost to himself.	8.09	8.09	±3 / 0	8.09
PERSONAL RELATIONS 1 Effectiveness in dealing with peers and others to achieve unit goals.	Inconsiderate; negative, hard to get along with.	Indifferent to needs of others; little effort to cooperate.	Maintains good relations; understands and is attuned to others.	Well-liked by others; encourages cooperation.	Very sensitive to human nature; skilled at securing cooperation.	7.38	7.38	±3 / 0	7.38

Category	1	2	3	4	5	
PROFESSIONAL ACTIVITIES 1 Activities in professional societies.	Inactive; does not participate locally or nationally.	Fairly active locally; attends meetings; not an officer.	Active locally; frequently a local officer; active attendee. Presents 1 paper/year nationally. 5.64	Occasionally holds national committee posts and presents at least 2 papers/year.	Very active nationally and locally with frequent offices, committees, papers.	±3
			5.64	5.64	5.64	0	5.64
UNIVERSITY SERVICE 1 Service on SMU or Institute Committees, in guidance, counseling, student societies, etc.	Avoids service on committees or guidance and counseling duties.	Seldom nominated for committee work or as a counselor, tends to grumble over "extra" duty.	Occasionally serves on committees, works effectively, but not enthusiastically, accepts assigned guidance/counsel. 7.09	Accepts duties in guidance and counseling or on committees in good spirit and works constructively.	Commonly nominated and serves with enthusiasm and effect.	±3
			7.09	7.09	7.09	0	7.09

Sub Total Personal Job Points = PJP = 43.80

Research Production

Category	1	2	3	4	5	
RESEARCH PRODUCTION 4 Effort and relative success in research proposals and funding.	Does not submit proposals; does not do research.	Submits few proposals; research on SMU funds.	Submits proposals, occasionally successful;	Submits many proposals, with frequent success; about	Prolific source of proposals; usually	±10

(continued)

Rating Scale 2-18 continued

Research Production	Unsatisfactory Lower 10% 0 1	Fair 20% 2 3	Good 40% 4 5	Superior 20% 6 7 8	Outstanding Upper 10% 9 10	Rating	Score Rating X Factor	Adjust Score by	Job Points = Score + Adjust
		Below $15K/year.	$25K/per yr. average. 4.51	$30K–40K per year.	successful, over $50K per year.	4.51	18.02	0	18.02
SCHOLARLY PRODUCTION 2 Refers to publication of books, in national "refereed" Journals, or serves as editor of such.	Does not publish at all, except for class notes.	Occasional paper, no books, no editorship.	Publishes regularly (1 paper + per year), perhaps 1 book. 5.47	Publishes steadily, one or two books, editor possibly.	20 or more publications, over 2 books nationally recognized.	5.47	10.94	±5	10.94
PH.D. PRODUCTIVITY 2 Actually produces or forecast because of enrollment in pipeline.	No Ph.D. students enrolled.	Occasional Ph.D. produced or in pipeline.	Produces about 0.5 Ph.D.'s per or pipeline forecast. 5.33	Attracts large numbers output over 0.5 per year.	Produces 1 or more Ph.D.'s per year.	5.33	10.66	±5	10.66

Sub-Total Research Job Points = RJP = 39.62

Rating Scale 2-18 continued

Teaching	Unsatisfactory Lower 10% 0 1 2	Fair 20% 3	Good 40% 4 5 6	Superior 20% 7 8	Outstanding Upper 10% 9 10	Rating	Score Rating X Factor	Adjust Score by	Job Points = Score + Adjust
STUDENT INSPIRATION 1 Motivation and inspiration of graduate students.	Negative reaction from students.	Deficient in motivating students.	Reasonably successful in motivating students.	Highly effective; good teacher. 7.34	Unusually effective; draws student acclaim.	7.34	7.34	±3 / 0	7.34
TEACHING EFFECTIVE- NESS 2 Results of the student evaluation or your impression.	Bad teacher, inconsiderate, ill-prepared, indifferent, unfair.	Poor teacher, limited grasp, appears indifferent, often not prepared.	So-so teacher, pedestrian, adequate, but not inspiring.	Good teacher, considerate, fair, well prepared, interesting. 7.58	Outstanding teacher, enthusiastic, communicates well, popular.	7.58	15.17	±5 / 0	15.17
TEACHING PRODUCTION 2 Total number SCH produced per academic year.	Below 100 SCH/year.	Approximately 200 SCH/year.	Approximately 300 SCH/year. 5.28	Approximately 350 SCH/year.	Over 400 SCH/year.	5.28	10.55	±5 / 0	10.55

(continued)

Rating Scale 2-18 continued

Teaching	Unsatisfactory Lower 10% 0 1 2	Fair 20% 3	Good 40% 4 5 6	Superior 20% 7 8	Outstanding Upper 10% 9 10	Rating	Score Rating X Factor	Adjust Score by	Job Points = Score + Adjust
EDUCATIONAL INNOVATION 2 Extent to which creativity and imagination, new approaches are utilized.	Teaches same course from same book every year.	Occasionally updates course and/or presentation technique when pushed.	Changes book and technique fairly often; every year; keeps course updated.	Willing to innovate, make course improvements but judiciously. 6.78	Makes every effort to bring in new material, new teaching technology, new approaches.	6.78	13.55	±5	13.55
								0	
ADEQUACY OF PH.D. STUDENT SUPERVISION 4	Students receive little or no direction, contact with advisor random/ineffective.	Minimally adequate faculty direction and supervision.	Students are adequately prepared for dissertation defense, well counseled.	Students well prepared and progress rapidly to degree objectives. 6.20	Vitally concerned with students on a continuing, informed basis.	6.20	12.40	±5	12.40
								0	

Sub-Total Teaching Job Points = TJP = 59.01

Developed by Southern Methodist University, Institute of Technology, Dallas, Texas 75275. Used by permission. See Resources, p. 124, for further information and restrictions.

Rating Scale 2-19. Greenfield Community College Faculty Committee

Departmental Evaluation Form for the File of _____

Since information from administration offers important insights into improvement of particular areas of professional performance, would you please rate the above named instructor according to the criteria listed below. Please omit those areas where you feel you have no basis for judgement. Place your responses in the space to the left of each numbered item, using the following rating scale:

4 = excellent   3 = good   2 = average   1 = fair   0 = unsatisfactory

_____ 1. Academic competence.
_____ 2. Ability to get along with others.
_____ 3. Participation in division or curriculum activities.
_____ 4. Participation in committee assignments.
_____ 5. Reliability in carrying out professional responsibilities.
_____ 6. Reliability in getting routine work (grades, book orders, etc.) in on time.
_____ 7. Meeting classes regularly and on time.
_____ 8. Concern for professional growth and improvement.
_____ 9. Accessibility to students.
_____ 10. Overall effectiveness as member of the faculty.

Additional remarks:
(Statements are often more helpful than any check list. Include here any information you think is pertinent or useful. This can be a summary or elaboration of any of the various categories above or a statement of additional information.)

Administrator _____

Title _____

Date _____

Developed at Greenfield Community College, Greenfield, MA 01301. Form 5. Used by permission. See Resources, p. 124, for further information and restrictions.

Sample Rating Scales: Self

Rating Scale 2-20.   Greenfield Community College Faculty Committee

Self Evaluation Form for the File of _____

Dear Colleague:

One means of up-grading professional effectiveness is self-evaluation. To facilitate the process we have devised the attached questionnaire, which we are asking you to fill out. Completing the questionnaire will be useful in two ways: First and foremost, it will get you to think about your own strengths and shortcomings. (You probably evaluate your own teaching continually, but the questionnaire should help you to do it in a more formal, perhaps more precise, way.) Second, it should add a dimension to the committee's understanding and appreciation of you as a teacher.

We would ask that you try to avoid two common pitfalls in your self-appraisal: First, do not let modesty keep you from being very explicit about your assets. Second, try to be equally candid about your shortcomings. As teachers and as students of particular disciplines we are well aware that individuals are less knowledgeable in some areas of a discipline than in others, just as they have both good days and bad days in the classroom. We also appreciate only too well that every teacher has certain methods and approaches with which he is very comfortable and adept, as well as those with which he is less proficient.

One final comment on the questionnaire: You will notice that it is divided into two parts. The first part, consisting of two sections, deals with those areas having a direct bearing on the committee's work. The first section, that which deals with subject area and classroom approach, is obviously the most important. The second section, dealing with your overall G.C.C. activities and experiences, asks for additional information which we feel can be of real help to us. The second part of the questionnaire is entitled *Supplementary Information*, and this title was deliberately chosen. We are asking that you complete this part of the questionnaire only if you feel the information will contribute to our picture of you as a teacher and member of the G.C.C. community.

Sincerely,

The Faculty Committee

Rating Scale 2–20 continued

FACULTY QUESTIONNAIRE

Section I—Subject Area and Classroom Approach

1. Within your own discipline, which area or areas do you regard as your strongest?

2. Which area do you regard as your weakest?

(continued)

Rating Scale 2–20 continued

3. What is your greatest asset as a classroom teacher?

4. What is your greatest shortcoming as a classroom teacher?

5. Do you feel that your discipline is best taught by a particular approach (method) and, if so, which approach and why do you feel it is the best?

6. As a teacher in a Community College, what is your goal with respect to your students?

(continued)

Rating Scale 2-20 continued

7. Describe what you have found most gratifying in your work at G.C.C.

8. Describe what you have found most disappointing or frustrating in your work at G.C.C.

Section II—G.C.C. Experience

1. List under *A* the courses you are presently teaching and under *B* any other courses you have taught in the past at G.C.C.

   A.

   B.

2. List the Committees on which you haver served or are now serving.

3. List any other activities you have engaged in at the College.

4. For how many years, including the 1970–71 school year, have you been teaching full-time at G.C.C.?

(continued)

Rating Scale 2–20 continued

SUPPLEMENTARY INFORMATION

If you think it appropriate, kindly give us a brief biographical sketch of yourself. Include any and all information which you think might help us to help you, items such as educational and professional background, honors received, articles published, community activities, general interests, etc. You may use the back of this sheet or make attachments.

Greenfield Community College, Greenfield, MA 01301. Form 4. Used by permission. See Resources, p. 124, for further information and restrictions.

(continued)

Sample Rating Scales: Resource

Rating Scale 2-20 continued

1. DESCRIPTIONS OF SELECTED BOOKS, ARTICLES, DOCUMENTS, AND TAPES

Topic	Format	Author, Title	Description	Available
General	Book	Eble, K.E., *Professors as Teachers*, 1973	A report of the Project to Improve College Teaching; Eble spent 2 years visiting 70 schools throughout the country. Comments include teaching from every aspect: in and out of the classroom, effective measures, training, evaluation and general current trends and practices.	Jossey-Bass Publishers 615 Montgomery Street San Francisco, CA 94111 Price: $8.95
General	Book	Miller, R.I., *Evaluating Faculty Performance*, 1972.	Presents a guide to evaluation of faculty in a variety of approaches, with advantages and disadvantages.	Jossey-Bass Publishers 615 Montgomery Street San Francisco, CA 94111 Price: $8.95
General	Book	Miller, R.I., *Developing Programs for Faculty Evaluation*, 1974	Designed to supplement preceding edition, further detail on programs, with sample forms for administrator, peers, etc., and evaluation of administrators included. Major portion of book is annotated bibliography on whole subject.	Jossey-Bass Publishers 615 Montgomery Street San Francisco, CA 94111 Price: $9.95
Teaching	Booklet	Astin, A.W. et al., *Faculty Development in a Time of Retrenchment*, 1974	In context of current declining resources, ways to encourage emphasis on teaching by training, rewards, grants, and evaluation. 96 pp.	Change Magazine NBW Tower New Rochelle, N.Y. 10801 Price: $2.95
Student Ratings as Feedback	Booklet	Centra, John A., *Two Studies on the Utility of Student Ratings for Improving Teaching*, SIR Report No. 2, 1972.	Two studies: 1. The effectiveness of student feedback in modifying college instruction. 2. Self-ratings of college teachers: a comparison with student ratings. Summarized in article in	Educational Testing Service Institutional Research Program for Higher Education Princeton, N.J. 08540

Topic	Type	Citation	Description	Source / Price
Teaching Evaluation	Booklet	Hildebrand, M., Wilson, R.C., Dienst, E.R., *Evaluating University Teaching*, 1971.	This study developed descriptive characteristics of effective teaching performance to provide a satisfactory basis for the evaluation of teaching. 52 pp.	Publications Department Center for Research and Development in Higher Education University of California 2150 Shattuck Street Berkeley, CA 94704 Price: $2.00
Teaching and Evaluation	Booklet	Eble, K.E., *The Recognition and Evaluation of Teaching* Project to Improve College Teaching, 1970.	A report of the Project to Improve College Teaching (PICT); clear description, example forms and programs, good bibliography. 112 pp.	Publications Office AAUP Bulletin One DuPont Circle, N.W. Suite 500 Washington, D.C. 20636 Price: $1.00
Characteristics of Programs and Instruments	Softcover Manual	Hodgkinson, H., Hurst, J., Levine, H., and Brint, S., *A Manual for the Evaluation of Innovative Programs and Practices in Higher Education*, Center for Research and Development in Higher Education, University of California, Berkeley, 1974.	Lists 60 innovations in higher education, institutions that are engaged in innovative practices, and characteristics of evaluative instruments for measuring effectiveness. 201 pp.	Publications Department Center for Research and Development in Higher Education University of California 2150 Shattuck Street Berkeley, CA 94704 Price: $5.00
Research Reviews on Student Ratings	Article	Costin, F., Greenough, W.T., and Menges, R.J., "Student Ratings of College Teaching: Reliability, Validity, and *Change Magazine* 5 (April 1973).	Careful examination of literature on student ratings and how they can be used. Sets limitations and situational controls and procedures.	Frank Costin, Dept. of Psychology University of Illinois Champaign, Illinois 61820 Price: $2.00 Also available, SIR Report No 1, *The Student Instructional Report: Its Development and Uses.* Price: $2.00

(continued)

Rating Scale 2–20 continued

Topic	Format	Author, Title	Description	Available
Research Reviews on Student Ratings	Article	Usefulness, *Review of Educational Research*" 41 (1971): 511–535.	Extensive references.	or other authors, same address Reprint, no charge.
Review of Research on Evaluation of Teaching	Book	Kulik, J.A., and McKeachie, W.J., "The Evaluation of Teachers in Higher Education," in F.N. Kerlinger, ed., *Review of Research in Education,* Vol. 3.	Clear list of factors affecting evaluation fo students, peers, and administrators; general review of research, with references.	J.A. Kulik Center for Research on Learning and Teaching University of Michigan 109 East Madison Ann Arbor, Michigan 48104 Reprint: No charge.
Review	Article	Frey, P.W., "The Ongoing Debate: Student Evaluation of Teaching," 1974.	Background and review of Northwestern's studies for their "Endeavor" instrument.	Center for the Teaching Professions Northwestern University Evanston, Illinois 60201 No charge.
Annotated Bibliography	Report	deWolf, Virginia A., *Student Ratings of Instruction in Post-Secondary Institutions: A Comprehensive Annotated Bibliography of Research Reported since 1968.* Vol. I, June 1974	Comprehensive annotated bibliography, 1968–1974.	Educational Assessment Center University of Washington 1400 Parkway PB-30 Seattle, Washington 98195 No charge.
Evaluation of Teaching	Article	Scriven, M., "The Evaluation of Teachers and Teaching," *California Journal of Educational Research* 25 (1974): 109–115.	Position paper on practices currently and the description of an alternative method and procedures.	California Journal of Educational Research Department of Psychology San Jose State University

Statements on Topics as Noted	Documents	AAUP: −*Academic Freedom and Tenure,* 1940. −*Statement on Teaching Evaluation,* 1974. −*Statement on Procedural Standards in Faculty Dismissal Proceedings,* 1968. −*1972 Recommended Institutional Regulations on Academic Freedom and Tenure.* −*Statement on Procedural Standards in the Renewal or Non-Renewal of Faculty Appointments,* 1971. −*Termination of Faculty Appointments Because of Financial Exigency, Discontinuance of a Program or Department, or Medical Reasons,* 1974. −*Statement on Faculty Workload,* 1970. −*On the Imposition of Tenure Quotas,* 1973.	Comprehensive statements covering many of the dimensions of faculty policy that provide guidelines for academic standards. Statements provide framework within which evaluation programs should fall.	San Jose, California 95192 $2.25 single issue. AAUP One DuPont Circle Suite 500 Washington, D.C. 20036 No Charge for documents.
Tenure Decisions, Grievance Procedures	Softcover Book	Peairs, Richard H., ed., *Avoiding Conflict in Faculty Personnel Practices,* #7 in New Directions Series, 1974.	Five papers on related topics describing procedures to avoid conflict and review faculty.	Jossey-Bass Publishers 615 Montgomery Street San Francisco, CA 94111 Price: $2.00.

(continued)

Rating Scale 2-20 continued

Topic	Format	Author, Title	Description	Available
Evaluation Procedures	Softcover Book	Pace, C.R., ed., Evaluating Learning and Teaching. New Directions in Higher Education, 1973.		Jossey-Bass Publishers 615 Montgomery Street San Francisco, CA 94111 Price: $2.00.
Survey of Practices, 1966	Article	Astin, A., and Lee, C.B.T., "Current Practices in the Evaluation and Training of College Teachers," *Improving College Teaching*, American Council on Education, 1967.	Extensive review of evaluation practices, sources and subjects in 1966.	American Council on Education One DuPont Circle Washington, D.C. 20036 Charges. $2.00 (single issue).
Survey of Practices, 1974, Compared to 1966 Study	Article	Seldin, Peter, "A Study to Determine the Current Policies and Practices Used in Liberal Arts Colleges to Evaluate Classroom Teaching Performance of Members of the Faculty," 1974, Fordham University; part published: "How Deans Evaluate Teachers, *Change* 6 (1974): 48–49.	Extensive review designed to parallel 1966 study and compare 1974 practices. Shows some dramatic changes. See under Survey on Evaluation Practices, below.	Entire study available (parts have been published) Dr. Peter Seldin Fordham University Office of the Asst. Dean College of Business Adm. Bronx, N.Y. 10458 Charge for Xeroxing: $15.
Critical Incident Technique	Artilce	Ronan, W.W., *Evaluating College Classroom Teaching Effectiveness*, PREP Report No. 34, HEW Publication No. (06)72–9, 1972.	Describes background and present study to cull incidents and CIT (Critical Incident Technique).	Superintendent of Documents U.S. Govt. Printing Office Catalogue HE 5.212:12089, 1972. Washington D.C. 20402 Price: 45¢ ERIC No. ED056 647

Information	Telephone Number	NEXUS, a project of The American Association of Higher Education, One DuPont Circle Washington, D.C. 20036	Telephone service: Staff answers questions about where to find resources. Expects explicit inquiries which cannot be easily found elsewhere.	To use the service call (202) 785-8480 between 1:00 p.m. and 6:00 p.m. Eastern time. Cost: The cost of the phone call only.
Faculty Evaluation	Audio and Video Tapes (7)	Audio 101, Video 201—*Faculty Evaluation and Development: An Overview*, Paul L. Dressel, Michigan State University.	Dressel discusses faculty roles and functions, the professor as a professional, and findings, assumptions, and questions concerning the evaluation of teaching.	To order: Bert R. Biles Division of Continuing Education 301 Umberger Hall Kansas State University Manhattan, Kansas 66506
		Audio 102, Video 202—*Facilitating Faculty Development*, John F. Noonan, Virginia Commonwealth University.	Noonan looks at faculty development from the perspectives of personal development, professional development, and organization development.	Audio Cassettes (price is for purchase. AAHE members eligible for 10% discount).
		Audio 103, Video 203, *Faculty Evaluation and Development: Comparative Viewpoints*, Paul L. Dressel, Michigan State University, Wilbert J. McKeachie, University of Michigan, et al.	Four distinguished educators discuss a wide range of faculty evaluation and development issues raised by the panel moderator, Sagen.	1-3 cassettes—$7.50 ea. 4 or more—$6.75 ea. Complete set of 7—$45. Video Cassettes (price is for five-day lease. AAHE members will receive scheduling priority).
		Audio 104, Video 204, *Measuring Teaching Effectiveness*, Wilbert J. McKeachie, University of Michigan.	McKeachie presents a rationale for the evaluation of faculty performance, how to set about measuring teaching effectiveness, and how and when to use evaluative data.	1-3 cassettes—$45 ea. 4 or more—$35 ea. Complete set of 7—$195.
		Audio 105, Video 205, *Evaluating Non-Teaching Faculty Performance*, Richard I. Miller, Illinois Board of Higher Education.	Miller considers five aspects of nonteaching faculty performance—advising, faculty service and relations, public service, professional status and activities, and administration.	

(continued)

Rating Scale 2–20 continued

Topic	Format	Author, Title	Description	Available
		Audio 106, Video 206, *The KSU Instructional Effectiveness Assessment Program: A Case Study*, Richard E. Owens, Joe Knopp, Donald P. Hoyt, Donald McGavin, Bert R. Biles (moderator); all from Kansas State University.	A panel of representatives presents an informative case study of the Kansas State University Instructional Effectiveness Assessment Program.	
		Audio 107, Video 207, *Implementing Faculty Evaluation and Development Programs*, Donald P. Hoyt, Kansas State University.	Hoyt describes the pressures for and the resistances to evaluation, and then explores how these forces may affect the implementation of specific evaluation efforts.	
Collective Bargaining	Book	Duryea, E.D., Fisk, R.S., and Associates, *Faculty Unions and Collective Bargaining*, 1973.	History and current state of collective bargaining and unions and their influence on higher education.	Jossey-Bass Publishers 615 Montgomery Street San Francisco, CA 94111 Price: $8.95.
List of Development Centers	Paper	Gaff, Jerry G., "A List of Instructional Improvement Centers and Programs," May 20, 1974 version and later list.	Simple listing in preparation for Jossey-Bass book in the fall, *Toward Faculty Renewal*.	Jerry G. Gaff Project on Teaching Improvement Centers 425 Spruce Street Berkeley, CA 94708 No charge.
Student Rating Scale Construction	Article	Menges, Robert J., "The New Reporters, Students Rate Instruction"—Reprinted from C.R. Pace, ed., *Evaluating Learning and Teaching, New Directions in Higher Education*, 1973. 16 pp.	Details of format and construction of rating scales for student use. Describes four approaches to item selection using examples of specific instruments (all of which are included in this book). Clear and understandable exploration.	Center for the Teaching Professions Northwestern University Evanston, Illinois 60201 Reprint. No charge.

Development Centers	Paper	Boyer, R.K., "Instructional Development Agencies: What are They? Models and Strategies," 1974.	Paper presented at a conference describing organization and function of a center with recommendations and examples.	Institute for Research and Training in Higher Education University of Cincinnati Cincinnati, Ohio No charge.
Student Evaluation	Paper	Pambookian, Hagop, "Discrepancy Between Instructor and Student Evaluation of Instruction: Effect on Instructor," 1973.	Paper from convention of American Psychological Association, 1973. Describes a study on feedback impact.	Hagop S. Pambookian Department of Educational Psychology Marquette University Milwaukee, Wisconsin 53233 No charge.
Survey on Evaluation Practices	Booklet	Seldin, Peter, "How Colleges Evaluate Professors," 1975.	Current policies and practices in evaluating classroom teaching performance in Liberal Arts colleges, based on a study.	Peter Seldin, Asst. Dean College of Business Adm. Fordham University Bronx, N.Y. 10450 Price: $3.50

2. CENTERS FOR DEVELOPMENT OR INSTRUCTIONAL IMPROVEMENT

Throughout the country, there are more and more centers that serve the faculty (and sometimes other personnel) in higher education. Most are established within institutions and are designed to serve primarily its own personnel. Others have independent status, though they may be associated with a particular institution. Most of these centers have attempted to collect articles, booklets, films, or other media on a variety of related topics. Many incorporate evaluation procedures, rating scale information, or even act as coordinators for a variety of such activities, including training workshops, meetings or conferences in this area. Some, such as the Center for Research and Development in Higher Education at the University of California at Berkeley, or the Center for the Teaching Professions at Northwestern University, Evanston, Illinois, publish lists of materials available and their prices, if any. They and others produce as well as collect materials, and offer a variety of aides to those requesting general or

(continued)

Rating Scale 2-20 continued

specific information regarding evaluation or development. The Institute for Research and Training in Higher Education, (IRTHE), University of Cincinnati, Cincinnati, Ohio, is unusual because it also focuses on administrator and organizational improvement. A reference to that center, as well as several others, are included in this resource list.

Many centers have been responsive and furnished materials and references contributing greatly to this project. Two centers at the University of Massachusetts were particularly helpful and were visited several times. They are the Center for Instructional Resources and Improvement (CIRI) under the direction of Sheryl Riechmann at 125A Graduate Research Center, Amherst; and the Clinic to Improve University Teaching, School of Education, directed by Michael Melnik. The former serves the university with consultative services and addresses both evaluation and improvement needs, while the clinic (described in Chapter 2) runs a diagnostic and training service for faculty both within and outside the University.

Two items in this Resource section refer to development centers. One by Jerry Gaff, which lists a large number of centers, and the other by Ronald Boyer, which describes and defines such centers. When developing programs for evaluation, many of these centers can serve as valuable resources.

The Center for Faculty Evaluation and Development in Higher Education at Kansas State University offers a faculty evaluation system that leads to improvement. Colleges and universities can participate in this program on a fee-for-services basis. Those seeking more information should write to the Center, 1627 Anderson Avenue, Box 3000, Manhattan, Kansas 66502.

3. RATING SCALES (RS)

Title		Source (for further information contact)
RS2-1:	Student Description of Teachers: Short Form	Robert C. Wilson
RS2-2:	Student Description of Teachers: Long Form	Evelyn R. Dienst
RS2-15:	Colleague Description of Teachers	Teaching Innovation and Evaluation Services
		University of California
		Berkeley, California 94720

(continued)

RS2-3:   Student Perception of Learning and Teaching

W.J. McKeachie
The Center for Research on Learning
   and Teaching
109 E. Madison
Ann Arbor, Michigan 48104

RS2-4:   Course Evaluation
RS2-5:   Course Evaluation, Written Form

Bruce Finnie, Registrar
Princeton University
3 West College
P.O. Box 70
Princeton, New Jersey 08540

RS2-6:   The Purdue Cafeteria System

S.M. Marks, Head, Copyright Section
Purdue Research Foundation
West Lafayette, Indiana 47907

The Cafeteria System consists of four parts:

1. Complete Systems Manual
2. Four computer programs on punched source decks
3. Two hundred item catalogue
4. Paper forms—Item selection and student response forms

The system has licensing options, where an institution, according to size, may purchase a license for a period of time from 1–15 years, with many plans available for forms, usage, services, etc. For example, if the institution has its own computer facilities, a fee could be initially $200 plus forms for 4¢ each, or as little as 1¢ for the institution developing its own form from Purdue's items. For longer time commitments, costs decrease. Licensees can provide services to other institutions with an agreement from the Purdue Research Foundation.

RS2-7:   Student Instructional Report, Instructors Cover Sheet
RS2-8:   Student Instructional Report

Student Instructional Report
Educational Testing Service
Princeton, New Jersey 08540

Rating Scale 2-20 continued

Title	Source
RS2-9: Student Reaction to Instruction and Courses (IDEA)	
RS2-10: Faculty Information Form (IDEA)	Bert Biles, Director Center for Faculty Evaluation and Development in Higher Education 1627 Anderson Avenue Box 3000 Manhattan, Kansas 66502
RS2-11: Endeavor Instructional Rating Form	Peter W. Frey 206 Cresap Laboratory Northwestern University Evanston, Illinois 60201
RS2-12: Instructional Assessment System, Forms A-E	Gerald M. Gillmore Educational Assessment Center University of Washington Seattle, Washington 98195
RS2-13: Critical Incident Technique, Instructor Evaluation	Professor Ronan School of Psychology Georgia Institute of Technology Atlanta, Georgia 30302
RS2-14: Teaching Analysis by Students (TABS)	Michael A. Melnik, Director Clinic to Improve University Teaching 329 Hills House North University of Massachusetts Amherst, Mass. 01002
RS2-15: (See RS2-1)	
RS2-16: Peer Evaluation Form	Professor Carleton P. Stinchfield Greenfield Community College 125 Federal Street Greenfield, Mass. 01301
RS2-17: Class Observation Report	
RS2-19: Departmental Evaluation Form	
RS2-20: Self Evaluation Form	
RS2-18: SMU Rating Scale	Peter Van't Slot Institute of Technology Southern Methodist University Dallas, Texas 75275

Chapter Three

Administrator Evaluation

CHAPTER USES AND AUDIENCES

This chapter summarizes existing practice and research on administrator evaluation. It is primarily intended to aid college and university administrators, board members, faculty, and students, who are interested in developing a formal program of administrator evaluation.

Our approach to administrator evaluation is comprehensive and untested. Those who are interested in applying it should understand the experimental nature of their undertaking. Developing an administrator evaluation program of the sort we describe, tailored to a specific institution, will demand a major investment of time and energy.

Where it is possible this chapter parallels Chapter 2 on faculty evaluation. Because of the overlap regarding certain aspects of faculty and administrator evaluation, such as rating scale characteristics, program acceptance, issues of disclosure, and legal factors, we will make cross-references to the faculty evaluation chapter rather than repeating what is there.

PURPOSES OF ADMINISTRATOR EVALUATION

Institutions of higher education vary dramatically in purpose, history, size, resources, student characteristics, and a host of other ways. The purposes for which they evaluate will also vary. Given the time-consuming and complex nature of administrator evaluation, the single most important step for any institution is to *make sure that there are compelling reasons for starting a formal program of administrator evaluation.* We cannot underscore this point enough. In the natural rush to action, inadequate attention to planning the purposes of an evaluation can create misunderstandings and frustration. An already threatening venture will be put on the defensive from the very beginning. If each constituency is to benefit, they must all be represented in the planning of an administrator evaluation program.

Administrator evaluation can be used for the following purposes:

1. Establishing and attaining institutional goals.
2. Helping individual administrators to improve their performance.
3. Making decisions on retention, salary, or promotion.
4. Increasing the effectiveness and efficiency of the administration as a team.
5. Keeping an inventory of personnel resources for reassignment or retraining.
6. Informing the governing body and administration of the degree of congruence between institutional policy and institutional action.
7. Sharing governance.
8. Informing internal and external audiences on administrative effectiveness and worth.
9. Conducting research on factors related to administrator effectiveness.

Establishing and Attaining Institutional Goals

Because the establishment and attainment of institutional goals is a primary function of administrators, we feature this purpose of administrator evaluation in this chapter.

Administrator evaluation should be a tool for institutional improvement, rather than a set of procedures that only describe static conditions at the end of a period of time. Administrator evaluation should be *goal-referenced,* illuminating the formation of institutional aims and charting progress toward them. To accomplish this purpose we use the logic of an approach called "management by objectives" (Likert, 1961; Odiorne, 1969; Brenneman and Black, 1973). But we broaden this approach to accommodate the organizational complexity of colleges and universities, and we base goal formation on an empirical assessment of the current state of the institution.

Helping Individual Administrators to Improve Their Performance

Individual administrators should be provided periodically with information regarding their performance in their areas of responsibility such as academic leadership, institutional communications, student registration, fund-raising, or building maintenance. But merely providing such information to administrators will rarely be sufficient to bring about improved performance. Some form of accountability and support among administrative peers or supervisors is required. The typical practice is for the administrator to review his or her evaluation with an immediate supervisor, and to plan on ways to make needed improvements. Some institutions will invest in on-site training, or send their administrators to workshops on specific subjects outside the institution. In other institutions a center for faculty development might include assistance for administrators (see Chapter 2).

Making Decisions on Retention, Salary, or Promotion

Retrenchment, faculty unionization, demands for accountability, and questions of institutional purpose, which are pressing for faculty evaluation, are contributing to increased interest in the evaluation of administrators. More and more, decisions regarding the retention, salary, or promotion of administrators will require performance evaluation information. If improved performance *and* personnel decisions are to be accepted as parallel and equally important purposes of an administration evaluation program, care must be exercised to keep separate the procedures for this purpose.

Increasing the Effectiveness and Efficiency of the Administration as a Team

Administrative team-building has been receiving increased attention over the past decade. Administrative teams have usually concentrated on collaborative assessment and planning improvements of particular aspects of the institution, such as communications, budget and financing, and program coordination. The efforts of individual administrators are frequently hidden in such team efforts.

The team spirit of mutual accountability, important though it is, may also mask individual strengths and weaknesses. It would do little good for a college or university to work globally toward improving "poor institutional communications" if the problems can be located in a specific subunit, or with a few administrators. Institutionwide measures can be used in the identification of goals for administrative teams. But these should be complemented by the goals of individual administrators, resulting in both shared and individual accountability.

Keeping an Inventory of Personnel Resources for Reassignment or Retraining

The increasing diversity and complexity of tasks facing college and university administrators requires that institutions find ways to increase the role flexibility of administrators. One means to this end is to include an experience/resource inventory in the evaluation dossier of each administrator. For example, an admissions officer may have had prior experience in institutional problem-solving outside the usual jurisdiction of his office. A dean of faculty, a building and grounds officer, and a vice president may share complementary capacities, in, say, institution/community relations. Without formal inventory procedures, such individual capacities and interests may be overlooked, and the institution might neglect the full utilization of its administrative resources. The administration should be built around the capacities of individual administrators, rather than trying to fit them into a rigid organizational mold.

Informing the Governing Body and Administration of the Degree of Congruence between Institutional Policy and Institutional Action

One of the functions of administration, especially of the president as chief executive officer, is to insure that policies established by the governing body are carried out. If policy statements are vague and general, they are open to a variety of interpretations. For example, the student aid officer may be allocated a certain amount of funds for "scholarship aid to recruit minority group students." His or her interpretation of the number and nature of students desired—ethnic and racial characteristics, educational preparation, geographical distribution—may be highly congruent, or widely divergent, from what the intent of the governing body was when it established its policy.

It is not always possible, or desirable, for the governing body to provide highly specific policy statements. But, in fact, the members of the governing body do have expectations about how policy should be carried out, and may well become frustrated when they learn of practices widely divergent from those expectations. And administrators, especially those several layers removed from the governing body, share in the frustration by not knowing those expectations. By participating in the evaluation of administrators, either as a whole group or by representation on review committees, members of the governing body will become more informed of administrative action, and discussion of expectations can become more routine.

The administrator evaluation program can therefore also be used to increase the congruence between governing board policy and administrative action. The increase in information and dialogue between administration and governing body should also influence the formation of new or revised policy based on a better understanding of the operating realities of the institution.

Sharing Governance

The inclusion of students and faculty in the governance of colleges and universities has been on the increase. One means of sharing governance is to include these various constituencies in periodic evaluation—evaluation of each other and of the total institutional enterprise. In general, such involvement will inevitably have *some* influence on institutional decisions.

Informing Internal and External Audiences on Administrative Effectiveness and Worth

Various external audiences—consumers, legislators, advocacy groups, government officials, parents, taxpayers—are increasingly questioning the need for administrative positions in colleges and universities. And faculty and students are demanding that administrative positions be justified.

Those external and internal audiences will only be satisfied by convincing data—not rhetorical appeals. Given the web of intervening variables, it will be very difficult to demonstrate a cause-and-effect relationship between administrative acts and student learning, but other performance results are demonstrable.

Conducting Research on Factors Related to Administrator Effectiveness

A cluster of institutions such as a state college system may undertake empirical research on factors related to administrator effectiveness in order to improve their own operations, and to contribute to the body of knowledge in this field. Or a single institution may pursue explorations into effective administration for similar reasons.

Administrator evaluation can also be started as a small research venture, out of which can grow a full, operational program. Those institutions for which administrator evaluation is particularly threatening may choose to pursue this course as a beginning strategy; it should be less threatening than a more comprehensive approach.

CURRENT PRACTICES

Research and practice in administrator evaluation is at a stage of infancy compared to the maturing adolescence of faculty evaluation. But the infant clamors for attention. In our survey of current practices we found few comprehensive programs, but there was considerable interest in administrator evaluation. Many faculty want their administrators to be evaluated, at least out of fairness to themselves. Many administrators are willing to be evaluated, but have not found current practices acceptable. Many administrative actions and the contexts of those actions are not visible to faculty, and administrators are justifiably concerned about being evaluated by those not completely familiar with their work.

As with faculty evaluation, the overall aim of administrator evaluation is the continual maintenance and improvement of the quality of teaching, learning, research, and service. Unlike faculty, most administrators (except those in student services) have little direct contact with students in the teaching/learning function, and administrative actions are typically defined by their effects on other aspects of the institution. The link between effective administration and student learning is intuitive, and without empirical verification.

Without adequate empirical links between administrative action and the quality of teaching, research, and service, administrator evaluation must concentrate on more immediate outcomes: leading, decision-making, budgeting, problem-solving, and internal coordinating. According to our survey, most administrator evaluation programs consist of a periodic use of a rating scale that lists functions like these, given to faculty, administrators, and sometimes students. Examples of these rating scales are on pages 153–166.

Rating scales of administrative processes such as leadership and decision-making are, by their nature, static. They do not tend to promote development or improvement. In addition, it is not known whether these instruments are *valid*, whether they actually indicate whether individual administrators have performed effectively. At best, scales such as these yield an approximate sense of the level of satisfaction of faculty, administrators, or students with the total administration.

We also found increasing use of management by objectives (MBO) (Likert, 1961; Odiorne, 1969; Brenneman and Black, 1973). In this approach an administrator, in conjunction with his or her supervisor, chooses several objectives to work toward over a specified time. The administrator is evaluated on the degree of attainment of those objectives.

MBO was developed and is most widely used outside of education—in business, in government, and in the military. In our view, MBO works best in those organizations whose goals and authority structures are relatively simple and clear. Colleges and universities that are experimenting with MBO on a large scale have frequently found it reductionistic and limited primarily to areas of bureaucratic authority. In addition, the selection of objectives within MBO is typically based on the perceptions of institutional need held by the staff member and supervisor involved, rather than on extensive empirical information. Thus it is easy to select goals that are safe (i.e., involve minimum risk), or are insufficiently related to priority institutional needs. But, unlike evaluation procedures which depend primarily on static ratings of administrative processes, MBO is developmental. It provides a forum for the discussion of specific objectives, a *sine qua non* for improvement.

ADMINISTRATOR AND INSTITUTIONAL EFFECTIVENESS

A program of administrator evaluation must be set within a unifying framework. Such a framework must relate administrators' actions to the effectiveness of the college or university as a total organization, and must allow for considerable variation in the characteristics of colleges and universities which are effective.

Four of the most commonly used criteria of organizational effectiveness are brought together as composite criteria by Helsabeck (1973). These are goal formation, goal attainment, resource acquisition, and membership satisfaction. The capacity of an organization to establish and accomplish organizational purposes that are acceptable to a majority of its members is one indication of its effectiveness. For an organization to attain its goals it must also be capable of acquiring necessary resources. An effective organization, as distinct from "fortunate" organization, is also one that acquires needed resources in a scarce environment. And an effective organization will achieve membership satisfaction: students, faculty, administrators, governing body, and alumni will be able to realize their individual goals within the collective enterprise. These criteria all appear to have a reciprocal effect on each other (Helsabeck, 1973). These four criteria of organizational effectiveness provide a framework for evaluating the *effectiveness* of administrators' actions.

In addition, the *appropriateness* of administrators' actions should be evaluated. Our approach, unlike most MBO programs, sets effective behavior within three overlapping institutional contexts: institutional climate, institutional authority patterns, and institutional stages of development.

Institutional climate refers to how students, faculty, and administrators perceive their college or university—the quality of instruction, program offerings, group attitudes, governance, and other important aspects of campus life. Administrators act appropriately when they keep abreast of these perceptions, and take them into account in forming their goals.

An effective college or university administrator also acts in ways that are appropriate to the authority pattern of the institution. Colleges and universities are hybrid combinations of three types of organizational authority patterns. They are part bureaucratic, characterized by a vertical authority hierarchy (Weber, 1947; and Stroup, 1966); they are part collegial, where authority is shared among individuals irrespective of position (Anderson, 1963; and Millett, 1962); and they are part political, where various forms of authority are exercised by various interest groups (Baldridge, 1971; and Tennebaum, 1968). Given the unique circumstances, history, and traditions of particular institutions, different patterns of dominance among these patterns of authority have emerged.

Some institutions, as a whole, can be described as predominately political in their operations. They tend to be more vulnerable to groups that articulate their interest to bring pressure on institutional decision-making. Other institutions are more accurately characterized by the legal/rational approach of bureaucracies. Still others continue to operate mainly by the trust and mutual respect of a community of scholars. But each characterization alone is too simplistic, for lurking in the background of the trait that dominates at any moment are the shadows of the other characteristics.

Furthermore, within each institution authority patterns are frequently different in various administrative areas. For example, the management of institutional support services, such as libraries, registration and admissions, building and grounds, and accounting, requires coordination that is accomplished most appropriately and efficiently by a bureaucratic hierarchy of specialists. Academic affairs require more collegial decision-making. And negotiating, mediation, confrontation, or mutual problem-solving are required in the allocation of limited resources among interest groups. The college motor pool is not run in the same manner as the English department or the community outreach program. And a president may find him or herself acting bureaucratically with a state budgeting process, collegially with his principal staff officers, and politically with several groups of protesting alumni.

These important variations in the ways in which authority is exercised in an institution demand different uses of authority by administrators for the attainment of institutional goals. A thorough evaluation program should therefore take account of the appropriateness of the administrator's actions in the context of diverse, and shifting, patterns of authority.

The appropriateness of administrator actions to form and attain goals, acquire resources, and achieve membership satisfaction also depends, in part, on the stage of development of the institution. For example, a new or developing institution with inexperienced staff may require a more autocratic, entrepreneurial president to establish institutional credibility and support. An established institution may need a more democratic president to maintain excellence. And a threatened institution that is fighting for survival may require a president who is particularly skilled in political maneuvering. Thus the needs of the institution at its stage of development must be considered as part of the context of administrator evaluation.

In summary, our framework for administrator evaluation focuses on administrator actions that contribute to the effectiveness of the college or university as a whole. The effectiveness and appropriateness of the administrator's actions are judged against certain dimensions of institutional context. An outline of this framework of areas of evaluation is shown in Table 3-1.

PROCEDURES FOR PRESIDENTIAL EVALUATION

In the preceding section we suggested that an administrator be evaluated by analyzing the *effectiveness* of his or her actions in four areas: goal formation, goal attainment, resource acquisition, and membership satisfaction. We further suggested that the *appropriateness* of these actions be judged within three contexts: institutional climate, institutional authority patterns, and institutional stage of development. We believe that a program of administrator evaluation that includes all of these factors will contribute to the improvement of the college or university as a whole, as well as the individual administrator. The procedures of data collection, and the data collected for evaluating administrators, can in fact be used by administrators to form goals.

For several reasons, we recommend that an institution start with an evaluation of the president and, perhaps, the president's immediate professional staff, to make the process of administrator evaluation acceptable. The first steps taken by an institution must be of manageable scope, and the top administrators must demonstrate their commitment to evaluation. Also, where some administrative functions are common among administrators (e.g., leadership, communications), others are role-specific (e.g., fund-raising admissions), requiring

Table 3-1. Dimensions of Administrator Evaluation

A. Administrator Actions to be Evaluated:

1. *Goal Formation:* The administrator systematically develops written, acceptable and attainable goals which, within his or her area of responsibility, aim at maintaining or improving aspects of the college or university.
2. *Goal Attainment:* The administrator attains his or her goals.
3. *Resource Acquisition:* The administrator secures the human and material resources needed for goal attainment.
4. *Membership Satisfaction:* The administrator facilitates the attainment of the goals of students, faculty, administrators, governing board members, and alumni.

B. Judged in the Context of:

1. *Institutional Climate:* The administrator's goals address the priority needs of the institution, such as excellence in instruction, diversity in opportunities, and vitality in atmosphere.
2. *Institutional Authority Patterns:* The administrator's goals are formed and attained in accordance with appropriate authority patterns.
3. *Institutional Stage of Development:* The administrator's goals are appropriate to the needs of the institution at its particular stage of development.

what can be a time-consuming analysis of role-specific functions if all administrators are to be evaluated at the same time. Goal-referenced evaluation at the lower levels of the organizational hierarchy requires the guidance and perspective of institutionwide goals, especially with regard to the possibilities and constraints within which the institution must operate. Such institutional goals can be formed as part of the process of evaluating the president, which can then be applied in evaluating other administrators.

The procedures for administrator evaluation that encompass the formation of administrator goals are described in the remainder of this section in eight steps. These eight steps illustrate an evaluation of the president, but are generally applicable to any administrative role.

Step One: Form Evaluation Committee

Responsibility for carrying out the presidential evaluation should be vested in a visible group. Depending upon the institution's usual decision-making processes, the group could be a committee of the governing board, or a committee already responsible for the faculty evaluation program. Forming such a committee to carry out the evaluation assumes that the institution has already decided to engage in a formal program of administrator evaluation. We strongly urge institutions to follow the procedures described in the Preface in making this decision in order to insure cooperation and empowerment by the campus constituents.

Step Two: Select Evaluation Purposes

As its first activity, the evaluation committee will need to identify the purposes of the presidential evaluation. This chapter highlights the first purpose enumerated above: administrator evaluation as a basis for establishing and attaining institutional goals. Other purposes—performance improvement, personnel decision, and so forth—can be accommodated within this central purpose.

Step Three: Identify Current Goals

The next task for the evaluation committee is to understand what the president's current goals are so that they may be evaluated. If the president has already developed explicitly stated goals, and presented them in writing, the evaluation committee can proceed to step four. If the president's goals are not explicitly stated in written form, they can be inferred from his or her recent activities. We suggest that the committee work with the president on this task, assisted by someone experienced in writing goals.

To identify the implicit goals of the president, first draw up a list of several of his or her *major* activities for the past one to three years. Next, decide what those activities were supposed to accomplish. Treat the activities as means toward ends called "goals." The goal statements should be specific enough to describe things people can understand and observe. They should also describe a degree of outcome that is judged sufficient. And, to indicate the priority of those activities and goals, estimates should be made of the percentage of time given to them. Examples of such a "role analysis" of the president are shown in Table 3–2. We recommend that the president's initial statements be as broad as those shown, especially where the evaluation committee is not experienced in writing goals.

Step Four: Evaluate Goal Effectiveness

Once the goals are understood and accepted, the president and the evaluation committee should discuss the consequences of the president's actions to attain those goals. At this point some committee members may question the appropriateness of certain activities, goals, or proportions of time spent, and their questions should be noted and taken into account for step six. For the task at hand, however, we are dealing with what was actually intended and accomplished in the past. If the committee or president is uncertain about the degree of attainment of certain goals, a fact-finding effort should be carried out by examining records, or interviewing samples of faculty, students, other administrators, or others with first-hand knowledge of the area in question.

The principal question to be asked in the evaluation of resource acquisition is whether the president was able to obtain the financial and personnel resources necessary to accomplish his or her goals. If there is no empirical performance data, the evaluation committee will have to make its best judgment regarding the adequacy of resource acquisition. Judgment must also be used (if effectiveness data is scarce) to estimate the effectiveness of personnel chosen to realize the institution's aims.

To gauge membership satisfaction, we recommend the use of a questionnaire to be completed by other administrators regarding the president's leadership,

Table 3-2. Partial Example of a Role Analysis of the President.

Activities	Implicit Goals	Percent Time (average)
1. Fund-raising (private sector)	a. Annual raising of $22 million: $7 million from alumni, $11 million in endowments, $4 million in grants to expand science facilities and dormitories.	30%
2. Academic leadership	a. Stimulate faculty in undergraduate programs to adopt testing and grading methods that will better reflect learning (e.g., grades have become inflated from B- to A- average in the past six years).	20-25%
	b. Facilitate the upgrading of humanities instruction in occupational and vocational programs.	
3. External relations (public sector)	a. Present regional board and legislature with information regarding students served (e.g., ratio of applicants; admittance, percentage graduates to graduate school, career patterns) sufficient enough to support budget requests.	20%
	b. Extend by 35 percent the number of student hours in course-related field experience in local hospitals, schools, businesses, etc., and increase the exposure of these service/learning activities via media.	

decision-making, communications, and the like. For most institutions we do not recommend that these kinds of questionnaires be given to students or faculty because their knowledge of specific presidential actions is usually limited.

Since questionnaires about administrator processes such as leadership and decision-making are the most often used method of evaluating administrators, more needs to be said about them. We wish to encourage further experimentation with such questionnaires, even though we advocate their use in gauging a unitary notion of membership satisfaction within our schema. Further research may in fact establish their validity in measuring dimensions such as leadership and decision-making of particular administrators, or of the total administration. A differentiation of members' satisfaction with such dimensions of the administration or of particular administrators would add information to be used in evaluation and new goal-planning. To illustrate what research is needed we turn to work done recently at Texas Christian University.

We have chosen to feature two Texas Christian University Administrator Evaluation Questionnaires (Rating Scales 3-3 and 3-4), which are the only research-derived questionnaires that we have found to measure such general administrative processes. Other questionnaires shown in this section (Rating Scales 3–5 through 3–8) show some similarities to the TCU instrument, but their technical qualities (e.g., validity, reliability, nonredundancy, powers of discrimination) have not been put to such a rigorous test. In fact, the trial-run version of the TCU questionnaire (Rating Scale 3–3) was revised because of undesirable technical properties revealed by a trial application. As can be seen, the 43 items were reduced to 28, and rearranged to form different scales on the basis of empirical information (Rating Scale 3–4). The trial questionnaire has what is called "face validity"—the dimensions such as decision-making and communications appear to a panel of judges (e.g., faculty, administrators, students) to contain items related to these dimensions. However, certain items from different scales are more related to each other, as shown by how respondents rate the items. This rearrangement of items, and the dimension so formed, are said to have empirical validity.

We advocate the use of either the TCU trial questionnaire or the TCU revised questionnaire, with the following qualifications. The revised questionnaire was derived from a trial application involving 1,392 people in a variety of roles at TCU in 1972. A replication of this trial today at TCU might produce different results, and the chances of different results are greater outside of TCU, especially in different types of institutions. Thus we advise the use of the TCU trial questionnaire by those to whom it appears more appropriate to their particular institution, and who are willing and capable of performing statistical analysis of the results. This involves essentially factor analytic and correlational techniques, for which most institutions with access to computer facilities and psychometric expertise should be equipped to handle.[a] These analyses will show where revision is called for, giving a questionnaire with technical qualities determined at the institution where it will be used.

Otherwise, use the TCU revised questionnaire if it appears more appropriate. In both cases at least one trial application with statistical analysis will be necessary to develop an instrument with known properties that will give meaning and confidence to the results of its use.

Other administrator evaluation questionnaires are included in this section, principally to illustrate the range of what is in use today. To our knowledge none has undergone the careful development and testing applied to the TCU questionnaires, and they are therefore of more limited value. Choose a questionnaire that makes the most sense for your setting, but whichever one you choose, make sure that you use it on a trial basis at least once, and revise (or reject) it on the results of statistical testing.

---

[a]For the details of the methods and results of the TCU experience, see: "The Evaluation of University Faculty and Administrators: A Case Study," Richard M. Fenker, TCU. This is an unpublished paper, and can be ordered at a cost by writing to Professor Fenker at: Texas Christian University, Psychology Department, Fort Worth, Texas.

To summarize step four, we recommend that the evaluation committee in discussions with the president make informed judgments about (1) the degree to which his or her current goals have been attained; (2) his or her effectiveness in acquiring the resources necessary to attain those goals; and (3) the degree to which subordinate administrators are able to attain their goals (i.e., membership satisfaction). We call this an evaluation of the president's "goal effectiveness."

Step Five: Describe Institutional Context

Next the evaluation committee should collect information that will help it to identify those aspects of the college or university which the president *should* be working to improve. General areas such as instruction, fiscal affairs, academic programs, external relations, and staff morale should be surveyed to give an approximate view of the areas of strengths and weaknesses of the institution as a whole. Such an institutional assessment will provide the context for evaluating the appropriateness of the president's goals.

In Table 3-1 we identified three interrelated institutional contexts: (1) institutional climate; (2) institutional authority patterns; and (3) institutional stage of development. For assessing institutional climate we recommend the use of tested questionnaires given to all or samples of students, faculty, and administrators, depending on the size and financial resources of the institution. In this work, the evaluation committee should have technical assistance from the department of psychology, the institutional research office, or the computer center.

We have selected two questionnaires described under Rating Scales 3-1 and 3-2 that measure general institutional climate on the basis of relevance to this schema, practical utility, and technical qualities.[b] We advise the committee to order and examine specimen sets. These questionnaires can be used intact, or selected items can be used with permission from ETS at a cost negotiated with them.[c] Institutions choosing to select items, rather than using intact questionnaires, must arrange for their own scoring of those items. ETS does offer scoring services and technical assistance such as choosing a sample, at a determined cost.

Six dimensions of campus life are described in Rating Scale 3-1 (from the Institutional Functioning Inventory of Educational Testing Service, Princeton, New Jersey). Figure 3-1 on page 152 shows sample responses to this questionnaire of students, faculty, and administrators in a public university. In this example, the students, faculty, and administrators agree strongly that either

---

[b]For other instruments available in this area, see H. Hodgkinson, *A Manual For the Evaluation of Innovative Programs*, CRDHE, Berkeley.

[c]For permission or additional information, write to Institutional Research Program for Higher Education, Educational Testing Service, Princeton, N.J., 08540.

undergraduate instruction stands relatively low as an institutional priority, or that the quality of undergraduate teaching is poor (i.e., from the low rating in the "Concern for Undergraduate Learning," or "UL" dimension). Such a low estimate of undergraduate learning would doubtless be known before administering this questionnaire, but the questionnaire results add credibility to the seriousness of this condition. With such empirical information, the presidential evaluation committee has legitimate reason to assess the president's leadership in improving undergraduate teaching as a major evaluation criterion. And if the president's leadership in this area is lacking, the improvement of undergraduate teaching might become a major presidential goal for the next goal-attaining/ evaluation cycle.

Next, the committee must deal with the appropriate use of authority by administrators. For example, another interesting result shown in Figure 3-1 is that students in that particular institution feel considerably less involved in institutional decision-making than do faculty (as shown in the ratings of the "Democratic Governance," or "DG" dimension). In our schema, we would interpret this as a discrepancy in institutional authority patterns, where students view the pattern as more bureaucratic (hierarchical) and faculty view the pattern as more collegial (shared). If collegial authority relations with students as well as with faculty are valued, again such empirical information gives the presidential evaluation committee legitimate reason to assess the president's role in improving this dimension.

Without questionnaires such as the IFI, the further description of institutional authority patterns can be done by the presidential evaluation committee by discussion, by interviewing, and by examining records. Further assessment of institutional climate, and an identification of the important needs of the institution at its particular stage of development, will rest essentially on *judgment*. The point of administering questionnaires to and interviewing students, faculty, and administrators is to base those judgments on empirical information. Such information about the institutional context of the president's actions will yield important criteria for evaluating his or her effectiveness in forming and attaining goals, acquiring resources, and satisfying institutional members.

Step Six: Evaluate Goal Appropriateness

Here the president's current goals (from step three) are evaluated against the institutional context (from step five). Two questions are at issue: (1) did the president form goals that address the most important needs of the institution at its particular stage of development; and (2) did the president form and attain those goals in accordance with appropriate authority patterns?

In the example given in step five, sample questionnaire results showed that students, faculty, and administrators concurred in an extremely low rating of the quality of undergraduate instruction at a public university. If the president had no current goals to improve this condition, or if his goals were tangential or otherwise insufficient, this would be inappropriate. Or if the president has a sufficient goal to improve undergraduate instruction, but was trying to do so by administrative fiat in an institution that values collegial action, this would also be inappropriate.

A president who showed a pattern of setting goals (or pursuing activities) in areas insufficiently related to priority institutional needs, or one who tries to attain goals through the inappropriate exercise of authority, should be given a negative evaluation. Whether or not such a president is retained or replaced, the information used in this evaluation can also be used in the appropriate formation of new goals that do address priority institutional needs.

Step Seven: Form New Goals

The information gathered from students, faculty, and administrators in the preceding steps, and used to evaluate the president, is also the basis for forming new goals. The president's goals, broadly stated, should address the priority needs of the institution, and as such can be considered institutional goals.

When goals are established for the institution and the president, the next task is to decide how the responsibility for goal attainment is to be divided. To refer to our previous example of poor undergraduate instruction (page 139) the president of that public university may take overall responsibility for the goal, but he or she certainly cannot attain the goal singlehandedly. The president must organize an effort that will involve all constituent groups, designating certain people to be responsible for certain tasks. When this is determined, the key personnel with responsibility for major subtasks can also use goal formation as a management and evaluation tool. The president's role may become one of facilitating the improvement of undergraduate instruction, and subsequent presidential evaluations would assess the degree of facilitation in attaining that goal.

Step Eight: Begin New Goal Attainment/Evaluation Cycle

When new goals are established and validated by broad participation of the members of the institution, and when plans have been developed for the means of implementing those plans, the institution acts on those plans. It is beyond the scope of this book to present a detailed approach to institutional planning and operations. Our focus on evaluation provides a foundation for institutional and administrative planning, and we assume that institutions either have sufficient planning and operational capabilities to carry out these functions, or can arrange for assistance.

Evaluation does, however, play an important part when institutional members are working toward the attainment of new or revised goals. First, the institution must devise procedures for the continual evaluation of progress toward the desired goals. We recommend that step eight involve a three-year cycle, and that all administrators be evaluated every three years against the goals formed. Annual, interim evaluations are recommended to chart progress and make revisions where necessary. The beginning of those three-year cycles for particular administrators should be staggered as a working convenience.

The technical requirements of goal-formation, goal-attaining, and goal-evaluation are considerable. Several good books and manuals are available that deal with these requirements, and the reader should certainly begin with those for general knowledge and to assess the type and scope of application appropriate to their institution. Next, talk with people experienced with goal-directed planning in a college or university. We advise that if you are inexperienced that you arrange for help with the training, planning, and implementation required. Among the resources listed on page 146 are references for those who want to explore the uses of goal-setting for their institution.

EVALUATION OF OTHER ADMINISTRATORS

If an institution chooses to evaluate its president first, it can use the new goals formed in steps seven and eight for evaluation of other administrators. They would be evaluated according to the degree they attain their responsibility for those goals, acquire resources, satisfy their members, and exercise appropriate authority. If an institution chooses to evaluate other administrators at the same time or before the president, it should follow the eight steps shown above.

The kinds and sources of information for the evaluation of other administrators will differ from those appropriate for the president. All administrators knowledgeable about the evaluatee's performance in the areas of goal formation, goal attainment, and resource acquisition, should participate in the evaluation. We suggest the following plan for participation in evaluation in the areas of membership satisfaction and the exercise of authority: faculty evaluate academic administrators; students evaluate administrators of student services; and other administrators evaluate administrators in finance and facilities areas. The procedures for evaluating institutional factors remain the same, with the information obtained being used as contextual information as it was in the evaluation of the president and for setting new goals.

There is one administrative role that requires special consideration here— the department chairperson. This role is at the intersection of collegial and bureaucratic or political authority, and often the role is filled by departmental faculty members on a rotating basis. Often the faculty member in this role is not comfortable in directing other faculty members. In our experience, when the department chairperson involves the faculty in establishing departmental goals he or she acquires the authority for attaining those jointly established goals. Thus, for department chairpersons we advocate that goal formation, which is part of our evaluation scheme, be done jointly with the faculty of that department.

Certain areas of administrative responsibility, such as budget development or academic planning, are the shared responsibilities of department heads, the academic dean, and other administrators. Other functions, such as budget control, may be assigned to one particular administrator, such as a financial officer. The location of responsibility of certain functions may be clear or ambiguous, but the evaluation of administrators in colleges and universities would not be complete without some assessment of role-specific functions, where possible. And involvement in the process of determining role-specific functions may, in itself, bring clarity to ambiguous areas of responsibility.

Some work has been done, however, that can be used or adapted, and will serve to guide those interested in determining role-specific functions themselves.

The most detailed delineation of role-specific functions we have found is in two separate self-audit manuals for registrars and admissions officers. Several pages from the registrars manual are shown in Rating Scale 3-9 (ordering information is shown under Resources, page 169). These manuals each contain over 100 questions designed for and used by registrars and admissions officers for self-evaluation. Without too much difficulty the more important questions could be posed to students, faculty, or other administrators, giving their views to be compared with the self-evaluation. The questions in these manuals could be used as they presently stand to establish what is done, or they could be put into a rating scale format to assess the effectiveness of what is done by questionnaire application.

The process for establishing role-specific areas of responsibility should involve at least two administrators—the one whose role is being defined, and the administrator to whom he or she is primarily accountable. It was found in one study (Callahan, 1971) that there was an average discrepancy of 25 percent between individual and supervisor lists of routine responsibilities for that individual. For more complex, innovative, or problem-solving areas of responsibility, the discrepancies averaged 80 percent. Since even small discrepancies may affect ratings, attitudes, expectations, or motivation, descriptions of role-specific areas of responsibility should be developed by at least the individual and supervisor involved, and reviewed by all administrative staff. A simple process for establishing role-specific areas of responsibilities for an administrator is:[d]

1. The individual and supervisor involved each independently list all of the areas of responsibility for that individual. The initial lists should show broad categories, such as those shown below.

Registrar's Responsibility Areas

   I. Registration
  II. Transcript Communication

---

[d]A more elaborate, empirical process that can be followed is described in Chapter 4.

III.   Student Record Maintenance
IV.   Course Credit Equivalency
V.   Student Progress Monitoring
VI.   Course Offering List
VII.   Office Administration

Financial Officer's Responsibility Areas

I.   Accounting
II.   Food Service
III.   Auxiliary Services
IV.   Purchasing
V.   Budget Development
VI.   Reports
VII.   Financial Planning
VIII.   Plant Supervision

Academic Dean's Responsibility Areas

I.   College Instructional Program
   A.   Curriculum Development
   B.   Instructional Evaluation
   C.   Staff Recruitment and Development
   D.   Instructional Support Equipment
   E.   Course Offering Schedule
   F.   Academic Program Effectiveness
II.   Academic Budgeting
   A.   Budget Development
   B.   Budget Negotiation
III.   Academic Policy and Procedures
IV.   Communication with Constituencies

2. The individual and supervisor involved compare and discuss each other's list and work out an agreed-upon resolution where discrepancies exist.
3. The revised list is shared among all administrators, and a final list is developed by consensus.
4. This process can be repeated to give more detailed descriptions of functions within each broad area, as in the Kentucky *Registrar's Manual* (Rating Scale 3-9).
5. For these functions, or responsibility areas, statements are written of the goals (purposes) within each area.

FEEDBACK: RECIPIENTS AND CONDITIONS

The general principles laid out regarding feedback in faculty evaluation also apply to administrator evaluation (see Chapter 2). The reader is referred to the section *Feedback: Recipients and Conditions* in Chapter 2 for a more detailed discussion of the issues involved.

One of the principles in Chapter 2 is that the various sources of evaluative information, particularly those who fill out questionnaires, are entitled to receive some feedback of the results of their efforts. Knowing that information will be fed back, and to what uses it will be put, contributes to the seriousness and useability of the respondent's information. We predict that any evaluation will fail without such feedback. Respondents should also be guaranteed the anonymity of their responses (see Disclosure, Chapter 2). The following discussion is concerned with feedback to the administrator evaluated (self) and those who participate in the evaluation.

To Administrator Evaluated (Self)

The administrator who is evaluated should receive, or have access to, all evaluative information except that which by *prior, mutual agreement,* is to be kept confidential. Completely open access is ideal, but an institution may at certain times have compelling reasons for keeping some administrator evaluation information confidential. For example, sensitive personal or political considerations that bear on the well-being of the person evaluated, or the institution as a whole, may be kept in confidence from the person evaluaated by those responsible for conducting the evaluation. This is obviously a controversial point that requires sensitive judgment, and it should be the exception to full disclosure only in extreme cases.

In general, the administrator should have access to all evaluative information about himself, and the general (not individual) sources of that information. Following our principle of multisource evaluation, our schema for comprehensive evaluation of administrators includes as sources of information presidential evaluation the president (self); the governing body; other administrators; faculty; and students. Each source evaluates selected aspects of the president's functions or activities, as described in the preceding section. Following the principle of individual anonymity, the president should receive or have access to a summary of the results of each group's evaluation. Where quantitative assessment is involved (e.g., with the results of questionnaires), means should be calculated and fed back to the president. Written or oral comments may either be summarized, or listed verbatim, without identifying their individual sources (see Format, Chapter 2).

To Others

As with feedback to the administrator being evaluated, those who provide evaluative information should receive, the overall results from their group, but not necessarily the results from other groups. Thus, other administrators who evaluate general administrative processes should receive a summary of the results of the total administrative group. But for those areas where they were not sources of information (e.g., goal formation) there is no reason why they should receive feedback, other than by prior mutual agreement. Similarly, students and faculty, if asked only to evaluate the general climate and conditions of the institution, should receive summarized feedback regarding the responses of their group in those areas.

There are exceptions to these general conditions of feedback which are tied to certain purposes of administrator evaluation. For example, if a purpose is to use the information for goal formation (Purpose 1), the information (always in summary, anonymous form) must be fed back to those involved in the goal-formation process. If the information is to be used for personnel decision-making (Purpose 2), it must be fed back to the person or group empowered to make those decisions. If the information is to be used for retraining or reassignment, it must be fed back to the person or group responsible for that function.

There are, however, compelling reasons to make full disclosure of all *summarized* information regarding administrator evaluation to all institutional members, within the bounds of privacy and disclosure in sensitive areas. First, such disclosure makes real the common principle of shared administrator accountability to the governing body, faculty, students, and others with a stake in the well-being of the institution. Second, it increases the visibility of the administration, which is often "hidden" to members of the governing body, faculty, and students. Third, it puts the same pressure of "consumer" concerns on administrators as is put on faculty by student evaluation, a pressure that should lead to more effective and efficient administration. Fourth, it may contribute to improved institutional morale, participation, responsibility, and coping capacity, by contributing to a climate of mutual trust and respect.

INDICATORS OF SUCCESS

None of the positive effects of full disclosure listed in the preceding section is guaranteed, however, and in fact the opposite effect may result. It is not only the fact of disclosure that is important, but also the *manner* in which disclosure—and other aspects of administrator evaluation—are done. Among those aspects of administrator evaluation which contribute to the success are: general climate of acceptance of the goals and procedures of administrator evaluation; visibility of goals and procedures; evaluation program administration; capacity to overcome resistance; grievance procedures and legal factors; affirmative action; stages of development; and maintenance and renewal. The reader is referred to Chapter 2, where a detailed discussion of these factors occurs.

SELECTED BIBLIOGRAPHY

Anderson, Lester F. "The Organizational Character of American Colleges and Universities," in Terry Lunsford, ed., *The Study of Academic Administration* Boulder, Colorado: Western Interstate Commission for Higher Education, 1963.

Baldridge, Victor J. *Academic Governance.* Berkeley, California: McCutcham Publishing Corporation, 1971.

———. *Power and Conflict in the University.* New York: John Wiley, 1971.

Brenneman, D. Saunders, and Black, Walter P. *Management by Objectives (MBO) Training.* Chapel Hill, North Carolina: National Laboratory for Higher Education, 1973.

Callahan, Daniel M. "Conformity, Deviation, and Morale among Educators in School Systems." USOE Cooperative Project in Educational Development, Contract OEG-3-8-0800069-043, 1969.

Clark, Burton R. "Faculty Organization and Authority," in Terry Lunsford, ed., *The Study of Academic Administration.* Boulder, Colorado: Western Interstate Commission for Higher Education, 1963.

Connellan, Thomas K. "Management by Objectives in Community Colleges." Michigan State University, Conference Paper, 1971.

Corson, John J. *Governance of Colleges and Universities.* New York: McGraw-Hill, 1960.

Dressel, Paul L. "Evaluation of the Environment, the Processes, and the Results of Higher Education," in Asa S. Knowles, ed., *Handbook of College and University Administration* New York: McGraw-Hill, 1970.

Gross, Edward, and Grambsch, Paul V. *Changes in University Organization, 1964-71.* New York: McGraw-Hill, 1974.

Helsabeck, Robert E. *The Compound System, A Conceptual Framework for Effective Decision Making in Colleges.* Center for Research and Development In Higher Education, University of California, Berkeley, California, 1973.

Henderson, Algo D., and Henderson, Jean Glidden. *Higher Education in America.* San Francisco: Jossey-Bass Publishers, 1974.

Katz, Daniel, and Kahn, Robert L. *The Social Psychology of Organizations.* New York: John Wiley, 1966.

Lawrence, Paul R., and Lorsch, Jay W. *Organization and Environment.* Homewood, Illinois: Richard D. Irwin, 1969.

Likert, Rensis. *New Patterns of Management.* New York: McGraw-Hill, 1961.

Miles, Matthew. *Innovation in Education.* Bureau of Publications, Teachers College, Columbia University, 1965.

Millett, John. *The Academic Community.* New York: McGraw-Hill, 1962.

Odiorne, George S. *Management Decisions by Objectives.* Englewood Cliffs, N.J.: Prentice-Hall, 1969.

Olive, Betsey A. "The Administration of Higher Education: A Bibliographic Survey," *Administrative Science Quarterly* 2, 1967.

Stroup, Herbert H. *Bureaucracy in Higher Education.* New York: Free Press, 1966.

Tennebaum, Arnold S. *Control in Organizations.* New York: McGraw-Hill, 1968.

Weber, Max. *The Theory of Social and Economic Organization.* New York: Free Press, 1947.

Wert, Robert F. "Leadership: The Integrative Factor," in Terry Lunsford, *The Study of Academic Administration* (Boulder, Colorado: Western Interstate Commission for Higher Education), 1963.

Winter, David G. *The Power Motive.* New York: Free Press, 1973.

Sample Rating Scales

Rating Scale 3-1.   The Institutional Functioning Inventory (IFI)

The student questionnaire consists of 72 items which measure six dimensions of campus life.[a] These dimensions are:[b]

(IAE) Intellectual-Aesthetic Extracurriculum refers to the availability of activities and opportunities for intellectual and aesthetic stimulation outside the classroom. Colleges with high scores are characterized by their deliberate efforts to encourage intellectual and artistic interests through appearances by leading intellectuals, informal discussion groups, student literary productions, art exhibits, musical presentations, and so forth. Low scores would mean a relative absence of extracurricular opportunities of an intellectual and aesthetic nature.

(F) Freedom has to do with academic freedom for faculty and students as well as freedom in their personal lives for all individuals in the campus community. High scores imply that respondents perceive themselves to be essentially free to discuss topics and organize groups of their own choosing, to invite controversial speakers, and to be relatively free of college restrictions on their personal conduct and activities. Low scores suggest an institution that places many restraints on the academic and personal lives of faculty and students.

(HD) Human Diversity has to do with the degree to which the faculty and student body are heterogeneous in their backgrounds and present attitudes. A high score indicates that the college is viewed as having attracted students and faculty of diverse ethnic and social backgrounds, of diverse political and religious attitudes, and of diverse personal tastes and styles. A low score suggests a campus community that is relatively homogeneous in terms of faculty and student backgrounds and beliefs.

(IS) Concern for Improvement of Society refers to a desire among people at the institution to apply their knowledge and skills in solving social problems and prompting social change in America. A high score implies that many faculty wish to, and do, consult with governmental agencies on social and economic matters, that programs dealing with contemporary social problems exist on campus, that campus authorities are committed to the view that the institution should be actively engaged in working to improve social conditions. Low scores imply some combination of disinterest, parochialism, or conservatism in relation to the existing American social order.

(continued)

Rating Scale 3-1 continued

(UL) Concern for Undergraduate Learning describes the degree to which the college—in its structure, function, and professional commitment of faculty—emphasizes undergraduate teaching and learning. A high score suggests a faculty generally disposed toward personalized teaching of undergraduates, encouragement of active student involvement in the learning enterprise, and institutional rewards for good teaching. A low score indicates either that undergraduate instruction stands relatively low as an institutional priority, or else the perception that, for whatever reasons, the quality of teaching at the college is generally somewhat poor.

(DG) Democratic Governance reflects the extent to which individuals in the campus community who are directly affected by a decision have the opportunity to participate in making the decision. High scores signify extensive and meaningful faculty and student involvement in institutional affairs, decentralized decision-making, and shared (horizontal) rather than hierarchical (vertical) organizational arrangements. Low scores suggest authoritarianism—authority and power tightly held, typically by an administrative clique, in a "top-down" administrative framework.

Figure 3–1 shows sample results from the 132-item questionnaire, which includes student results on the six dimensions ("scales") described above. This sample profile shows that students' ratings were:

—*High* for (IAE) Intellectual-Aesthetic Extracurriculum (82nd percentile), and (HD) Human Diversity (82nd percentile).
—*Medium/high* for (IS) Concern for Improvement of Society (71st percentile).
—*Medium/low* for (F) Freedom (46th percentile).
—*Low* for (UL) Concern for Undergraduate Learning (3rd percentile), and (DG) Democratic Governance (8th percentile).

One advantage of using the IFI questionnaire with faculty and administrators, as well as with students, is that it shows where there is agreement or disagreement. In this case, the sample profile shows amazing agreement in all areas except (DG), Democratic Governance. Where there is agreement regarding weaknesses, a joint improvement is possible. Where there is disagreement, joint debate and consensus building may be a necessary precursor to improvement efforts.

Available IFI materials and their costs are:

—Specimen Set which includes Technical Manual, questionnaires and answer sheet	$ 4.00
—Technical Manual only	$ 3.50
—IFI questionnaire (132 items), reuseable	$ .40
—IFI Student questionnaire (72 items), reuseable	$ .25
—IFI answer sheets	$ .06

IFI scoring and reporting services, and their costs are:

Faculty, administrators, other non-student answer sheets (Items 1-132):

Computer Print-Out Service—$1.20 per answer sheet scored (institutional summary, subgroup analysis, scale scores, and tabulation of local option and information questions).

(continued)

Rating Scale 3-1 continued

Combined Scoring Service–$1.45 per answer sheet scored (computer print-out service plus data cards with scale scores).

Student answer sheets (Items 1–72 only):

Computer Print-Out Service–$1.10 per answer sheet scored (institutional summary, sub-group analysis, scale scores for scales 1–6, and tabulation of local option and information questions).
Combined Scoring Service–$1.20 per answer sheet scored (computer print-out service plus data cards with scale scores for scales 1–6).
There is a $50 minimum charge for scoring each group of answer sheets included in one computer print-out.
IFI is available from: ETS College and University Programs, Box 2813, Princeton, New Jersey 08540

---

[a]A longer questionnaire of 132 items and 11 dimensions of campus life is available for use with students (Sections 1 and 2), faculty, administrators or governing board members.
[b]The descriptions of the dimensions and profile shown were taken from the ETS Technical Manual on IFI, 1970, and are used by permission. See Resources, p. 169, for further information and restrictions.

A public university:

——————   Faculty

— — —   Administrators

— — — — —   Students (first six scales)

INSTITUTIONAL MEANS

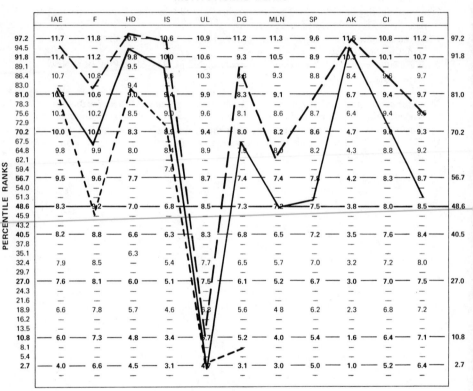

Figure 3-1.   Mean Score Profile
From Educational Testing Service, Princeton, N.J. 08540. Used by permission. See Resources, p. 169. for further information and restrictions.

Rating Scale 3-2. Student Reactions to College (SRC)

Almost a third of the 171 items in this questionnaire are concerned with some aspect of the students' classroom instruction. Smaller numbers of items deal with student goals and planning, student activities, administrative problems, out-of-class studying, various aspects of daily living such as housing and transportation, financial concerns, and student-staff contact. Colleges will be able to learn from the ways students respond to these items what student expectations are not being met, what instructional procedures are causing difficulty for students, which kinds of students need particular kinds of help, what program changes would be well-received by the students, and in general a variety of ways in which the college's programs and the students' needs are and are not congruent.

The results of administering the questionnaire to a sample of students will be reported to a college broken down by groups of items and groups of students. Those issues identified by the college as of primary importance will be emphasized in the report to prevent the users from having to deal with a large body of unorganized information. Secondary analyses of the results will be possible after the initial report has been examined by the college. Procedures for administering the questionnaire and for making the most effective use of the results are presented in a user's manual.

SRC Booklet and Scoring Charges: $ .35 per SRC Booklet; $1.25 per each SRC Booklet scored.

There is a $350 minimum charge for scoring booklets included in one report. *Magnetic tape:* For institutions wishing to do further analysis of their data, a magnetic tape containing the institution's data can also be ordered. The tape is 9-track 800 or 1600 BPI. Cost for the tape is $100. Additional reports for more than five subgroups can be made available at additional cost.

Educational Testing Service utilizes SRC data in continuing research studies. No disclosure identifying such data with an individual institution is made. For complete information on these or other questionnaires, either call or write to:

Director, ETS Community and Junior College Program
Educational Testing Service
Princeton, N.J. 08540

Used by permission. See Resources, p. 169, for further information and restrictions.

Rating Scale 3–3. Administrator Evaluation Questionnaire

TRIAL RUN FORM

Individual Evaluated: _____   Position _____

On the average I have contact with him: Daily___Weekly___Monthly___Bimonthly___

Occasionally___

I am: A student___A faculty member___An administrator___A professional staff member___

Listed below are a number of statements which describe aspects of administrator behavior. Rate the above administrator on each of these items by marking the appropriate response category. In making your rating the administrator should be compared with other administrators at TCU that you have known. If you are uncertain about a particular item or feel that it is not applicable in describing the administrator's behavior then mark the category labeled "uncertain".

CODE

L - Low Score
BA- Below Average Score
A - Average Score
AA- Above Average Score
H - High Score
U - Undecided, Not Applicable

Evaluate the above administrator in terms of the degree to which he:

SCALE 1. COMMUNICATIONS

1. Communicates with you in a timely and responsive manner	L BA A AA H U
2. Conducts decisive conferences and interviews	L BA A AA H U
3. Balances and validates conflicting information effectively and fairly	L BA A AA H U
4. Writes letters or makes statements that seldom need clarification	L BA A AA H U
5. Is duly sensitive to your needs for information	L BA A AA H U
6. Has sufficient contact with you	L BA A AA H U
7. Shares important data willingly and in an organized manner	L BA A AA H U

SCALE 2. DECISION MAKING

8. Makes sound and timely decisions	L BA A AA H U
9. Gathers pertinent facts before acting	L BA A AA H U
10. Consults with others on important decisions	L BA A AA H U
11. Applies policy consistently and fairly	L BA A AA H U
12. Strives to identify as specifically as possible all alternatives before making a decision	L BA A AA H U
13. Is skilled in participatory decision making	L BA A AA H U

SCALE 3. PLANNING

14. Plans ahead for those activities under his cognizance	L BA A AA H U
15. Makes time for planning by delegating routine work	L BA A AA H U
16. Keeps goals up to date and clearly stated	L BA A AA H U
17. Is receptive to constructive suggestions for change	L BA A AA H U
18. Encourages initiative and innovation	L BA A AA H U

SCALE 4. OPERATIONS/ACTION

19. Initiates and sustains action toward defined goals	L BA A AA H U
20. Assigns duties so as to maximize capabilities of those involved	L BA A AA H U
21. Is skilled in those specialities demanded by his assignment	L BA A AA H U
22. Appoints effective committees	L BA A AA H U
23. Works well with committees	L BA A AA H U

(continued)

Rating Scale 3-3 continued

24. Sustains momentum of effort toward difficult goals	L BA A AA H U
25. Has a sense of quality and standards	L BA A AA H U
26. Encourages initiative and performance by delegating tasks effectively to others	L BA A AA H U
27. Demonstrates a clear understanding of the role and scope of his assignments and responsibilities	L BA A AA H U

SCALE 5. PROBLEM SOLVING

28. Is alert to potential problems because plans are not working out in practice	L BA A AA H U
29. Is able to cope with unanticipated events	L BA A AA H U
30. Gathers all pertinent facts before acting on a problem	L BA A AA H U
31. Knows how to use the special talents of others as an aid to solving problems	L BA A AA H U
32. Approaches problem solving on a systematic basis	L BA A AA H U
33. Is able to arouse a spirit of dynamic response to a problem without alarming or depressing others unduly	L BA A AA H U

SCALE 6. HUMAN/PUBLIC RELATIONS

34. Buoys morale and instills enthusiasm	L BA A AA H U
35. Gives proper and generous credit to others for their contributions	L BA A AA H U
36. Strives to help those under his supervision develop their full potential	L BA A AA H U
37. Is available for counsel when needed and appropriate	L BA A AA H U
38. Understands the university well enough to refer matters to the proper offices for effective action	L BA A AA H U
39. Constantly strives to broaden both the internal and external perception of the goals and accomplishments of the university	L BA A AA H U
40. Establishes rapport easily and is approachable for counsel	L BA A AA H U
41. Takes positive steps to counteract destructive rumors	L BA A AA H U
42. Commands positive results and does not harp about the negative ones	L BA A AA H U
43. Inspires you with a sense of purpose and direction	L BA A AA H U

Developed by Texas Christian University, Fort Worth, Texas 76129. Used by permission. See Resources, p. 169, for further information and restrictions.

Rating Scale 3–4. Administrator Evaluation Questionnaire

REVISED FORM

Individual Evaluated: _____ Position _____

On the average I have contact with him: Daily___ Weekly___ Monthly___ Bimonthly___

Occasionally___

I am: A student___ A faculty member___ An administrator___ A professional staff member___

Listed below are a number of statements which describe aspects of administrator behavior. Rate the above administrator on each of these items by marking the appropriate response category. In making your rating the administrator should be compared with other administrators at TCU that you have known. If you are uncertain about a particular item or feel that it is not applicable in describing the administrator's behavior then mark the category labeled "uncertain".

CODE

L - Low Score
BA- Below Average Score
A - Average Score
AA- Above Average Score
H - High Score
U - Undecided, Not Applicable

Evaluate the above administrator in terms of the degree in which he:

SCALE 1. INFORMATION/COMMUNICATIONS: refers to the accumulation of pertinent information before acting, or communicating important information.

1.	Communicates with you in a timely and responsive manner	L	BA	A	AA	H	U
2.	Writes letters or makes statements that seldom need clarification	L	BA	A	AA	H	U
3.	Is duly sensitive to your needs for information	L	BA	A	AA	H	U
4.	Has sufficient contact with you	L	BA	A	AA	H	U
5.	Gathers pertinent facts before acting	L	BA	A	AA	H	U
6.	Consults with others on important decisions	L	BA	A	AA	H	U
7.	Applies policy consistently and fairly	L	BA	A	AA	H	U
8.	Has a sense of quality and standards	L	BA	A	AA	H	U
9.	Understands the university well enough to refer matters to the proper offices for effective action	L	BA	A	AA	H	U

SCALE 2. GOAL COMPLETION: refers to the planning activities, and initiating and sustaining action toward a goal.

10.	Conducts decisive conferences and interviews	L	BA	A	AA	H	U
11.	Makes sound and timely decisions	L	BA	A	AA	H	U
12.	Plans ahead for those activities under his cognizance	L	BA	A	AA	H	U
13.	Initiates and sustains action toward defined goals	L	BA	A	AA	H	U
14.	Assigns duties so as to maximize capabilities of those involved	L	BA	A	AA	H	U
15.	Is skilled in those specialties demanded by his assignment	L	BA	A	AA	H	U
16.	Is alert to potential problems because plans are not working out in practice	L	BA	A	AA	H	U
17.	Is able to cope with unanticipated events	L	BA	A	AA	H	U
18.	Takes positive steps to counteract destructive rumors	L	BA	A	AA	H	U

SCALE 3. DELEGATION OF RESPONSIBILITY

19.	Is skilled in participatory decision making	L	BA	A	AA	H	U
20.	Makes time for planning by delegating routine work	L	BA	A	AA	H	U
21.	Appoints effective committees	L	BA	A	AA	H	U

(continued)

Rating Scale 3-4 continued

22.	Encourages initiative and performance by delegating tasks effectively to others	L BA A AA H U
23.	Approaches problem solving on a systematic basis	L BA A AA H U

SCALE 4. PERSONAL SKILLS: refers to ease in establishing rapport, success in working with committees, and sensitivity to the contribution of others.

24.	Is receptive to constructive suggestions for change	L BA A AA H U
25.	Encourages initiative and innovation	L BA A AA H U
26.	Works well with committees	L BA A AA H U
27.	Gives proper and generous credit to others for their contributions	L BA A AA H U
28.	Establishes rapport easily and is approachable for counsel	L BA A AA H U

Developed by Texas Christian University, Fort Worth, Texas 76129. Used by permission. See Resources, p. 169, for further information and restrictions.

Rating Scale 3-5. Rating Scale for Academic Administration

Part I

Directions: Following is a list of personal and professional *qualities* generally considered to be desirable in administrators of colleges and universities. To obtain information that may lead to the improvement of administration, you are asked to rate the indicated administrator on each of these qualities. On the basis of your own experience and judgment, rate the administrator as high, fairly high, moderate, fairly low, or low in each quality by marking a cross (x) in the appropriate square on the right-hand side of the page.

[*Note:* Any Item which you regard as not applicable to this administrative position may be omitted.]

Administrator's Name and Title_____Date_____

	High	Fairly High	Moderate	Fairly Low	Low
1. Interest in the Progress of Education	☐	☐	☐	☐	☐
2. Educational and Cultural Background	☐	☐	☐	☐	☐
3. Sympathetic Attitude Toward Students	☐	☐	☐	☐	☐
4. Fairness in Dealing with Students	☐	☐	☐	☐	☐
5. Considerate Attitude toward Faculty	☐	☐	☐	☐	☐
6. Fairness in Dealing with Faculty	☐	☐	☐	☐	☐
7. Self-adjustment and Sense of Humor	☐	☐	☐	☐	☐
8. Tolerance of New Ideas	☐	☐	☐	☐	☐
9. Trustworthiness (Honesty, Reliability)	☐	☐	☐	☐	☐
10. Skill in Securing Group Action	☐	☐	☐	☐	☐
11. Ability to Inspire Confidence	☐	☐	☐	☐	☐
12. Ability to Organize	☐	☐	☐	☐	☐
13. Ability to Evaluate Faculty Performance	☐	☐	☐	☐	☐
14. Ability to Maintain Faculty Morale	☐	☐	☐	☐	☐
15. Appearance (Appropriate Dress, Grooming)	☐	☐	☐	☐	☐

Part II

Directions: Following is a list of activities that relate to the methods employed by the administrator in performing his or her administrative work. You are asked to rate the administrator on the relative degree to which you consider that he or she engages in these activities or applies these methods.

	High	Fairly High	Moderate	Fairly Low	Low
16. Encourages Democratic Participation	☐	☐	☐	☐	☐

(continued)

Rating Scale 3–5 continued

17. Communicates Effectively with Group Members	☐	☐	☐	☐	☐
18. Presents Appropriate Materials for Group Action	☐	☐	☐	☐	☐
19. Adheres Faithfully to Group Decisions	☐	☐	☐	☐	☐
20. Respects Professional Rights of Faculty	☐	☐	☐	☐	☐
21. Assigns Work Fairly and Suitably	☐	☐	☐	☐	☐
22. Makes Fair Decisions on Promotions and Salary	☐	☐	☐	☐	☐
23. Makes Contributions to His Academic Field	☐	☐	☐	☐	☐
24. Uses Generally Appropriate Administrative Methods	☐	☐	☐	☐	☐
25. Overall Rating of Administrator	☐	☐	☐	☐	☐

Rating Scale 3-6.   Evaluation of Administrator

Name of administrator: _____

Directions: Please circle the appropriate number for each item. Forward this evaluation to the Dean of Instruction when completed.

5 = Superior
4 = Above average
3 = Average
2 = Below average
1 = Poor
0 = Not applicable or not observed

Communications

1. Keeps staff informed of institutional policies, procedures, and activities.   5 4 3 2 1 0
2. Explains rationale for administrative actions and decisions.   5 4 3 2 1 0
3. Acknowledges and considers faculty questions, complaints, suggestions, and requests.   5 4 3 2 1 0
4. Creates uninhibited atmosphere of free communication— upward from faculty.   5 4 3 2 1 0
5. Creates uninhibited atmosphere of free communication— downward from administrator.   5 4 3 2 1 0

Management

6. When appropriate, takes action upon faculty questions, complaints, suggestions, and requests.   5 4 3 2 1 0
7. Involves individuals or groups in decision making related to their working conditions, including scheduling, physical plant, class size, team composition, etc.   5 4 3 2 1 0
8. Knows and makes effective use of talents and interests of his staff.   5 4 3 2 1 0
9. Acknowledges and rewards competence and dedication with praise and support.   5 4 3 2 1 0
10. Helpful in the procurement of educational materials.   5 4 3 2 1 0

Instructional Leadership

11. Objectively counsels staff members on instructional problems in a professional manner.   5 4 3 2 1 0
12. Stimulates experimentation and innovation by presenting recommendations of his staff for consideration by the Instructional Dean's Council.   5 4 3 2 1 0
13. Helpful and constructive in evaluations of faculty based on classroom observations.   5 4 3 2 1 0
14. Allows and encourages staff members free exchange of ideas and professional discretion in teaching activities.   5 4 3 2 1 0
15. Commitment to the institutional philosophy.   5 4 3 2 1 0

Comments

(continued)

Rating Scale 3-6 continued

16. What do you think makes this person an effective administrator?

17. How do you feel this administrator could increase his effectiveness?

Developed by Moraine Valley Community College, Palos Hills, Illinois 60565. Used by permission. See Resources, p. 169, for further information and restrictions.

Rating Scale 3-7. A Questionnaire for Department Faculty Evaluation of Chairman or Department Head

A Preliminary Draft Compiled for Discussion by the Faculty

1. How would you rate the leadership abilities of the present chairman or department head in terms of the academic profession as a whole (statewide, national and international)?

1	2	3	4	5	6
very superior	superior	average	mediocre		very mediocre

2. How would you rate the leadership abilities of the present chairman or department head in terms of stimulating scholarly activity by the faculty of this department?

1	2	3	4	5	6
very superior	superior	average	mediocre		very mediocre

3. How would you rate the leadership abilities of the present chairman or department head in terms of curriculum development within this department?

1	2	3	4	5	6
very superior	superior	average	mediocre		very mediocre

4. How would you rate the present chairman or department head in terms of the procurement of improved physical plant (teaching classrooms and laboratories, research and office facilities)?

1	2	3	4	5	6
very superior	superior	average	mediocre		very mediocre

5. Do you believe that the present chairman or department head commands the respect of most of the faculty members and staff of this department?

1	2	3	4	5	6
very superior	superior	average	mediocre		very mediocre

6. Does the present chairman or department head have abilities to develop and manage budgets and finances for the successful operation of this department?

1	2	3	4	5	6
very superior	superior	average	mediocre		very mediocre

7. Do you believe that the present chairman or department head is seriously committed to the professional goals of this department?

1	2	3	4	5	6
To a maximum extent		To a moderate extent			To a minimum extent

8. Has the present chairman or department head been seriously committed to the pursuit of scholarly and professional activities during his term of office?

1	2	3	4	5	6
To a maximum extent		Only to a moderate extent			To a minimum extent

9. Does the present chairman or department head encourage controversy in areas pedagogical and scholarly?

1	2	3	4	5	6
To a maximum extent		Only to a moderate extent			To a minimum extent

10. Do you believe that the present chairman or department head has the ability to delegate authority to his colleagues in this department with confidence and respect?

1	2	3	4	5	6
To a maximum extent		To a moderate extent			To a minimum extent

11. Do you believe that the present chairman or department head is seriously committed in assisting the scholarly and professional growth and development of most members of this department?

1	2	3	4	5	6
To a maximum extent		To a moderate extent			To a minimum extent

(continued)

Rating Scale 3-7 continued

12. Has the present chairman or department head encouraged evaluation of current curricula by colleagues in other institutions of higher learning in the United States or other English speaking countries?

1	2	3	4	5	6
To a maximum extent		To a moderate extent			Not at all

13. Does the present chairman or department head encourage sabbatical leaves or leaves of absence to enhance the professional enrichment and growth within the faculty of this department?

1	2	3	4	5	6
To a maximum extent		To a moderate extent			To a minimum extent

14. Do you believe that the present chairman or department head is seriously committed to the scholarly growth and development of the university?

1	2	3	4	5	6
To a maximum extent		To a moderate extent			To a minimum extent

15. Has the present chairman or department head operated successfully under the rules established in the "bylaws" of his college as well as those established by the university as a whole?

1	2	3	4	5	6
To a maximum extent		To a moderate extent			To a minimum extent

16. Do you believe that the present chairman or department head has enjoyed his position as it has been constituted during the past five years?

1	2	3	4	5	6
To a maximum extent		To a moderate extent			To a minimum extent

17. In comparison with other department chairmen or department heads under whom you have served, how would you rate the present chairman or department head?

1	2	3	4	5	6
very superior	superior	average	mediocre	very mediocre	

18. Do you believe that there are any members of the department faculty as now constituted who could perform as well as, or possibly better than, the present chairman or department head?

1	2	3	4	5	6
More than 5	5	4	3	1-2	none

19. In cases involving non-reappointment of faculty members, has the present chairman or department head operated according to the rules and procedures established by the "bylaws" of the university?

1	2	3	4	5	6
To a maximum extent		To a moderate extent			To a minimum extent

20. To your knowledge how many member of the faculty of this department have resigned to accept positions at other institutions during the tenure of office of the present chairman or department head?

1	2	3	4	5	6
More than 10	8-9	6-7	4-5	1-3	none

21. To your knowledge how many members of the faculty and staff of this department have been "fired", not reappointed, or forced to resign, during the tenure of office of the present chairman or department head?

1	2	3	4	5	6
More than 5	4-5	3	2	1	none

(continued)

Rating Scale 3-7 continued

22. To your knowledge has the present chairman or department head exhibited examples of behavior toward members of this faculty or staff that could in any way be interpreted as "unethical"?

1	2	3	4	5	6
Frequently		On some occasions			Absolutely not

23. To your knowledge has the present chairman or department head exhibited any examples of behavior that indicates a vindictive attitude toward any members of the faculty and staff of this department?

1	2	3	4	5	6
On numerous occasions		On some occasions			Never

24. Do you believe that the present chairman or department head behaves in a humane and gentlemanly fashion in relations with most faculty members and staff of this department?

1	2	3	4	5	6
To a considerable extent		To a moderate extent			Not at all

25. Do you believe that the present chairman or department head is seriously concerned and committed to an impartial treatment of all members of the faculty and staff of this department?

1	2	3	4	5	6
To a maximum extent		To a moderate extent			Not at all

26. Do you believe that the present chairman or department head has behaved in a manner favoring certain members of the faculty to the exclusion of other members of the faculty?

1	2	3	4	5	6
To a maximum extent		To a moderate extent			Not at all

27. Has the present chairman or department head established, or advocated the establishment of well defined "rules of procedure" for the conduct of business and operations of this department?

1	2	3	4	5	6
To a maximum extent		To some extent			Not at all

28. Do you believe that the present chairman or department head would behave independently in behalf of any member of this department's faculty and staff when faced with a situation which could involve the Dean of the College or other members of the higher administrations of this university?

1	2	3	4	5	6
To a maximum extent		To a moderate extent			Absolutely not

29. Overall, do you believe that the present chairman or department head has performed satisfactorily in this position during the past five years?

1	2	3	4	5	6
Excellent		About average			Unsatisfactory

Developed by Benjamin H. Banta at the United States International University, San Diego, CA, 1974. Used by permission. See Resources, p. 169, for further information and restrictions.

Rating Scale 3–8.   Professional Staff Evaluation of Assistant Dean for Student Programs

Instructions: Please rate from 1 to 5 (5 being the highest rating) the Assistant Dean in the areas listed by circling the appropriate number.

I.   Communication

   A. To what degree does he keep you informed about developments within the Student Affairs area and in other areas of the University?

             1   2   3   4   5

   B. How effectively does he communicate with you about matters affecting your area within the scope of the total program?

             1   2   3   4   5

   C. With what degree of proficiency does he represent you by communicating your concerns and needs to the Vice-President and other appropriate officials?

             1   2   3   4   5

   D. How well does he promote and facilitate communication among staff in the Student Programs area?

             1   2   3   4   5

   E. How would you rate him with respect to his initiative, openness, and interest in communicating with you as an individual staff member?

             1   2   3   4   5

II.   Budgeting and Financial Management

   A. How closely does he consult with staff in your area regarding budget?

             1   2   3   4   5

   B. With what degree of understanding does he explore, recognize and assess the budgetary needs of your area?

             1   2   3   4   5

   C. How effective is he in obtaining an adequate budget for your program?

             1   2   3   4   5

   D. How thoroughly and promptly does he process requests for expenditures?

             1   2   3   4   5

   E. To what extent does he follow up on pending budgetary matters?

             1   2   3   4   5

   F. With what degree of effectiveness does he provide feedback on budgetary decisions?

             1   2   3   4   5

III.   Staff and Program Development

   A. To what degree does he demonstrate interest in you as an individual professional staff member, encourage your professional development, and recognize your progress?

             1   2   3   4   5

   B. How effectively does he encourage and facilitate the development of a comprehensive, sound and consistent philosophy for the area?

             1   2   3   4   5

   C. How receptive is he to proposals for new programs and revisions of existing programs and practices?

             1   2   3   4   5

(continued)

Rating Scale 3–8 continued

D. With what degree of effectiveness does he promote the formulation of appropriate goals and objectives for the area, utilizing the resources of the total staff as well as making contributions to the process?

1   2   3   4   5

E. How effective is he in the selection, orientation, and evaluation of staff members?

1   2   3   4   5

F. To what extent does he plan and encourage others to provide opportunities for staff and program development?

1   2   3   4   5

IV. Implementation of Programs

A. How knowledgeable is he about people, policies and processes in the University?

1   2   3   4   5

B. To what degree does he encourage and facilitate coordination:
   1. Among the sections of Student Programs?   1 2 3 4 5
   2. With other areas of Student Affairs?   1 2 3 4 5
   3. With other parts of the University?   1 2 3 4 5

C. How effectively does he administer programs keeping in mind identified goals, the good of the area and the institution, valid principles of student personnel administration, and the welfare of students?

1   2   3   4   5

D. How fully and efficiently does he utilize the staff and other resources in implementing evaluation of programs?

1   2   3   4   5

E. To what degree does he encourage, facilitate and implement evaluation of programs?

1   2   3   4   5

F. How fairly and equitably does he make decisions?

1   2   3   4   5

V. Comments regarding your overall evaluation of the Assistant Dean, including any suggestions for improvement you may wish to offer:

Developed by Ball State University, Muncie, Indiana 47306. Used by permission. See Resources, p. 169, for further information and restrictions.

Rating Scale 3-9. Self-Audit For Registrars

	Yes	No	Undecided	Unknown

II. Scheduling and Sectioning

A. The Class Schedule

1. Is the schedule of courses made available in sufficient time for all students to adequately plan their schedule of classes? ( ) ( ) ( ) ( )

2. Are schedules distributed to faculty and students? ( ) ( ) ( ) ( )
   a. from one location? ( ) ( ) ( ) ( )
   b. several locations? ( ) ( ) ( ) ( )
   c. mail? ( ) ( ) ( ) ( )
   d. other? ( ) ( ) ( ) ( )

3. In building the class schedule, is the Registrar:
   a. actively involved? ( ) ( ) ( ) ( )
   b. partly involved? ( ) ( ) ( ) ( )
   c. rarely involved? ( ) ( ) ( ) ( )

4. Is there provision for student input to the scheduling process? ( ) ( ) ( ) ( )

5. Is production of the class schedule:
   a. completely computerized? ( ) ( ) ( ) ( )
   b. manual with computer assistance? ( ) ( ) ( ) ( )
   c. completely manual? ( ) ( ) ( ) ( )

6. Could the class schedule be done better if it were computerized? ( ) ( ) ( ) ( )

B. Registration

1. During the registration period, does your office continue to provide its normal service? ( ) ( ) ( ) ( )

2. Is your registration period:
   a. too long? ( ) ( ) ( ) ( )
   b. too short? ( ) ( ) ( ) ( )
   c. just right? ( ) ( ) ( ) ( )

3. Do you feel it takes a student too long to complete the registration process including payment of fees, making of I.D., etc.? ( ) ( ) ( ) ( )

4. Do you have long lines of students:
   a. picking up registration materials? ( ) ( ) ( ) ( )
   b. registering for classes? ( ) ( ) ( ) ( )
   c. receiving counseling? ( ) ( ) ( ) ( )
   d. paying fees? ( ) ( ) ( ) ( )
   e. making I.D.'s? ( ) ( ) ( ) ( )
   f. other? ( ) ( ) ( ) ( )

5. Must a student receive his advisor's approval to register for his courses? ( ) ( ) ( ) ( )

(continued)

Rating Scale 3-9 continued

	Yes	No	Undecided	Unknown
B. Registration				
6. Does the student pay his registration fees prior to submitting his registration materials to you?	( )	( )	( )	( )
7. If a new section or a new class is opened during registration, are you adequately geared to inform students and faculty?	( )	( )	( )	( )
C. Forecasting, Planning, Facilities Utilization				
1. Are classroom assignments made:				
a. by the Registrar alone?	( )	( )	( )	( )
b. by division or school?	( )	( )	( )	( )
c. by an office of facilities?	( )	( )	( )	( )
d. by the Registrar in cooperation with one of these other officials?	( )	( )	( )	( )
2. Is the Registrar's enrollment data used to influence course offerings?	( )	( )	( )	( )
3. Does the Registrar participate in facilities utilization studies?	( )	( )	( )	( )
4. Does the Registrar's enrollment data influence curriculum development?	( )	( )	( )	( )

BASIC PRINCIPLE: The Registrar, by reason of the data obtained through various activities, is an authority on matters of schedules and curriculum management. Hopefully, he will be included in the development of these activities.

NOTES:

	Yes	No	Undecided	Unknown
C. Transcripts				
1. Are transcripts:				
a. issued to students upon request?	( )	( )	( )	( )
b. usually mailed within one working day?	( )	( )	( )	( )
c. self-explanatory?	( )	( )	( )	( )
d. a reflection of all classes attempted?	( )	( )	( )	( )
e. validated by hand process?	( )	( )	( )	( )
f. validated by use of a machine?	( )	( )	( )	( )
g. denied to a student if he has unpaid bills at the school?	( )	( )	( )	( )
h. reproduced by a permanent type copying process?	( )	( )	( )	( )
i. reproduced with in-progress course work listed?	( )	( )	( )	( )
j. available to faculty for advising purposes?	( )	( )	( )	( )

From *Self-Audit Manual for Registrars,* prepared under the sponsorship of the Kentucky Association of Collegiate Registrars and Admissions Officers, 1974. Used by permission. See Resources, p. 169, for further information and restrictions.

RESOURCES: RATING SCALES

Title	*Source (for further information contact)*
RS 3-1: The Instructional Functioning Inventory (IFI)	Nancy Beck, Associate Director Institutional Research Program for Higher Education Educational Testing Service Princeton, New Jersey 08540
RS3-2: Student Reactions to College (SRC)	Director, Community and Junior College Programs Educational Testing Service Princeton, New Jersey 08540
RS3-3: Administrator Evaluation Questionnaire, Trial Run Form RS3-4: Administrator Evaluation Questionnaire, Revised Form	Richard M. Fenker, Jr. Psychology Department Texas Christian University Fort Worth, Texas 76129
RS3-5: Rating Scale for Acacemic Administration (Revised)	Eugene D. Koplitz Psychology, Counseling and Guidance College of Education University of Northern Colorado Greeley, Colorado 80639
RS3-6: Evaluation of Administrator	Nelson W. Diebel, Adm. Asst. Moraine Valley Community College 10900 South 88th Avenue Palos Hills, Illinois 60465
RS3-7: A Questionnaire for Department Faculty Evaluation of Chairman or Department Head	Benjamin H. Banta 421 Santa Helena Solana Beach, California 92075
RS3-8: Professional Staff Evaluation of Assistant Dean for Student Programs	James Marine Assistant Dean for Student Programs Ball State University Muncie, Indiana 47306
RS3-9: Self-Audit for Registrars ($3.00) (Also available for $3.00 is a Self-Audit Manual for Admissions Officers)	James R. Sehr Sec./Treas. KACRAO Director of Admissions and Records Bellarmine College 2000 Norris Place Louisville, Kentucky 40205

Chapter Four

Faculty Evaluation in Competency-Based Educational Programs

PURPOSES AND BACKGROUND

The purposes of this chapter are as ambitious as its subject matter: a summary of the state of the art of faculty evaluation in educational programs that are competency-based. The chapter is intended to provide some answers and ask some questions about competency-based education in general, and faculty instructional performance in particular. Hopefully the reader will get some information regarding the purposes, sources and methods of faculty evaluation in competency-based programs, and will have increased access to reference materials related to faculty evaluation in competency-based education (CBE).

To deal with such a broad and complicated educational area as CBE, and the evaluation of faculty performance in CBE in the limited space of this book means unavoidable sacrifice of issues, concepts, and examples concerning this new, growing, and confused movement in American education. Readers, whether they be students, faculty, administrators, psychometricians, or interested others are encouraged to do CBE as well as to know it, and are invited to use the references in the appendix to learn more about this educational enterprise that has fascinating implications for all who teach and learn.

This chapter was developed by Mark T. Munger and his associates at McBer and Company of Boston, Massachusetts. Mr. Munger is Senior Associate of McBer and Company, an organization which promotes the theory and practice of Competency Based Education (CBE) in colleges, universities, and other institutions. Mr. Munger and other colleagues, working with David C. McClelland, Chairman of McBer and Professor of Psychology at Harvard University, have explored the utility and promise of assessing and "teaching" competence in a number of institutions of higher learning across the country. Mr. Munger, who holds degrees from Princeton and Harvard Universities, has evaluated instructional performance in schools and universities in the United States and abroad, and is interested in educational programs for adults which improve performance. He has served as consultant to a variety of competency-based educational efforts and hopes that both research in the assessment of competence, and the development and implementation of competency-based programs will be helpful for educators and educatees.

For our purposes, a competence is that combination of knowledge, skills, values and attitudes a person can be certified to possess, based on set of criteria critical to the performance of a task.[a] Competency-based educational programs by and large identify areas in which faculty and administrators think students should be competent, and then try to teach students to become competent.[b]

By definition, a competence is a broad mix of skills and represents a range of behaviors. Competence in a task, job, or role often demands the integration of a number of abilities. Although the list which follows does not represent empirical research into the competencies of the most successful faculty members in competency-based programs, it is at least a partial estimate, and illustrates what is meant by competence:

Competencies Related to Faculty Performance

Competency	*Tasks for which needed*
Listening skills	Meeting with, advising, counseling students
Presentation skills	Lecturettes, lectures, information sharing
Problem-solving skills	"Contracting" with, working with students on learning paths
Empathy	Making contact with non-traditional, as well as traditional students
Skill in diagnosing student learning styles	Supervising student progress, designing learning experiences/curricula
Perseverance	Dealing with adversity in new situation, new and unfamiliar problems
Positive expectations of people	Advising, counseling, teaching students, working with colleagues and administrators in difficult situations
Analysis of argument	Problem-solving situations, class meetings, meetings with individuals for evaluation

The movement toward CBE is full of conflicting theories and perceptions about what a competency is, how to measure it, and how to develop it. While it is difficult to evaluate faculty performance in more traditional arenas of education, the task is complicated enormously by the newness of the field. The scientific and research base of this kind of educational endeavor is small

[a]For another perspective, see Chickering (1974).

[b]How one assesses, measures, or teaches the mix of skills and abilities that underlie competence raises important and provocative issues as more and more educators look to competency-based education as an alternative methodology to meet alternative educational needs.

but developing, but at this early stage is inconclusive. In a broad context of disagreement over terms, procedures, and outcomes of CBE, there is agreement only on the need to evaluate student and instructor performance, with widely disparate opinions on how that might or should be done.

At the heart of CBE is the desire to produce specific kinds of performance linked to real-life situations and opportunities, such as speaking a language. The Berlitz schools of language have operated for some time as an example of a commercial competency-based program. Contrast these statements from the Berlitz brochure, with statements about language learning in most university, college, or community college catalogs: "You begin speaking your new language from the first minute of instruction." "You learn to think in your new language." These are performance measures related to *doing,* with the specific outcome of speaking a language.

In this context CBE is perceived as a route towards the relevance of education, often missed by students, faculty, and administrators who are unable to see clear connections between what they do and important life outcomes. The competency-based movements fits neatly into the current press for educational accountability on the part of educators, state legislators, and the general public, including, of course, students as consumers of educational programs. This press for accountability, linked to politicized attention to fiscal issues in education, is particularly apparent in the efforts of numerous state departments of education to develop more effective certification procedures and standards for teachers. With roots in the teacher education programs, CBE has expanded into a variety of educational settings.

In its present and evolving form CBE has a number of historical antecedents and modern educational cousins. The apprenticeship form of learning, practiced in some forms of professional education, deals with doing as well as knowing. Whether the mode be union apprenticeships or internships the rationale is similar: people can often learn by doing, and can demonstrate what they can do. The movement towards increased experiential learning supports the notion of different kinds of competence necessary for performance of differentiated tasks. Although CBE is not career, or vocational, education in the strict sense of the word, there is some similarity in their objectives such as being able to conceptualize performance standards, and the route taken is sometimes similar to those found in cooperative education programs, or in more recent shifts to modular curricula.

It is also expected that an increasing number of community colleges will develop competency-based programs because of prior activity in the area of individualized instruction, career education, and continuing education.

Before dealing with the issues of evaluation of instructional performance in competency-based programs, it may be useful to look at the characteristics of CBE and explore some of the differences between CBE and more traditional educational programs described elsewhere in this book.

In most competency-based programs, emphasis is placed upon students meeting standards related to general performance in jobs and life. Students progress at different rates, on individual routes toward competence. The criteria applied in the assessment of student competencies are public, explicit, and sometimes negotiable. Instruction appears to be quite individualized, as training and instructional decisions are related to the successful attainment of competence, and individual programs are designed for students in passage toward being able to do something, Finally, while students are held accountable for meeting criteria in order to be certified as competent, faculty members are held accountable for the effectiveness of their planned programs to assist students in the development of competence.

It may be necessary here to make a distinction between competency-based instruction and performance objectives. Competency-based programs are designed to promote the ability to do in global terms, in regard to a broad mix of skills, rather than the accomplishment of one particular task. For example, one might be interested in developing the ability to persuade an audience, which might be considered a competency, rather than the ability to organize thoughts on a three-by-five card, which is a specific objective. Competencies reflect a mix of skills, and are open to a broad range of evaluation techniques. Finally, a competency-based program is centered on the learner and the tasks required to attain a certain level of performance, while objectives suggest a focus on the teacher and the tasks required to bring a learner to a certain level of performance.

The following list attempts to illustrate the difference between a competence (a broad mix of skills, integrated into a whole), and a performance indicator (a more specific, observable commodity).

Competence	Performance indicator
Listening skills	Accurate paraphrase of a student's statement, accurate perception of *affect* (i.e. feeling) as well as content.
Problem-solving skills	A student learning contract, with obstacles accurately anticipated.
Empathy	Number of nontraditional (or traditional) student advisees who seek out and maintain contact with faculty member in advisory relationship.

Educators familiar with the field have seen promise in competency-based educational programs. When asked about advantages, they sepak in terms of the connection between competency attainment and life outcomes not normally associated with or related to education, such as learning how to solve problems or use resources. Students and faculty often make a specific contract around performance. With a sharper focus on objectives than found in many traditional curricula, competency-based programs often try to match the training of students with their own personal and professional goals. They argue that it is possible to pay more attention to individual differences in learning styles and focus energy on performance rather than exposure to materials. Because of the degree of individual assessment and feedback essential to competency-based programs, a learner of any age should be able to attain competence. Instructional routes are highly flexible with teacher and learner sharing responsibility for competency attainment. Evaluation deals with performance and not just the acquisition of a knowledge base. The evaluation process may be said to be less arbitrary and mysterious than some traditional evaluation procedures, since the competencies are public knowledge. In this context assessment and evaluation can be used as a tool in a management information system to help determine the allocation of institutional resources. However, as in more traditional educational programs, the evaluation problem still surfaces: to date, in the field of CBE, there is no demonstrated relationship between teacher behavior and performance and student behavior and performance—the educational outcomes.

Disadvantages present but not necessarily inherent in CBE are problems of cost (at this point start-up costs seem to be at least 25 percent more expensive than traditional programs), support for and training of faculty to new roles and responsibilities, scheduling and other administrative problems, and protests from teachers, unions, and others who argue that CBE is reductionistic, simplistic, and not real education. Not only are basic maintenance costs higher, but multisource, multimethod forms of evaluation will be more costly as well. One can also predict that some students will become upset if they find that their performance in a competency-based program has the consequences that they do not or cannot become competent, and are evaluated more strictly than in the more ambiguous realm of degree programs based on some level of content mastery. Finally, there is the problem of the definition of competence. Individuals, faculties, and institutions differ on what is meant by competence and how competence might be assessed. This difference in definition may be thought of as the difference between a rational approach to competence and an empirical approach. Briefly stated, a rational competency is that set of skills or abilities that a well-intentioned and qualified individual (or group of individuals) thinks is critical to the performance of a certain task. It may go beyond the guesswork that surrounds the estimation of abilities required for successful performance in a number of occupations, but it is basically an informed prescription about what a person *should* be able to do to perform with competence.

Opposed to this is what one might call an empirical competency, a set or mix of skills and abilities that are actually evidenced in performance, through observation, analysis, and self-description, and which distinguish superior performers from average or poor performers. An empirical competency is the behavior exhibited which matches the criteria drawn from what superior performers actually do in the completion of a task.

The lack of unanimity among faculty members, students and administrators about the rational or empirical definition of competence has led to some misunderstandings and fragmentation in the competency-based movement. Lack of agreement clearly hinders faculty evaluation, as will become apparent.

FACULTY EVALUATION

At the present time, evaluation methods and procedures used in competency-based educational programs vary among institutions and, as one might expect, are not standardized. Most of the procedures resemble those evaluation methodologies used in more traditional settings, and to date educators have not been able to devise new ways of measuring performance in this setting. If one concept were picked to describe the common theme of evaluation methodologies in CBE, that concept would be joint effort. In many if not most of the institutions experimenting with competency-based programs, evaluation is conducted by faculty, administration, and, indirectly, students, as all are engaged in learning more about the system in which they try to function.

A number of competency-based institutions have postponed decisions related to the evaluation of faculty performance for the present, because of the difficulties of the measurement process for both students and faculty. Instead they have concentrated on staff and faculty development programs to provide support and training for faculty members who find themselves moving through strange and uncharted waters without proper navigational equipment.

One can guess that a certain amount of evaluation takes place, at least for administrative, career, and professional reasons related to salary, promotion, and tenure. In the absence of clear guidelines about new evaluation techniques for a new situation, decisions about salary and promotion are probably based on the assumptions and information that have been used and continue to be used as bases for decision-making in more traditional post-secondary academic institutions. Whether or not new forms of evaluation will influence hiring and firing remains, of course, to be seen.

Responses to the problem of evaluation have been as varied as the institutions themselves are widespread. In California, many of the state institutions engaged in teacher training and education have tried to enhance the kinds and amounts of resources available to instructors in those programs. In Ohio, Bowling Green University has instituted a competency-based faculty development program. In Massachusetts, Hampshire College has used federal funds to develop faculty competencies in the assessment of students. McAlester College in St. Paul, Minnesota, has tried to increase cross-disciplinary cooperation among its faculty members, and improve instruction by incorporating new competencies into instructional methodologies. The University of California at Riverside is in the process of developing a competency-based certification program in human services, education, and public safety, for which faculty retraining will be essential.

As each institution develops its competency-based program it comes to grips with the issue of faculty performance. At this point in time there is no prototype, no one example to which others in the field may look for guidance, and each institution is proceeding primarily on its own, although some efforts at coordination have been made. As mentioned, one reason for this eclectic approach is the difficulty in coming to agreement on the nature of competency assessment.

Use of an empirical competency model would help individuals and institutions to reach a kind of agreement. However, there is a preference—and a useful one—within the CBE movement for multimethod, multisource evaluation, of which the empirical competency model is one choice, and a choice not yet widely known or adopted. It differs from others in that it ends potentially endless discussion about what a rational competency is. That rational competency, like beauty, exists in the mind of the beholder, and is subject to change according to the nature and inclinations of the beholder(s). An empirical competency model is data-based, easily tested, and also can be used to predict performance. If applied to faculty performance it might help deal with some of the questions that now prove so troubling.

PURPOSES OF FACULTY EVALUATION

The purposes of evaluation in CBE remain vague but important. Most colleges and universities using CBE in one form or another are anxious to learn from experience, and one clear purpose of faculty evaluation is institutional research—the institution trying to learn about itself. How good is the teaching? Are student needs being met? Is the institution really helping people become competent?

A second broad purpose is related to client needs. As many of the competency-based programs address professional and semi- or paraprofessional concerns, individuals involved in such programs evaluate faculty to help determine the quality of the outcomes they deliver—students. There is an assumption that in order for the students to be competent, the faculty must be able to judge them as competent, and accordingly the faculty must be competent to do that. Accordingly, much of the evaluation of faculty has to do with how well or how poorly faculty members can assess rather than necessarily instruct.

A third *de facto* purpose of faculty evaluation is to enable students to be influential in determining some of the routes of their educational progress. Many of the competency-based programs are designed for older, or nontraditional students who are more accustomed to exercising influence than younger and less experienced undergraduates. Evaluating faculty both helps students get more or better attention from the faculty, and helps to equalize the faculty-student relationship.

Because CBE is so new, evaluation of faculty performance is conducted both to determine program effectiveness and suggest training needs. As will develop later in this chapter, the faculty role changes in most competency-based programs, and evaluation of performance in the new role helps faculty and administrators to assess departments in order to provide training or support.

Individual faculty members can initiate different forms of evaluation or different application procedures as they consider their own professional development. Many faculty members in CBE are determined to scrutinize their own performance, particularly if they are working in pedagogical areas in which they lack familiarity or experience.

Lastly, questions of promotion and tenure occur in the competency-based world as well as in more traditional academic groves, and the situation is perhaps even more charged because, as mentioned previously, there is little agreement about what competent performance in CBE means. Time-honored academic benchmarks—such as publications—still exist, but new task functions have been added, and the politics of tenure are now called accountability in competency-based programs.

Many of the institutions, being relatively new, are just beginning to deal with promotion. At older institutions, where some faculty are already tenured, evaluation has more institutional then personal meaning. There are no easy alternatives, as accountability has many faces. Here again, an empirical model of competency is directly related to the stated goals and objectives of most competency-based educational programs, particularly in the context of faculty competence. Applied to an entire faculty, the information collected would suggest the allocation of scarce resources for faculty training and development in areas of weakness, and also identify areas of strength for individuals and groups alike. It is a more useful diagnostic tool for faculty and student self-development. Finally, because of a scientific base and methodology, the procedure begins to shed some light on the basic ingredients of teaching and learning, namely: How does instructor behavior influence learner behavior?

SOURCES OF EVALUATION

Sources for faculty evaluation have widened in most competency-based educational efforts. For example, there is a group of what might be called authority sources currently evaluating performance related to the development of the rational competencies. Those sources are the individual; the recipients of competence (patients, students, etc.) practitioners of the competence (patients, students, etc.) practitioners of the competence (other faculty members, employers, experts in the field, and government, state boards and agencies, etc.).

This pattern is somewhat similar to the traditional sources of faculty evaluation: peers and colleagues, students, administrators, and the profession or discipline at large. The broadening of this base for evaluation puts additional demands on faculty members, and raises methodological questions.

For example, many of the individuals who are called in to comment directly or indirectly on student or faculty performance may not speak a common language of competency, and in fact may be using points of reference far different from the criteria employed by others to evaluate the same performance. It is difficult to understand or demonstrate the relationship between courses (materials, readings, writings, experiences, etc.) and the development of competencies in students which will be critical to the performance of minor or major tasks in real-life situations.

Individuals responsible for faculty and staff development in some of the more innovative competency-based programs in different parts of the country allege that CBE is too new, too experimental, to have developed faculty evaluation measures. They indicate that there appear to be major differences between the roles, tasks, and abilities associated with superior performance in more traditional academic settings, and the roles, tasks, and abilities that have surfaced in speculation about superior instruction in competency-based programs. In the new mix of skills required of an instructor, key abilities seem to include the capacity to design new instructional formats or paths to competence, the ability to accurately assess and diagnose student progress toward competence, and the ability to assist students, in a variation of the counseling role, to set goals and use resources available to them. Faculty members in some competency-based programs have been asked to expand their repertoires of teaching styles, and in some cases faculty members have been cautious and wary of moving into instructional areas in which they have little background or training.

What are these new faculty abilities desirable in the climate of CBE? It is important to examine the set of tasks and responsibilities that appear to be inherent in most of the competency-based programs that have been developed.

THE COACH/MENTOR ROLE

A significant role change common to most competency-based educational programs is apparent. Whatever the faculty person did before, in terms of teaching, research, and service, it now seems that the faculty member is required to take on and master an additional set of abilities. With all the varying definitions of what an instructor was asked to be or do in a traditional setting of a college, community college, or university, that person is now asked to be a *coach/mentor.* Indeed, much talk related to evaluation of faculty performance centers on how well the faculty member can perform in that role.[c]

[c]The coach/mentor role is challenging because of differences in assumptions about teaching and learning that differentiate CBE from more traditional liberal arts, professional

In terms of specific differences, coach/mentors tend to lecture less and deal less with large groups of students. Instead they have more one-to-one contact with students, and evaluate students in areas in addition to content mastery. They need interpersonal skills because of the advising and counseling required in the role: it is important to be an effective and empathic listener.

They must be flexible themselves, to match teaching styles with learning styles. For example, if the instructor is trained to lecture with wit and wisdom, and yet very few students attend lectures or find lectures a useful learning experience, that instructor will have to reassess one of the things he or she does well, but without reward.

The coach/mentor role requires that instructors possess diagnostic skills, to help students assess their levels of mastery of a particular competence. In order to diagnose accurately the coach/mentor may need some observational skills not often taught in graduate schools. From that diagnosis the instructor may then be asked to design and recommend a learning experience that will facilitate student attainment of competence.

Because emphasis in CBE is on student performance rather than exposure to faculty, the coach/mentor role demands a fair degree of tolerance and ability to use feedback about personal performance, to better meet student needs. It is an ability to make contact with students, to set moderate goals that are realistic and can be measured and time-phased, which may distinguish superior instructors from those individuals who also teach in competency-based programs but fall back on styles and methodologies that were successful for them in more tightly structured or traditional educational settings, but in CBE might block change in students and in themselves. The bias here is clear, and should be stated clearly: a coach/mentor plays a less directive, less judgmental role than traditional instructors play in their direction and evaluation of student learning. The coach/mentor has the task of helping students find learning experiences that help them to develop broad bands of skills related to real-life performance. It is no easy order.

Separate perhaps from the coach/mentor role, but important in the process of CBE, are tasks related to measurement and assessment. To return for a moment to the distinction between rational and empirical competencies, it is possible for an individual or a jury, or some other unit to make determinations about the presence or absence of a rational competence in a student's performance—"I know it when I see it." The measurement issues associated with empirical competencies are more elaborate, and require a new technology. Because the process of determining the validity and reliability of testing instru-

---

or vocational educational programs. Interestingly, educators interested in the training and support of coach/mentors suggest that certain attributes of the role would be beneficial for individuals now teaching in a wide range of post-secondary institutions. The value of the role, and some of the benefits inherent in the role, should not, in other words, be limited just to those engaged in CBE.

ments to determine competence requires sophisticated statistical analysis, it is unrealistic to think that individual faculty members will be able to either construct test instruments or analyze data that would have general applicability. One can think, however, of an assessment department that could provide such technical expertise to individuals, groups, or departments in a college or university, who were interested in the development of empirical competency mea- or faculty.

METHODS OF EVALUATION

What seems to be most common in the evaluation methodologies developed in competency-based programs is the use of many different sources and many different methods to derive a common vision of faculty performance. Student rating scales, peer ratings, administrator ratings, and self-ratings are all employed, and sometimes simultaneously. Some institutions are complementing direct observation with videotaped recordings of faculty performance, while other encourage colleagues to sit with one another and comment on performance. Before an enumeration of common practices, it is worth an examination of three different institutions practicing CBE to get a specific idea of some of the evaluation procedures currently in use.

These three colleges—Empire State College in New York, Alverno College in Milwaukee, and the College for Human Services in Nw York City—have taken quite different approaches to CBE, and yield some interesting information as examples of what is being done regarding the evaluation of faculty instructional performance.

At all three of the institutions, faculty evaluation is at a rudimentary stage. The institutions themselves are too new, still in fact in experimental stages, for a great deal of data on faculty performance to be available or systematically scrutinized. While faculty evaluation is important, as an issue it ranks somewhere in the middle of the range of issues each college has established as most deserving of attention. Each college, too, has had a preparation period of some duration to deal with new and unfamiliar aspects of CBE, and one would guess that there has been a self-selection process regarding the kinds of faculty members who are interested in being part of such a program or such an institution.

At Empire State, faculty training has involved an introduction to skills required in the practice of CBE in that particular institution. Faculty members are viewed as mentors and there have been attempts both to study and describe the mentor role for incoming faculty. While the competencies desirable in faculty members many are not necessarily aritculated and are subject to perceptual differences in interpretation, faculty members are expected to be adept at negotiating a contract with a student, and to be sensitive listeners to students' needs and agendas as they collaboratively design an individualized program of learning experiences. While it is assumed that faculty members will bring with them some traditional academic skills, the college believes that training and support are necessary for faculty members to acquire new skills, such as being able to assess experiential learning by students in nontraditional settings. There is a faculty effort now to develop cases in the areas of contracting, evaluation, and assessment, and to supplement those cases with videotaped recordings of mentor-student interactions. These exist for modeling purposes, however, rather than as part of an evaluation system. As Empire State College evolves and acquires a history, a more formal process of evaluating faculty instructional performance will probably surface.

At Alverno College in Milwaukee there is similarly no systematic evaluation of faculty at present. Members of the faculty and administration do look at faculty activities, how faculty members spend their time, and there is evaluation of faculty performance with indirect feedback; i.e., inferences are made about faculty in relation to outstanding student performance, but to date there is no formal evaluation process. Like other colleges there is some assessment made from inputs—how many students take courses, how many students pass their competencies, etc., but there is little direct control over assessment procedures, either of students or of faculty.

Alverno has instituted a series of faculty development workshops to help faculty members expand their repertoires of teaching skills and styles, and to develop additional resources to assist faculty in areas, intellectual or behavioral, in which they are unfamiliar. Like Empire State, Alverno hopes to make videotape recordings of faculty performance, to observe behavior, and to begin to make links between the kinds of learning experiences that appear to be related to the development of competencies in students. At Alverno there is a continuing effort to be explicit about skills that are necessary, and the activities that enhance those skills. Alverno's definition of mentor differs somewhat from that in practice at Empire State, with more emphasis on key characteristics desired in each faculty member—the abilities to design learning experiences, assess students, and be of assistance to students. While faculty evaluation does not yet rest on the development of these characteristics, it seems likely that individuals at Alverno will continue to regard these areas as fundamental to successful performance as an instructor.

At the College for Human Services in New York City there is a great deal of awareness of major differences between traditional teaching and teaching in a competency-based educational program, characterized in diagnostic terms as the separation of what a faculty person thinks a student *should* know, or wants the student to know, and empirical evidence as to what a student *needs* to know. Faculty development efforts are centered on assisting a faculty member to respond to the needs, but there is feeling that the assessment system is too new to provide much information about faculty performance. The mix of skills now articulated for faculty, that of mentor, assessor, and practitioner may be peculiar to the preparation and training of human service workers, and the college is paying attention to assessment of students by clients of the students as an additional perspective on faculty performance. There are questions, also common to more traditional programs, as to how much weight to assign to student performance, whether it be outstanding or inadequate, and how much weight to give to student feelings for or perceptions of faculty members. There is the realization that in order for faculty members to become successful and competent in their new roles they will require training and support. In this respect evaluation of faculty will probably be linked directly to training needs.

As these examples suggest, evaluation of faculty has not traveled very far. Faculty members, peers, and students offer their assessment of faculty performance, and individual faculty members make educated guesses about what they do well or not so well, based on their contact with students and groups of students. In contrast to the documentation, references, and suggestions of other chapters in this book, the measures, instruments, or procedures for evaluation in CBE are simply not as available as they are in more conventional academic programs.

In part, an assessment of faculty performance depends on faculty task. There is considerable debate if faculty members can or should be evaluated on student performance, a debate not dissimilar to that taking place in other educational settings. In New York State, the Board of Regents has developed a policy to hold faculty accountable for student performance, but has then hedged its bet by indicating that it may not be possible to determine levels of student performance at this time. In the absence of empirical outcomes for students, and with a host of factors that cloud the process, the desirability of evaluating faculty on student performance diminishes until underlying issues can be settled. This lack of empirical outcome measures of student performance hinders faculty assessment, because as of now one person's notion of competence may be another's idea of dysfunctional behavior; but there is little way of connecting curricular or pedagogical practice, no matter how innovative, with specific performance outcomes. It will be some time before the development and use of empirical competency measures become widespread.

A NEW APPROACH TO EVALUATION

If new measures are not yet available, it is still desirable to evaluate faculty performance in competency-based instruction. At present, administrators, faculty, students, and others are placed in the familiar but still embarrassing position of trying to evaluate one set of behaviors, or desirable behaviors, with tools and methodologies designed for another situation or climate. Unfortunately, some of these evaluation procedures may not be particularly informative or useful, even in settings which then were developed or practiced.

In the position of an evaluator of performance, consider the job and role of a filling station attendant. A group of drivers could sit down, and without a lot of difficulty list off the kinds of tasks such a person is asked to perform in the average filling station. One can think of pumping gas, wiping windshields, and checking oil, as some of the jobs an attendant does. In order to do those jobs, one might make the rational assumption that a person would have to be able to unscrew a gas cap, make change, distinguish between different types of automobiles, etc., and the list can go on and on, until it is highly reductionistic. Given the list, one could then design an instructional program to train potential filling station attendants. A question remains, however. Would a person trained this way be a superior filling station attendant?

A different way to look at the competencies inherent in the tasks completed by a filling station attendant would be to go out and talk to owners/managers of filling stations, drivers of cars which patronize filling stations, and filling station attendants. One might devise a rating system to discriminate between superior attendants and fair to poor attendants, and then observe the superior attendants to see what they actually do. One could also ask them to describe the things they do, and specifically demonstrate behaviors they feel to be successful. It might turn out that what separated superior attendants from average to poor attendants was the quality of friendliness implicit in the grins or smiles with which they welcomed customers, or the ways in which they answered questions about gasoline or engines. In any event, one would have a different, and empirical understanding of the role and tasks of a filling station attendant, which might or might not match the list devised in the rational process. If there were discrepancies between the lists, there would clearly be implications for the training and evaluation of those individuals who wished to become attendants.

Although this discussion of filling station attendant competence has centered on an occupation, it is possible to apply this technology to instructional performance. Most people, in or out of the profession of education, can distinguish between good and bad teachers, because they have experienced teaching which has or has not met or matched their learning styles and needs. This intuitive evaluation is not helpful on a broad programmatic scale, nor does it assist the selection or training of instructors. In the field of CBE, therefore, one would hope for two developments. The first would be the identification of superior instructional performance, empirically. The second would be development of test instruments for both students and instructors which would reliably and validly measure the competencies to which they aspired. While these developments lie some years ahead, there is work being done at present on both fronts.[d] The technology to develop such outcome measures is known and perhaps will become increasingly practiced. For example, the College for Human Services in New York City has reliable and valid information about the characteristics that distinguish superior human service workers from average-to-poor

---

[d]Psychologist David C. McClelland and colleagues at McBer and Company, in Boston, are presently at work in this area.

human service workers, and can make curricular changes and adaptations accordingly.

In light of the filling station example, how might one go about evaluating the performance of an instructor who attempts the coach/mentor role, or for that matter, any instructor participating in a program that is competency-based? The procedure which follows is new and different. It is costly, designed to produce outcome measures of faculty performance, and determine competence in a broad band of skills, against which faculty members in CBE might be measured.

The process is expensive in terms of time, money, and expertise. It demands a certain level of technical sophistication in terms of test design and data analysis. A serious and complex process, it requires both thoroughness and good will on the part of those who use it. It differs from most evaluation procedures in that once it is established it can be used to predict performance.

This procedure is designed to distinguish between superior instructional performance and average-to-poor instructional performance. Not only may it serve as a base for evaluation, but may also be used diagnostically to assess training needs for a faculty.

If one were to apply it, what would be the steps? What would it look like and what could one expect from it?

To begin, teaching is clearly a complicated task and profession. Instruction at any level, for any purpose, involves different mixes of skills and abilities. The focus here will be on the tasks and role-related aspects of instruction in a competency-based educational program, specifically on the coach/mentor role. Although an investigation of the competencies associated with superior instructional perfomance should of course be exhaustive, complete, and empirical, what follows is a brief outline of the process, to be considered for purposes of illustration. Both the description of the step, and the implications of taking it, are presented here.

Step One in the identification and development of competency measures involves a job analysis. Using first a conventional job analysis of tasks required to be performed in a certain job, and second, a methodology involving systems analysis, observation, and interview, one builds a product—a job description inventory. For the case of instructors in competency-based educational programs, such an analysis would involve examination of how instructors interact with students, with other faculty, with administrators, within the context of the coach/mentor role, and some of the tasks mentioned previously, such as advising, counseling, diagnosing student progress, and designing new learning experiences. If one were to attempt this type of job analysis, one could expect:

a. different perspectives among faculty members,
b. some traditional tasks,
c. some new and unanticipated tasks (dealing with state agencies, etc.)

d. argumentation about generalization

e. support from faculty

f. resistance from faculty

This job description inventory summarizes what a faculty thought it was about. Hopefully it would represent most of the things (jobs) faculty actually did. Clearly, within a faculty some individuals would do more of one and less of another. Some of the tasks included in the inventory would represent functions common to the process of teaching, while others would be content-specific in regard to the delivery of a certain body of information.

Step Two is a procedure in which faculty members are identified as superior, average, or less than average, or at least three different sets of ratings. Three groups of observers—most likely administrators, other faculty, and students—are asked to describe faculty people in terms of the job task inventory just completed. The purpose here is to identify superior performers, people who stand out as superior, on all three lists. The object of the exercise is to examine these individuals, and examine those regarded as less than average, and attempt to determine what accounts for the difference.

Why are some individuals universally regarded as outstanding, or competent, while others are seen as inferior performers? The three-factor rating establishes a group regarded as being competent. If a faculty or institution chose to establish this procedure, and rank faculty members into three groups, one might expect that:

a. some faculty would question the process as biased or unreliable

b. others would welcome it as an opportunity for feedback

c. still others would fear the uses to which the information was put

Individuals who have participated in this process are generally intrigued with it, and come to appreciate its operational definition of competence. One can, of course, suggest that it is possible to perform a certain function in a way better than that currently employed by the best performers within a given context. While that may be true, it does not detract from the notion that competence exists, empirically, as well as in more rational analyses.

Step Three is concerned with an interview procedure in which the individuals identified as superior performers are asked, in a standardized interview, to give reports of incidents in which they felt they were particularly successful, or incidents in which certain behaviors stood out or were called into play. Using this structured methodology, interviewers help these individuals flesh out incidents or events that illustrate success in the job. For instructors, such an incident might involve advising a student reluctant or unable to develop a contract in a certain competency area, or require the development of an off-site apprenticeship for a student interested in city planning, etc. A series of these illuminating incidents is collected.

These structured interviews, usually lasting an hour or so, flesh out differences in the ways individuals approach situations or other individuals. For example, some people, identified as superior leaders of groups, tend to remember more about what has happened in groups in which they have participated than other individuals judged as less adept in group leadership skills. It is that kind of information, whether it be the manifestation of an attitude, or a specific detail, which often differentiates people. One can think of degrees of patience related in the telling of a story or the kinds of regard or expectations toward others, which surface in a story-telling, or recreation of an event. These rigorous and in-depth interviews are conducted on tape, and then transcribed. If one were to conduct these interviews with a faculty, one would discover that:

a. most individuals enjoy the process and learn something from it
b. others are concerned that they won't perform well in the interview
c. still others regard the process as a kind of learning unfamiliar to them
d. others see it as an opportunity to consider differences in teaching and learning styles

As most people in academic life are articulate and adept in conversation, the interview process is not unlike some collegial encounters.

Step Four is the analysis of those incidents, to derive common traits among those individuals who reported. This analytic process scrutinizes the behaviors reported in the critical incidents, and teases out what a person does in terms of actual performance—superior, or average. For example, an individual working in the coach/mentor role might distinguish himself through an empathic listening style, while an individual rated as average-to-poor might be characterized by an inattentive, hurried listening style. The overall purpose of this analysis is to distinguish between the behaviors of those individuals rated as superior, and those rated as average-to-poor.

Both tone and detail separate the individuals who have been interviewed for illustrative incidents. The analysis of the material matches the traits or qualities found in the interviews of those described as superior performers with the characteristics or behaviors of those described as less than average performers.

If one were to continue in this process of empirical competency derivation, it is at this step where the services of a skilled and experienced evaluator or psychologist are required. Many characteristics have face validity in regards to assumptions about effective teaching, and it takes a sophisticated perspective to actually discover fundamental differences between teaching styles or characteristics that make one individual more competent—in the eyes of three different sets of people—than another.

Many institutions have individuals skilled in assessment procedures on their faculties, and while they might not be familiar with such a procedure, it is one they could learn.

Step Five is a selection process, the selection of assessment instruments to measure the behaviors that separate superior performers from average-to-poor performers. Some of these instruments may already be validated, while others are being developed. One such instrument, which is designed to measure empathy, is called the Profile of Non-Verbal Sensitivity, and uses content-filtered speech to get at the message or feeling that lies underneath much communication. This selection process, too, requires the assistance of psychologists, psychometricians, or educators with a background in measures of evaluation.

Other faculty, however, through the use of videotape and diagnostic observation, have helped colleagues develop instruments to measure their own performance as well as that of students. Such devices as adjective checklists, instruments to measure positive bias toward others, and programmed case analysis, have all been used in assessment.

In instances in which these measures have been used, faculty and administrators response has first been tentative and curious, and then supportive. Most faculty people are not accustomed to having their performance scrutinized in what they often regard as unconventional ways, and can become resistant if they do not understand the process.

Step Six is the administration of the assessment instruments. The tests are administered to a sample population matching the population from whom the critical incidents were derived. In this case the instruments would be given to faculty members identified as both superior and average-to-poor, in a competency-based educational program.

The test administration of these instruments is relatively uncomplicated, particularly in situations in which a faculty understands and supports the development of this type of competency model, the object is to determine, in statistically meaningful ways, if superior faculty members do, in fact, possess the mix of skills identified as a competence, and if those measures of competence can distinguish between those previously identified as superior and those identified as less than average performers. For reasons of design, it is important that the measures be administered to comparable groups of faculty members.

If one were to anticipate obstacles, one would guess that faculty being given the tests or assessment instruments might wonder into which of the two or three categories they might fall. If this became an issue, and the costs of administration were not too great, one might involve an entire faculty in such a procedure, as a learning experience as well as a validation procedure that did not outwardly signal which person was "superior."

Step Seven, the final step, is data analysis. The task is to analyze the data collected and to cross-validate it. One would ask the following questions at this stage in the process: Do the tests discriminate between instructors identified as superior performers and those instructors identified as average-to-poor performers? Do the assessment measures reflect real-life outcomes, i.e., do they assess a broad band of skills necessary to superior performance in this instructional or coach/mentor role, or rather, are they limited to the measurement of a specific set of abilities? For example, do the tests measure skills and abilities such as communication skills, the ability to set moderate goals, to be patient, etc.? Finally, do the tests sample operant as well as respondent behavior? Do they ask the instructor to behave in the coach/mentor role, or do they ask the instructor to answer questions about the coach/mentor role? If these questions, and questions like them, can be answered satisfactorily, one has the beginnings of a process to assess faculty competence in a competency-based instructional program.

Again, this analysis requires a somewhat sophisticated technical capacity. One performs statistical analysis and determines relationships between the factors underlying the definitions of competence. While most faculty members would not be intimately involved in this task, one can predict that:

a. they will eagerly await the outcomes
b. they will regard some of their teaching habits, mannerisms, or styles in new ways in light of the information they receive
c. they will be imaginative and creative in both their doubts on the process and their support of it

It is important to reemphasize that the purpose is to strengthen faculty members, not to weaken them; to assist them in difficult roles and responsibilities rather than evaluate and leave them. One might find that certain faculty excel in areas they had not known; that other faculty demonstrated strengths more suitable for instructional programs which were not competency-based, but who were skillful at what they did.

While the procedures might highlight the qualities and skills associated with the coach/mentor role, in different institutions one might uncover a different mix of skills which would be more appropriate. The critical point, however is to address and answer the questions related to the evaluation of faculty performance in a CBE program. The process itself, as mentioned previously, is complex and requires a great deal of technical ability and support. Its reward lies in the empirical nature of the competency measures it derives, the fact that those measures can be validated, and that they can predict future performance in the task. If, for instance, a candidate to be an instructor in a competency-based program were shown to be lacking in empathy—one of the qualities determined to be essential—that individual would have the choice to try to develop that quality (and there is some research that shows it is possible to become more empathic), or perhaps to choose to become an instructor in an alternative setting, in which the ability to be empathic was not so necessary.

As will become apparent at the end of this chapter there are problems associated with the implementation of this procedure, and as promising as it might be, the application of this technology has been limited to a few settings. It has by no means been universally welcome, as empirical measures are threatening to those who have doubts of their own competence, worry about the relation between assessment of performance and job security, and prefer to deal in political terms, or the rational model of competence, rather than subjecting the process to scrutiny, which might prove uncomfortable.

FEEDBACK

In most competency-based programs, feedback to instructors on their instructional performance is available, but methods of delivery are unsystematic and often unstructured. Again, the system or culture of CBE is so new that attempts to codify or structure feedback are in rudimentary stages. As mentioned previously, there are attempts to provide faculty members with information about their performance, but these attempts follow patterns that emanate from more traditional academic settings, and sometimes instructors are left without much certainty—old standards don't really apply, but new standards have not yet been developed.

Central to the problem of feedback in CBE are the following considerations: for faculty, there are doubts and questions which take the form of: What am I really supposed to be doing? For students there are different levels of understanding and commitment to competency-based programs, and many students are uncomfortable with the differences between CBE and education with which they have been familiar. For peers and colleagues there are genuine concerns about the nature of effective teaching within competency-based programs. They know the experience is different, and realize that it is meant to be different, but they are left without some of their old norms or anchors to evaluate their own or their colleagues' performance. Administrators encounter the same difficulties. They know intuitively that the nature of the instructional process has changed, but their experience in evaluating instructors in terms of lecture delivery, research, or the grading of papers falls down when they try to make the connections between instructor competence and student competence. Experts in the field or others are not necessarily particularly good at analyzing preparation for life performance, because they draw largely from their own experience, which is bound to be dissimilar from that of a competency-based program. In summary, for all parties involved in the feedback process, the traditional support system for both assessment and the communication of that assessment is often lacking. How can feedback be collected and delivered?

A variety of sources are used. The empirical competency model does not really exist yet, so that procedure and the use of its information is eliminated. At present, the use of feedback is handled in ways similar to those discussed in the other chapters of this book. Recipients are largely the same, conditions for disclosure are largely the same, and the forms the feedback takes are essentially the same.

Multiuse, multimethod forms of evaluations produce multiple kinds of feedback. If one of the goals of the feedback process is to assist faculty in self-development, then individual faculty members should receive information collected by, for, and about them. Hopefully this information will be coded and available in such ways and at such times that it encourages faculty to change, rather than promoting feelings of defensiveness or lack of efficacy. If the information is being collected to use in making decisions concerning personnel, other faculty should have access to those aspects of the feedback which are not confidential. If students have participated in some kind of evaluation process, the information collected from them should be available to them, as well as to faculty members.

In CBE students are often the primary source for feedback for faculty, particularly in the one-on-one counseling, advising, or diagnostic sessions between instructor and student. Instructor and student monitor the student's progress towards competent performance, and instructor helpfulness or ability is implicitly assessed. Reference earlier to a joint effort of evaluation was based on the assumption that faculty and students would provide each other with feedback, based on agreed-upon criteria.

Feedback about individual and group faculty performance should be provided, at least in summary form, if the feedback is to be used for training or staff development purposes. If a faculty is to have a commitment to improvement, it may want to structure a system by which it learns about itself. In that case, individual faculty members should have access to their own data and collective profiles.

Administrators and supervisors who use information about faculty performance for purposes of promotion, salary level, job enrichment, or advancement, will want to have information from as many sources as possible. Again, within the contraints of confidentiality, an administration can develop a situation in which feedback becomes a tool, and not necessarily a reward or a punishment.

Feedback to faculty, as feedback to students, will take different forms, and forms often difficult to document. Emphasis is on performance, on a broad band of instructional skills, and those skills are not easily identified.

The role change to coach/mentor outlined above means a departure from more traditional formal or informal evaluation measures. This role change is apparent in the areas that receive less emphasis in CBE—lecturing, for example, where instructors are used to rewards or feedback, whether it takes the form of yawns or applause. The new tasks—counseling and advising—are less susceptible to feedback, as they are more private and less public. Other students, peers, and colleagues, and administrators have less opportunities to develop an awareness of individual faculty performance.

It is more difficult to assess skills and performance than to test a knowledge base or mastery of content. Assessment procedures are less well known, are more costly, and all involved operate with less comfort and certainty about what they are doing. Other judges, or sources of feedback, such as potential employers for students, experts, or government agencies who oversee certification procedures, all provide instructors indirect feedback in their responses toward students, but there is little with which the faculty member can connect.

Finally, the stakes may be higher for individual instructors in the sense that the areas in which they will be increasingly evaluated are interpersonal. It is one thing to receive feedback on an article, a lecture, or the grading of an exam. It is quite another to receive feedback on one's listening style, one's empathy, one's ability to provide direction. Academicians are not necessarily trained either to giving or receiving such feedback, and may need to develop or acquire special skills to do so. If a person is being evaluated, not on research or teaching in the broad sense, but rather on how he or she facilitates another person's growth toward competence, the task, and perhaps the importance of the task, have changed, and faculty and administrators will need support to make the changes.

INDICATORS OF SUCCESS

The embryonic state of the competency-based movement also influences whatever indicators of success might be available to those interested in issues endemic to evaluation of faculty performance. So few evaluation systems are systematic or formalized in any way that it is difficult to draw conclusions about support available for evaluation processes from any of the parties involved. It is clear that there is strong support for programs to evaluate faculty performance from granting institutions, from administrations, from faculty, and from students. Institutions apparently vary in terms of institutional commitment and the purposes to which they put the evaluation. Most of the evaluation systems are in the first stage of development, and their jerry-built nature suggests not a lack of support, but rather a matter of timing. The institutions, or the competency-based programs, are simply not mature. With chronological assistance the programs will become more formal. There appears to be little if any resistance to evaluation of faculty, as most faculty participating in CBE are in a sense pioneers, and entered the field with an awareness of what they might encounter. If competency-based programs become mandatory, or spread to institutions in which there is resistance, there will undoubtedly be increased resistance, on the order of that demonstrated by the American Federation of Teachers in New York City who oppose CBE on philosophical, political, and practical grounds.

Other factors that influence the success or failure of evaluation of faculty performance in CBE are common to more traditional programs, factors that are mechanical, administrative, political, and fiscal. Unlike the proprietary schools—some of which are competency-based—colleges, community colleges, and universities do not hire and fire instructors based on client perfornance or satisfaction. Relationships between insturctors and students have in some cases taken on contractual elements, but in most programs evaluation and indications of its implementation continue to operate within older and more traditional administrative forms and norms.

The training programs for faculty and staff that have been developed after efforts at evaluation are probably the most concrete indicators of success one can find. Competency-based programs which support and follow evaluation with training demonstrate a committment to competency-based principles in the education of their own instructors.

IMPLEMENTATION ISSUES

It is important to anticipate and address some of the issues that arise in implementation of faculty evaluation in CBE. In order to carry out successfully the process, faculty members and administrators need a high level of commitment, to first understand and develop objectives and then to take the time to participate in meetings and discussions to clarify what action steps they wish to take. Individuals will need to consider the possibility that a competency-based program, and effective performance within it, will ask an instructor to alter a teaching style to conform more fully to the coach/mentor role. Although there is debate over the nature of the tasks to be performed by instructors in widely varying CBE programs, there is enough in common to suggest that change is necessary.

Another issue to be raised in advance of implementation of programs to evaluate faculty performance is the desire of the institution, or individuals in or out of the institution, to conduct institutional research. The empirical competency model described earlier provides information about teaching and learning outcomes quite different from softer data, or achievement on national tests, which appear largely unrelated to larger life outcomes. Institutional accountability takes on new meaning when there is the capacity to assess student or faculty performance empirically. When faculty members can be assessed in regard to a set of competencies judged necessary for successful performance in their instructional roles, a set of political and professional questions arises.

In order to have an empirical competency model, an institution requires the technical expertise to develop it. This expertise is in short supply, and while one can anticipate that those capable of performing this analysis will grow in number, particularly in response to government suits about affirmative action programs and competence, the psychometricians who are able to conduct such a process are few in number and their services are expensive. Other costs of this kind of faculty evaluation have to do with the time and energy required to build the model and then test against it, time that might be better spent in other ways.

It seems only fair that if such a faculty evaluation program were implemented the administration and faculty would wish to build training and development programs in the areas of need identified in the evaluation process. Faculty retraining, particularly in light of promotion and tenure concerns, seem inevitable. That poses additional organizational and budgetary problems.

Finally, there is the issue of student understanding and commitment to the empirical competency model, either applied to themselves or applied to the faculty. If students have participated in a faculty evaluation process by filling out rating sheets or through other methods, formal or informal, a new technology to evaluate may seem strange for them, particularly if their input is restricted to one level of judgment. A faculty member who is not popular, for example, could be found empirically to be particularly effective in the performance of his or her tasks, and students would have to reconcile their perceptions of this individual with data that is contrary. Clearly the opposite would also be true, where an especially popular faculty member, popular for whatever reasons, could be assessed as less than competent.

As an illustration of problems that arise in the implementation of competency-based performance evaluation, one may consider the following example, or case. As suggested earlier, the process of deriving outcome measures that underlie superior performance can be applied to students as well as to faculty. An attempt to do that has been underway at a community college in Massachusetts.

Faculty members who are charged with the responsibility of providing professional and paraprofessional training to a group of older, nontraditional students have made attempts to use the technology to determine what the students should be able to do in order to exit; in short, to identify the competencies needed for their already chosen occupation. These faculty members have started to establish a certification process, by identifying outstanding members of the profession and determining the competencies that underlie their effective performance. After they have identified the basic competencies critical to the performance of tasks in this occupation, they will assess students in their progress toward the development of those competencies.

At this writing these faculty members, in collaboration with members of the administration at the college, have finished stage one, or the job analysis required in this procedure. Moving from a variation of task analysis, they have identified superior performers, those individuals already active in the field who have been judged by the three rating sources described in the procedure. Staff at the college, with some outside assistance, may conduct interviews to collect illustrative incidents and then analyze the competencies that enable those individuals to perform effectively.

The process is moving slowly for a variety of reasons. First, it involves a large number of administrative details, and requires tight scheduling for a variety of individuals. Second, those who participate in such a process need to understand it fully, and that requires sharing of information, a basic educational task. Third, it takes time to build faculty commitment to a process not easily understood in the beginning, and which may have serious implications for them and for their instructional styles. A knowing-versus-doing debate also traditionally surfaces in competency-based programs, and consumes discussion time. Lastly, there is the task of building student commitment to what appears to be an abstract and arbitrary process at first glance. Students need to know what's in it for them, and to change some of their own expectations about teaching, learning, and the development of competence.

When and if the process is completed, the department in the community college undertaking this task may have a number of products—some tangible, and some intangible. The first will be an evaluation instrument and evaluation process against which faculty can measure student performance. This will enable faculty to make some calculations and adjustments about the connections between their teaching and educational objectives, and the kinds of abilities students will need to develop in order to perform well in their chosen occupation. One way of thinking about CBE is that it permits both students and teachers to "teach to the test." In other words, if the competencies are public knowledge, and how to get them is public, then students and instructors can work together to develop the mix of skills which will enable them to be certified as competent. The process also suggests that faculty may be able to do away with aspects of the curriculum which do not seem essential to the development of those broad band abilities, and concentrate instead on objectives directly related to student performance.

As this community college has invested substantial time and energy in the development of self-paced programs, the empirical competency model will give administrators, faculty, and students a more precise understanding of what is needed to attain a certain level of mastery, and students will be able, in some cases, to move independently toward that attainment. Two other factors recommend this procedure. The first has to do with accountability. The students either become competent or they do not, and the faculty will be able to predict who will function with entry-level skills. This ability to predict will influence potential employers of competent performers and will also help faculty members and administrators who need to make decisions about the allocation of resources, time, and energy within the college. Both can use performance indicators as outcome measures more accurately than they could with less precise means of assessment. Second, this procedure may result in greater satisfaction for both instructors and students, as both will be able to perceive more clearly the connection between instructional objectives and real-life outcomes. The word relevant becomes more meaningful, as students will actually be able to *do,* in most cases, what they have set out to do, whether that means speaking a language, learning how to solve problems, thinking critically, or analyzing arguments, all competencies that are indirectly addressed in more traditional forms of post-secondary education. If, however, this type of evaluation either proves too costly, or is not an institutional priority, potential benefits may not be realized, either for students or faculty.

A summary of the current state of the evaluation of faculty performance in CBE would be incomplete and unrealistic if it did not indicate that problems abound. There is much of merit in this new form of evaluation for a new form of teaching and learning experience, but the development of the process has been slow and incremental. Evaluation measures need development and support, both institutional and governmental, with energy, expertise, and monies. Still in the process of experimentation, there is a danger that results may be too necessary, too soon, to get a real understanding of what such an approach to evaluation might offer. Conflicts between theories of evaluation and implementation of evaluation practices, this or any other, make it difficult for an individual, a department, or a total faculty to see a way clear to use the process in an easily conceptualized, easily digested form. It is difficult if not impossible at this point in time to say, "These are the skills of a good economics professor in a competency-based program." The day may come when that statement and many others are readily available, for those who work with issues of evaluation in CBE display a sense of excitement as they confront their tasks.

As competency-based programs proliferate and mature, the art of performance evaluation will hopefully advance. Until then, those interested in the evaluation problem of new wine in old bottles will have to use their ingenuity, common sense, and good will to figure out what it means to perform effectively in CBE.

BIBLIOGRAPHY

American Association of Colleges for Teacher Education. *PBTE Series,* Nos. 1-12. Washington, D.C.: The Association, written in 1974-75.

(1) "Performance-Based Teacher Education: What is the State of the Art?"
(2) "The Individualized, Competency-Based System of Teacher Education at Weber State College."
(3) "Manchester Interview: Competency-Based Teacher Education/Certification."
(4) "A Critique of Performance-Based Teacher Education."
(5) "Competency-Based Teacher Education: A Scenario."
(6) "Changing Teacher Education in a Large Urban University."
(7) "Performance-Based Teacher Education: An Annotated Bibliography."
(8) "Performance-Based Teacher Education Programs: A Comparative Description."
(9) "Competency-Based Education: The State of the Scene."
(10) "A Humanistic Approach to Performance-Based Teacher Education."

(11) "Performance-Based Teacher Education and the Subject Matter Fields."
(12) "Performance-Based Teacher Education: Some Management and Decision-Making Considerations."

A useful collection of descriptive and think-pieces related to the competency-based education movement in the field of teacher education. Provides different perspectives on the nature of competency-based education for professional preparation. Also contains valuable references and bibliographic materials.

Chickering, Arthur. "Developing Competency," in *Education and Identity* (San Francisco: Jossey-Bass Publishers, 1974.

In this first chapter of Education and Identity, Chickering likens competence to a "three-tined pitchfork." Intellectual competency, physical-manual skills and interpersonal competence are the tines and sense of competence are analyzed separately, with Chickering maintaining that colleges have the responsibility to systematically and rationally respond to these components as separate elements of a larger whole. (The entire book is recommended).

Elam, Stanley. "What is the State of the Art?" *AACTE Pamphlet #1 of PBTE Series.*

This is an initial statement by the Committee on Performance-Based Teacher Education to clarify PBTE concepts, to examine their potential and identify related problems, issues, ambiguities, differences of opinion, and unanswered questions. Elam describes the five essential elements necessary for any PBTE program, states the characteristics implied in these essential elements, discusses the impact of the PBTE movement as it ranges through teacher education institutions, state departments of education, professional organizations and communities they serve, and finally identifies a number of advantages of PBTE.

Hodgkinson, Harold. "Issues in Competency-Based Learning." Keynote Address at the National Conference on Competency-Based Learning, Cincinnati, Ohio, February 15, 1974.

Hodgkinson attempts to define competency-based learning and suggests that the impetus for it stems from a prevailing mood of lack of faith in higher education. He deals with the development of Mastery Learning as Bloom and Carroll have articulated it, and discusses six levels of general competence which provide a basis for many competency-based education programs. Hodgkinson outlines some of the problems that arise from competency-based education as: the need to establish some norm-referenced criteria with acceptable levels of difficulty, role problems of the faculty, poor measures of assessment, the need to develop an additive program rather than an array of self-contained courses with no direction, and the need to know more about the consequences of competency-based programs for institutions.

Klein, Robert, and Babineau, Raymond. "Evaluating the Competence of Trainees: It's Nothing Personal," *American Journal of Psychiatry* (July 1974).

This article attempts to explore some of the factors that affect the participants in an evaluation process of professional competence of trainees in the mental health field. The authors draw on personal experiences with mental health trainees to delineate some of the rational and irrational components of the process, the dilemmas and conflicts for both the evaluator and the trainee, and recommendations for clarifying roles and responsibilities for the individuals and the institutions involved.

McClelland, David, "Testing for Competence Rather Than Intelligence," *American Psychologist,* January, 1973.

In this article, McClelland questions the validity of standard intelligence and aptitude tests as well as the predictability of them in relation to job performance and other worldly behavior. He proposes that we should test for competence rather than intelligence through the use of criterion-sampling tests, and that the assessment criteria be grouped in clusters of life outcomes (communication skills, patience, moderate goal-setting, ego development). He suggests that this new testing movement should lead to a different profile of an individual inclusive of ego and moral development and that tests should become a device for the mutual redesigning of the teaching/learning process.

McDonald, Frederick J. "The Rationale for Competency-Based Programs." (Unpublished paper).

McDonald traces the roots of competency-based education to behavioral psychology and systems analysis and suggests that these origins account for three characteristics common to all competency-based education programs. He maintains that competency-based education programs should be developed in an analogous way to models that already exist, and that the choice of the model be based on very specified criteria. In conceptualizing a competency-based education program, *teaching* and the nature of the *acquisition process* by which teaching competence is learned. According to McDonald, the rationale for competency-based education programs derives from a conception of the nature of what is to be learned and from a model of a system most likely to influence this acquisition. He points out that the model of competency-based education programs is basically a cybernetic one with a modular design as the technological device for implementing the model.

———. "The Research and Development Strategy of the National Commission on Performance-Based Education." Educational Testing Service, Princeton, New Jersey, March 1974.

A description of the Commission's on-going efforts to describe and assess teaching competence. McDonald outlines a variety of problems faced by the commission in its multitude of tasks. Touches on research design for faculty evaluation.

Merrow, John G.G., II. "The Politics of Competence: A Review of Competency-Based Teacher Education." A Report to the National Institute of Education, July 4, 1974, OE Vendor Code 541253.

An inquiry into the current condition of CBTE with particular reference to the origins and problems of competency-based programs. Merrow makes a candid assessment of some of the costs and benefits of CBTE and speculates about its future. Also contains useful bibliography.

Schmieder, Alan. "The State of the Scene." *AACTE Pamphlet #9 of PBTE Series.*

This document outlines the competency-based education movement in the United States. It covers the roots of CBE; distinguishing characteristics; degree of participation by states, higher education, teachers, administrators and community; current resources; a bibliography of significant publications; major issues; and a profile of competency-based education by state.

Faculty Evaluation Program Inventory

This inventory is designed to help those who are interested in improving an existing faculty evaluation program. The inventory lists and briefly describes many aspects of a faculty evaluation program, such as : purposes, sources and kinds of information, rating scales, feedback, legal factors. The categories are somewhat artificial, yet they are based on a current review of research and practice nationally, and they do provide a working convenience. It has been shown in pilot trials that these categories are relevant to a variety of colleges and universities, and are useful in idenfitying which aspects of a faculty evaluation program need attention first.

This is the sole purpose of the inventory—to help the users to establish priorities. It is difficult and frustrating to try to work on everything at once. Also, faculty evaluation programs will vary in how well or how poorly certain aspects are going, or whether they are attended to at all. You will be asked to give your opinion regarding how much attention each aspects of your faculty evaluation program needs at this time. The completed inventory is intended to serve as a basis for focused discussion and the development of an improvement plan.

DIRECTIONS

1. If your institution has a single uniform set of faculty evaluation procedures, you should fill out this inventory with those procedures in mind. If your institution has procedures that vary among departments or other units, then those filling out the inventory for mutual discussion should make a common decision regarding the specific unit and procedures which are the subject of this inventory.
2. If certain items in the inventory seem unclear, you may turn to the page reference shown in Chapter 2 for further explanation.

3. Your opinion regarding the amount of attention needed in each category should be based on whatever is presently practiced, not on what is intended, planned, or held to be ideal.
4. The provision for "comments" at each step should allow you to note reasons for your ratings, for later reference.

The Purposes of Faculty Evaluation

Several common purposes of faculty evaluation information are listed below. These uses may or may not be a part of the program at your institution. For each purpose listed below, circle the *one* number in each horizontal row which best describes your view of that purpose in your institution now.

Reference Pages in Ch. 2	Purposes	Does not need attention, or not applicable	Need for attention low	Need for attention medium	Need for attention high	Urgent need for attention
9	1. Helping faculty to improve their performance	5	4	3	2	1
9	2. Making decisions on retention, tenure, salary, or promotion	5	4	3	2	1
9	3. Guiding students in their selection of courses and instructors	5	4	3	2	1
9	4. Keeping an inventory of personnel resources for reassignment or re-training	5	4	3	2	1
10	5. Evaluating curricula, sequences, programs, departments, units	5	4	3	2	1
10	6. Informing external audiences on faculty performance	5	4	3	2	1
10	7. Conducting research on factors related to faculty performance	5	4	3	2	1
	Comments:					

Sources and Kinds of Information

Faculty evaluation procedures generate information. Because each source of information (self, students, other faculty, administrators, outsiders) has limited insight into any faculty member's performance, the objectivity and completeness of faculty evaluation in enhanced if multisource information is collected from those who are most knowledgeable about particular aspects of faculty performance. Circle the *one* number in each horizontal row which best describes your view of the amount or kinds of information collected from those sources in your faculty evaluation program.

Reference Pages in Ch. 2		Does not need attention, or not applicable	Need for attention low	Need for attention medium	Need for attention high	Urgent need for attention
12	1. *Students*: Teaching skills (pedagogy), course structure (materials, exams, text, readings, papers), work load, level of difficulty, instructor/group interaction, advising and supervision, course interest, the attainment of course and instructional objectives.					
16	2. *Peers*: Appropriateness of course and instructional objectives, reading lists, texts, exams, sequences, subject matter mastery, service to institution and community, research and scholarly publications, rapport.	5	4	3	2	1
20	3. *Administrators*: Service to institution and community, course load and other responsibilities, course enrollment factors, long-term evaluation and improvement patterns, market view of course and instructional objectives, inventory of resources.	5	4	3	2	1
21	4. *Self*: Course and instructional objectives, instructional activities, committee	5	4	3	2	1

		5	4	3	2	1
23	work, service to community, situational factors, use of student instrument to rate self.	5	4	3	2	1
	5. *Weighting:* Kinds and sources of information can be weighted, for example, research, service, teaching with percentages of value in total evaluation; or student, peers, etc., with percentage of weight identified.	5	4	3	2	1

Comments:

Rating Scales: Student

Methods of faculty evaluation vary from elaborate to simple. Instruments (rating scales, questionnaires, or forms) can be derived from research, or derived from practice. Research-based instruments for student evaluation of faculty are abundant, but most forms used for peer, administrator, and self-evaluation are based on practice. The quality and hence usefulness of information obtained from any instrument—research-based or practice-based—is affected by the several factors shown below. Circle the *one* number in each horizontal row which best describes your view of these several qualities of your student rating scale.

Reference Pages in Ch. 2		Does not need attention, or not applicable	Need for attention low	Need for attention medium	Need for attention high	Urgent need for attention
26	a. *Flexibility:* Allows for diversity in courses and teaching styles, (e.g., by having generally applicable items, a large pool of items to draw from, or alternate forms of the instrument).					
27	b. *Length:* Not too long; 10–30 items at most; takes 10–20 minutes to complete.	5	4	3	2	1
28	c. *Format:* No more than two pages; ratings next to each question.	5	4	3	2	1
28	d. *Scale Range:* Scales with a 1–5 or a 1–7 point range (to yield a wider band of ratings).	5	4	3	2	1
28	e. *Validity:* It has been demonstrated statistically that the instrument actually measures what it intends to measure, or it has face-validity.	5	4	3	2	1
29	f. *Reliability:* The instrument has been verified to be reliable over time, e.g., the same or different students will rate a faculty member the same over time (assuming no change in the faculty member's performance).	5	4	3	2	1

		5	4	3	2	1
29	g. *Situational Factors:* The instrument includes questions about student characteristics, and teaching conditions which influence evaluators (e.g., class size, major or minor, level, and student's attitude toward instruction and courses generally).	5	4	3	2	1
30	h. *Interaction Effects:* The fit between student orientation, and class structure and student-teacher interactions which may include "Teaching to the bright students" are variables to be considered.	5	4	3	2	1
30	i. *Acceptance:* Faculty members and students consider the instrument, and the uses to which the results are put, to be relevant and useful. Both take the process of filling out the instruments, and using results seriously.	5	4	3	2	1
31	j. *Timing and Procedures:* Students fill out instructor rating scales one or two weeks before classes end—not on the last day or two of classes. These questionnaires are sealed and locked until after final grades are issued, when they are then processed.	5	4	3	2	1

Comments:

Rating Scales: Peer or Other Faculty Member

Circle *one* number in each horizontal row which best describes your view of these several qualities of your peer or other faculty member rating scale.

Reference Pages in Ch. 2		*Does not need attention, or not applicable*	*Need for attention low*	*Need for attention medium*	*Need for attention high*	*Urgent need for attention*
33	a. *Format:* Both specific or quantitative and open-ended or qualitative information is requested.	5	4	3	2	1
33	b. *Flexibility:* Provision is made for including description of unique or special talents or contributions.	5	4	3	2	1
33	c. *Appropriateness:* Information is requested which evaluator has direct access to (e.g., course materials only if evaluator has reviewed them; classroom teaching only if evaluator has observed it).	5	4	3	2	1
34	d. *Acceptance:* Faculty members, administrators, and students consider the form and the uses to which the results are put to be relevant and useful. All take the process of filling out the form, and using the results, seriously.	5	4	3	2	1

Comments:

Ratings Scales: Administrator/Supervisor

Circle the *one* number in each horizontal row which best describes your view of these several qualities of your administrator/supervisor rating scale.

Reference Pages in Ch. 2		Does not need attention, or not applicable	Need for attention low	Need for attention medium	Need for attention high	Urgent need for attention
34	a. *Format:* Both specific or quantitative and open-ended or qualitative information is requested.	5	4	3	2	1
35	b. *Flexibility:* Provision is made for including description of unique or special talents or contributions.	5	4	3	2	1
35	c. *Appropriateness:* Information is requested which evaluator has direct access to (e.g., course materials only if evaluator has reviewed them; classroom teaching only if evaluator has observed it).	5	4	3	2	1
35	d. *Acceptance:* Faculty members, administrators and students consider the form and the uses to which the results are put to be relevant and useful. All take the process of filling out the form, and using the results seriously.	5	4	3	2	1
35	e. *Overview:* Administrative levels indicate perspective available to see faculty talents and interests in overall institutional needs. Trends over time also administrative responsibility.	5	4	3	2	1

Comments:

Rating Scales: Self

Circle the *one* number in each horizontal row which best describes your view of these several qualities of your self rating scale.

Reference Pages in Ch. 2		Does not need attention, or not applicable	Need for attention low	Need for attention medium	Need for attention high	Urgent need for attention
37	a. *Activities:* Faculty self-evaluation provides opportunity for all activities to be listed in all areas of performance (research, teaching, advising/supervisory and service).	5	4	3	2	1
37	b. *Goals:* Provision is made for individual's own goals to be identified as to priorities in these areas, or personal values in the institutional context.	5	4	3	2	1
37	c. *Purpose:* If results are to be used for any purpose *other than* decision about tenure, promotion or salary, etc., the individual's judgment of his own strengths and weaknesses is requested.	5	4	3	2	1
37	d. *Acceptance:* Faculty member and administrators accept the form and the uses to which the results are to be put, as relevant and useful. They take the process of filling it out and using the results seriously.	5	4	3	2	1
37	e. *Format:* Form has explicit requests and guidelines, yet allows for additional open-ended comments for unique or special talents, interests or contributions.	5	4	3	2	1

Comments:

Feedback: Recipients and Conditions

To a large extent, the purposes of doing faculty evaluation dictate who should receive what information, and in what form. Issues of disclosure, privacy, and confidentiality must be worked out among students, faculty, administrators, and, above all, the faculty member evaluated. Factors related to feedback are listed below. For each factor, circle the *one* number in each horizontal row which best describes your view of that factor as it relates to your faculty evaluation program.

Reference Pages in Ch. 2	*Recipients of Information*	*Does not need attention, or not applicable*	*Need for attention low*	*Need for attention medium*	*Need for attention high*	*Urgent need for attention*
38	1. *Self:* The faculty member evaluated receives results from all other persons or groups which evaluate him.	5	4	3	2	1
39	2. *Students:* Students receive results of their evaluation of faculty.	5	4	3	2	1
39	3. *Peers:* Other faculty who act as evaluators receive results of this peer evaluation.	5	4	3	2	1
40	4. *Administrators:* Administrators responsible for making decisions about faculty members (e.g., retention, tenure, salary, promotion, reassignment, retraining) receive results which pertain to the decisions they have to make. This includes the interpretations and recommendations of legitimate review committees.	5	4	3	2	1
40	5. *Others:* With prior agreement among students, faculty, and administrators, results may be sent to review committees, clinics, or centers for helping faculty to improve, or to prospective employers.	5	4	3	2	1

Comments:

General Conditions of Feedback

Reference Pages in Ch. 2		Does not need attention, or not applicable	Need for attention low	Need for attention medium	Need for attention high	Urgent need for attention
40	1. *Disclosure:* Prior agreements have been formally established among students, faculty, and administrators regarding the acceptable kinds and forms of information to be released to evaluators, evaluatees, and others.	5	4	3	2	1
42	2. *Timing:* When and in what order feedback is given to all constituents must be established before program begins.	5	4	3	2	1
42	3. *Format:* All results are in a composite, or interpreted format (to insure anonymity and to present a normative context).	5	4	3	2	1
	Comments:					

Indicators of Success

The quality of the procedures that characterize a faculty evaluation program are as important—if not more important—than the details of who evaluates what, how, and who gets feedback. The successful faculty evaluation program provides information that contributes to the establishment and continual improvement of quality in faculty performance. The exact measurement of the part faculty evaluation plays in achieving this end is impossible, given the complex web of other factors involved. However, approximate indicators of a successful faculty evaluation program are identifiable. For each of the approximate indicators of success listed below, circle the *one* number in each horizontal row which best describes your view of that indicator as it applies to your faculty evaluation program.

Reference Pages in Ch. 2		Does not need attention, or not applicable	Need for attention low	Need for attention medium	Need for attention high	Urgent need for attention
42	1. *Acceptance:* Students, faculty, and administrators follow procedures and fill out forms completely and on time.	5	4	3	2	1
43	2. *Visibility:* Students, faculty, and administrators can accurately describe the purposes and procedures of the faculty evaluation program.	5	4	3	2	1
43	3. *Program Administration:* One person or group assumes responsibility for the uniform, timely and effective collection, processing, and reporting of faculty evaluation results, following established guidelines.	5	4	3	2	1
45	4. *Overcoming Resistance:* Those responsible for administering the program are successful in finding ways of resolving or diffusing the complaints or passive resistance of students, faculty, or administrators.	5	4	3	2	1
46	5. *Grievance Procedures and Legal Factors:* Specific mechanisms exist for the resolution or grievances.	5	4	3	2	1

Indicators of Success continued

Reference Pages in Ch. 2	Does not need attention, or not applicable	Need for attention low	Need for attention medium	Need for attention high	Urgent need for attention
47					
6. *Affirmative Action:* The evaluation procedures are considered fair and objective, but allow for affirmative action concerns.					
48	5	4	3	2	1
7. *Stages of Development:* The faculty evaluation programs have been established and improved through planning, pilot testing, gaining acceptability, wide-spread adoption, and review and replanning.					
49	5	4	3	2	1
8. *Maintenance and Renewal:* Strong sponsorship exists from top administrators who provide adequate financial support and advocacy for the long-term maintenance and renewal of the faculty evaluation program.					
Comments:					

Preface to MACE/TDR Prototype Handbook

The folly of that impossible precept, "Know Thyself";
till it be translated into this partially possible one,
"Know what thou canst work at."—Thomas Carlyle

A college of university exists to provide educational service. That service is provided to people by people. Therefore the quality of the service can be best judged and then improved with a strong, helping system of personnel evaluation. If any college ignores or offers only superficial attention to this reality, the institution will not provide the best possible service to its constituents. It is more apt to become the victim of conflicting effort and, in the worst instances, public censure. This should not be allowed to happen. Human resources are too precious to waste in this way.

This handbook does not recommend that a system of evaluation be based on a statewide collection of information on individual performance. To the extent that this happens, the vitality and flexibility of management in individual institutions will be lowered by management behavior on the state level. Rather, the state through its boards of higher education should clearly insist that each institution of higher learning have a strong system of personnel evaluation in every department of its operations.

The main purpose of this handbook is to provide a statewide resource, not a statewide system. Each public and private college and university can use the information provided here to avoid the all too common practice of separate institutions doing the same research on the same critical management topic—reinventing the wheel, so to speak. The colleges can use this resource in making the decisions necessary to shape personnel evaluation systems to the unique missions, resources, and readiness levels of individual institutions. In this regard we recommend that each college and university make the handbook available to committees engaged in the tasks of:

1. Defining the exact purposes of the institution's personnel evaluation system.
2. Selecting or designing the processes and materials for the evaluation system.
3. Implementing, evaluating, or renewing the personnel evaluation system.

Finally, we express our deep appreciation to the dedicated Advisory Committee members and many other persons who helped to give thie project direction. The final product was made much better by the frank expressions of agreement, disagreement, and advice from project advisors. Special appreciation is extended to the presidents of the regional community colleges and Professor William Scott who first suggested the project.

Ronald J. Fitzgerald
Director of Research
Massachusetts Advisory Council on Education

Appendix C

MACE/TDR Project
Advisory Committee

William Baker, Director of Personnel and Management Services, Massachusetts Board of Regional Community Colleges

James Brennan, Faculty, Bridgewater State College

Barbara Dunn, Student, Worcester State College

John Fitzgerald, Chairman, Philosophy Department, Southeastern Massachusetts University

Ronald Fitzgerald, Director of Research, Massachusetts Advisory Council on Education

Ruth Ferguson, Office of the Speaker of the House, Massachusetts

John Griffin, Resident, Lexington, Massachusetts

Robert Grose, Registrar, Amherst College

William P. Haas, Associate Director for Academic Affairs, Massachusetts Board of State Colleges

James F. Hall, President, Cape Cod Community College

Douglas L. Johnson, Faculty, Clark University

Baheej Khleif, Collaborative, Massachusetts Board of State Colleges

Walter Mayfield, Faculty, Springfield Technical Community College

William Moore, Massachusetts Board of Higher Education

Leonard Paolillo, Faculty, North Adams State College

William Scott, Faculty, Quinsigamond Community College

Harold Shively, President, Bunker Hill Community College

Carleton P. Stinchfield, Faculty, Greenfield Community College

Frank A. Tredinnick, Executive Vice President, Association of Independent Colleges and Universities of Massachusetts

Ingeborg Uhlir, Massachusetts League of Women Voters

Mary E. Warner, Chairman, Massachusetts Advisory Council on Education

John Warren, Massachusetts Senate President's Office

Alan Weisberg, Office of the Commissioner of Education, Massachusetts

Brunetta Wolfman, Assistant Vice President for Academic Programs, University of Massachusetts

Appendix D

The Massachusetts Advisory
Council on Education

The Massachusetts Advisory Council on Education is an independent state agency created by special legislation (General Laws, Chapter 15, Section 1H) for the purpose of recommending policies designed to improve the performance of all public education systems in the Commonwealth. As such, the Advisory Council provides support for studies that will recommend policies promoting and facilitating the coordination, effectiveness and efficiency of these educational systems.

MASSACHUSETTS ADVISORY COUNCIL ON EDUCATION
Members of The Council
Mary Warner, Chairman; Engineer, Sunderland
Benjamin D. Fleet, Vice Chairman; President, Fleet Tire Co., Sandwich
Alford Dyson, Textile Workers Union of America, Westport
Oliver W. Kerr, Accounting Manager, New England Telephone Co., Springfield
Elaine Kistiakowsky, League of Women Voters, Cambridge
Milton Paisner, General Manager, Electronic Products, Inc., Newburyport
Nina E. Scarito, M.D., Obstetrician, Methuen
Verne W. Vance, Jr., Attorney, Foley, Hoag and Eliot, Boston
Gregory R. Anrig, Commissioner of Education, ex officio
Roy Keith, Chancellor, Board of Higher Education
Legislative Consulting Committee
Walter J. Boverini, State Senator, Lynn
Nicholas J. Buglione, State Representative, Methuen
Edward L. Burke, State Senator, Framingham
Michael J. Daly, State Representative, Brighton
Mary L. Fonseca, State Senator, Fall River
Ann C. Gannett, State Representative, Wayland
Frank J. Matrango, State Representative, North Adams
William L. Saltonstall, State Senator, Manchester

Staff

Ronald J. Fitzgerald, Director of Research
Ronald B. Jackson, Associate Director of Research
Allan S. Hartman, Associate Director of Research
Joan Fitzgerald, Administrative Assistant
Mary S. Gammons, Head Clerk
Joy A. Fitzgerald, Secretary
Janet F. Flemming, Secretary
Catherine O'Neill, Secretary

About the Authors

William J. Genova

William J. Genova is President of TDR Associates, Inc., of Newton, Massachusetts, a consulting firm offering services in training, organizational development, and research and evaluation. Mr. Genova is a specialist in the combined fields of evaluation and development as applied especially to organizations concerned with teaching and learning. He has directed numerous program and personnel evaluation projects at the local, state, and federal levels.

Prior to founding TDR in 1969, Mr. Genova was Director of Research and Development, in a joint appointment with the Harvard Graduate School of Education and the Brookline Massachusetts Public Schools. He is Adjunct Professor, Boston University, and has taught graduate courses in personnel evaluation, research design, organizational development, and leadership.

Marjorie K. Madoff

Mrs. Marjorie K. Madoff is a Research Associate of TDR Associates, Inc., specializing in evaluation. Mrs. Madoff has conducted and participated in evaluations of programs, curricula, personnel, and performance contracting in education, including a three-year evaluation of the Institute for Learning and Teaching at the University of Massachusetts/Boston. She was a Research Assistant for Information System for Vocational Decisions, a federally funded project at the Harvard Graduate School of Education.

Robert Chin

Robert Chin is Professor of Psychology, and Director of the Doctoral Programs in Social Psychology, Boston University, where he has been a faculty member since 1947. He is also Faculty Associate, Human Relations Center, Center for Applied Social Sciences, Boston University; Fellow, National Training Labs, and Staff Trainer, NTL Institute of Applied Behavioral Sciences in Organization Development; Director and Trainer of Organization Development Labs; Regional Coordinator of the International Association of Applied Scientists; and President of the Association of Asian American Psychologists. He is a Senior Associate of TDR Associates, Inc.

Mr. Chin is past President, Division Nine, Society for Psychological Study of Social Issues, American Psychological Association, 1969–70. He taught as Fulbright Research Scholar at Tiwan National University, 1973, and was Visiting Professor and Director of the Social Research Center, Chinese University of Hong Cong, 1971. He has been a prominent consultant to business, education, and religious organizations in the area of organizational and community change, and is co-author of *The Planning of Change,* with Bennis, Benne (Holt Rinehart & Winston, 1969).

George B. Thomas

George B. Thomas is a Senior Associate, TDR Associates, Inc., directing and participating in evaluation and development projects. For two years he directed the education and social planning for a new town in upstate New York. Prior to this, he was Associate Dean, Director of the Office of Field Activities, and Lecturer at the Harvard Graduate School of Education. His recent activities include assistance in planning and evaluation to Campus Free College, Berea College, and the National Institute for Campus Ministries.

Mr. Thomas is the author of "Tension: A Tool for Reform," *Saturday Review,* August 1969, and "Learning at a Conference," *Phi Delta Kappa,* April 1968.